MILENA
AND
MARGARETE

MILENA
AND
MARGARETE

A Love Story
in Ravensbrück

GWEN STRAUSS

ST. MARTIN'S PRESS
NEW YORK

First published in the United States by St. Martin's Press, an
imprint of St. Martin's Publishing Group

MILENA AND MARGARETE. Copyright © 2025 by Gwen Strauss.
All rights reserved. Printed in the United States of America.
For information, address St. Martin's Publishing Group,
120 Broadway, New York, NY 10271.

www.stmartins.com

Design by Meryl Sussman Levavi

The Library of Congress Cataloging-in-Publication Data is
available upon request.

ISBN 978-1-250-28574-4 (hardcover)
ISBN 978-1-250-28575-1 (ebook)

Our books may be purchased in bulk for promotional,
educational, or business use. Please contact your local
bookseller or the Macmillan Corporate and Premium Sales
Department at 1-800-221-7945, extension 5442, or by email at
MacmillanSpecialMarkets@macmillan.com.

First Edition: 2025

1   3   5   7   9   10   8   6   4   2

For my mother, Kate Cowles Nichols
(1940–2024)

Milena   Margarete

One has to press one's head between one's hands
and ardently, ardently love life,
so that it will be appeased by such a great love, and
redeemed from damnation.

—Milena Jesenská,
from "Mysterious Redemption,"
Tribuna, February 25, 1921

CONTENTS

PART ONE

1940

Passionate Friends

Ravensbrück camp

THE NOTE WAS WRITTEN ON A STOLEN SCRAP OF PAPER AND FOLDED carefully into a tiny square. It was small enough to be slipped surreptitiously into Grete's palm by a friend as they passed each other on the dusty camp street. Grete felt its delicate edges in her hand, then slid it quietly into an inner pocket that she had made for hiding just such things. She had to wait until the right moment, when it would be safe to examine the note. When there were no hostile eyes watching her. There were those in the camp who were waiting for a chance to catch Grete and get her thrown out of her job and sent to the punishment block.

She was struck first by the handwriting, bold and assured. And the words were simple, yet almost like an imperial summons: "Milena from Prague requests a meeting." She didn't even use her family name, just her city; where she came from was what mattered.

Grete arrived at Ravensbrück concentration camp, fifty miles north of Berlin, in August 1940, when she was thirty-nine. From a middle-class family in Potsdam, Germany, she had spent the previous two years imprisoned in the brutal Soviet Karaganda Gulag, on the steppes of Kazakhstan. Milena arrived in Ravensbrück two months later, in October 1940, after fifteen months in Gestapo prisons.

GRETE WOULD REMEMBER her first encounter with Milena as the turning point of her life. They met during the brief exercise period allowed to prisoners, when they could walk in a narrow oblong path between the backs of the housing blocks and the high gray wall topped with electrified wires. "The Wailing Wall," Milena would sardonically name it.

At age forty-four, Milena's pallid, ashen face was marked by the months she had spent in various prisons. She had deep circles around her eyes, but Grete remarked that they shone with intelligence. Milena had gorgeous shapely lips and a dimple in her chin. Her delicate, weary face was crowned with a mass of reddish-blond curls. She was tall with wide shoulders and a statuesque frame. Though she had a hitch in her gait, she still moved gracefully, gliding through crowds where she easily stood out.

Grete was more solidly built and muscular. Next to Milena, Grete saw herself as plain. The years in the Gulag had roughened and darkened her skin. But she had full eyebrows that accented her half-moon eyes the color of the bluest sky. With her blond hair and blue eyes, Grete had the Germanic beauty that her enemies, the Nazis, so adored. What Milena saw immediately in Grete was her honest open face.

"You must be Margarete Buber-Neumann," Milena said, smiling.

"Please call me Grete."

Milena reached out her hand and playfully warned, "Please not a firm German handshake, my fingers are too frail to withstand that."

They were blocking the path for the other prisoners trudging zombie-like in a circle along the wall. But Milena didn't seem to care. Even in a concentration camp, she acted as if they were meeting to chat on a busy city boulevard. She spoke excellent German with a Czech accent. She was carried away with the pleasure of the moment, and this infuriated Grete. Didn't she know where she was? She wanted Milena, the newcomer, to do as everyone else, to follow the unspoken rules. This was not how you behaved in a camp, especially when you were a newcomer. But as much as the others muttered angrily and jostled them, Milena ignored them; she stood her ground and continued talking. She had heard some of Grete's story, and wanted to know if it was true: Had Stalin really traded Grete, along with other anti-fascist prisoners, to Hitler?

Slowly Grete realized that here was a real free woman. Milena's curiosity remained unbroken by the harshness all around them. What at first bothered Grete was exactly what she would fall in love with: Milena's innate sense of freedom.

After their parting *"Auf Wiedersehen,"* Grete returned to her block. Later she would write, "All the rest of the day I was blind and deaf to everything. I was full of the name 'Milena,' drunk on the sound of it."[1]

THE ROMANI TRAPEZE artist Katharina Waitz, like Milena, never lost her innate sense of freedom. She never gave in to being a prisoner. It was celebrated how Katharina swung on her trapeze and flew through the air. She made leaps across the void of two swings that no one else would dare. She traveled in circus caravans and performed across Europe in those years leading up to the war. A nomad of both earth and air, she was Romani, and for that the Nazis arrested her. As a so-called *Asoziale*, she was put in "protective custody," which meant the society needed to be protected from her. But Katharina Waitz would not be held in a cage. Her first escape attempt was from the Lichtenburg Castle prison. It was a mystery how she had managed to scale the high castle walls.

Her second attempt occurred only days after the opening of Ravensbrück, the only camp just for women. It was an embarrassment for the new camp commander to almost immediately have an escapee, which led to a nationwide manhunt. By the time Grete and Milena arrived, Katharina was back, held permanently in the prison block. They would have learned about her soon after arriving. She was a legend. Much later, on her third and final escape attempt, she would mark the memory of everyone who was there to witness it, including Grete and Milena.

Ravensbrück's location had been chosen in 1938 by Heinrich Himmler, the SS *Reichsführer*, or head of the Nazi SS police force. It was deep in the Mecklenburg forest near a property he owned, where he eventually built a home for his former secretary, and mistress, Hedwig Potthast. There, not too far from Berlin, he could see Hedwig and inspect the camp while also visiting other Nazis in the area. His friend Oswald Pohl was breeding chickens on a nearby farm, and this idea of breeding the perfect race, chickens or humans, was close to Himmler's heart. He was a zealot about eugenics. This area north of Berlin was popular among Nazi officials for hunting, but Himmler abhorred hunting as "the cold-blooded murder of innocent and defenseless animals."[2]

As the SS *Reichsführer*, Himmler oversaw the entire concentration camp system, which would expand over the course of the war to include fifteen thousand camps across German-occupied territories, putting him in charge of a vast and lucrative network of slave labor. Ravensbrück would become one of the twenty-seven main concentration camps, with up to seventy subcamps administratively annexed to it.

The spot Himmler chose was in a wooded area near a lake across from the town of Fürstenberg, on the same train line as the male camp of Sachsenhausen. It conformed to several of Himmler's criteria: a site of natural beauty, hidden from view, and yet near a railroad. Ravensbrück opened on May 15, 1939, just a few months before the start of the war. The first 867 women came from the Lichtenburg Castle prison. A few were political prisoners such as communists, and former Reichstag members who had opposed the Nazi rise to power. They were given a red triangle to sew onto their prison outfits when they arrived.

A sizable group were Jehovah's Witnesses, who wore lavender triangles. They were a persistent thorn in the Nazi Party's side. They saw Hitler as the Antichrist and refused to make any oath of loyalty to the party or the country. Their men refused to fight, and the women refused to participate in auxiliary war efforts. In a country so deeply policed by National Socialism, and with all the pressures to conform, the Jehovah's Witnesses stood out.

The initial prisoners transferred to Ravensbrück included a large group who had been in prison for mostly petty crimes. They wore green triangles. In the early days of the camp, the green triangle prisoners were given the special functionary jobs, such as room elders and block elders, the prisoners in charge of the individual blocks, as well as jobs in the kitchen and other positions of privilege.

There was a small number of Jewish women who had been charged with *Rassenschande*, "race defilement," or having had relationships with so-called Aryans. At this stage, before the war and before the official adoption of the Final Solution, the German government was not imprisoning Jewish nationals in large numbers. Instead, they encouraged German Jews to emigrate. Many more Jewish men and boys, feeling they were in greater danger than Jewish women, emigrated during this period.[3] If a Jewish family had the means, they would buy their way out of Germany, usually sending the male members of the family first. Some of these early women prisoners wearing the yellow triangle could hope for release if they had money, a place to go, and someone working to get them a visa. But this potential getaway would soon end with Himmler's crucial order in March 1940, banning all further releases of Jews.

The largest group, the group that the trapeze artist Katharina came from, were the so-called asocials, or *Asoziale*. These were prostitutes, the destitute, vagrants, lesbians, and "Gypsies." Most of the "Gypsies" in Germany and Europe before and during World War II were from the Romani and Sinti nations or tribes. The Nazis believed that they were protecting the racial purity of the rest of society, the pure blood of the so-called Aryan race. The *Asoziale* group wore black triangles.

By separating the women into groups, the Nazis created a caste system, with a clearly delineated hierarchy of value. The black triangles were at the bottom of the camp hierarchy, hated by the Nazis and scorned by the other prisoners. Prison societies, it has been noted, are especially keen to control and police status. Perhaps when one is living in an extreme environment, when survival is precarious, it becomes important to have someone beneath you, *the other*, the one who is even worse off than you. Perhaps there is comfort in knowing that your situation is not as bad as *the other*. The *Asoziale* served that role in Ravensbrück.

At the opening of Ravensbrück, Johanna Langefeld was the head guard, or *Oberaufseherin*, and Max Koegel was the head SS commandant. They had very different ideas about how a camp for women should be run. The power struggle between the two would lead to numerous conflicts and clashes. And later their battle would explode, placing Grete's life in the crosshairs.

Johanna Langefeld had previously worked in welfare houses for prostitutes, a system that had developed out of the 1927 anti–venereal disease law aimed at abolishing prostitution through social reform. She saw herself as a social worker, there to reeducate and rehabilitate the women prisoners. Grete would later describe Lange-feld as someone conflicted and haunted by her religious beliefs. She believed she was there to "help" the women, but this motivation was incompatible with the reality of what would become the efficient Nazi killing machine of the camp system. Langefeld was also a loyal fol-lower of Hitler, fervently antisemitic, and believed in strict discipline and order. There were endless precise rules for everything. Beds had to be made in the "Prussian style," pillows had to be placed so that corners pointed at right angles with the bed, and the mattress of wood chips had to lie absolutely flat. The blue-and-white-checked blanket had to be folded so that the line of checks was perfectly straight, and not overlapping the mattress. The slightest deviation led to a torrent of screams, an extra work detail, standing at attention for hours, or an official written report, which could lead to more punishment and a record of bad behavior. And yet Langefeld did not believe in beat-ing women. She never hit or kicked, though she might slap a woman when listening to a report. Initially, there were no plans for a punish-ment block in Ravensbrück. Order and control could be maintained by other means, Langefeld believed. Female prisoners should be treated more gently than male prisoners.

Max Koegel, a coarsened right-wing extremist, had been trained at Dachau, the first concentration camp to be built in Germany. To him, there was no difference between a camp for men or women—all prisoners should be treated with unfaltering ruthlessness. Before the camp was even completed, Koegel was calling for the construction of a prison block, a *Strafblock*, like in the men's camps. As commandant of Lichtenburg Castle, he arrived with the first group of women. At the castle, he had dealt with the stubborn resistance of the Jeho-vah's Witness prisoners by turning fire hoses on the women as they prayed. They were then beaten by guards and attacked by dogs. The incident had turned into a riot, an unpleasant moment that Koegel hadn't forgotten. He felt a special animosity toward the "Bible Students" and wanted a place to put those "hysterical women."[4] Like so many of his SS colleagues, he was a sadistic man who, according to prisoner witnesses, took pleasure in beatings. One prisoner recalled that on Easter Sunday, he had beaten three naked women "until he could go on no longer."[5]

Random beatings occurred every day, but Koegel wanted permission to use the official method of the *Prügelstrafe* employed in the male camps. This form of torture involved strapping prisoners stomach down over a wooden horse and giving twenty-five lashes on their bare backside with an ox-hide whip.

Against Langefeld's softer methods, Koegel would have used as evidence the fact that within a few days of opening the camp, the trapeze artist Katharina Waitz had managed to scale the walls of this new prison and escape. Koegel wanted to be sure she became an example that would teach all the prisoners a lesson. Langefeld felt that Koegel was a brute who was not in line with her beloved Führer's ideals; she believed Hitler, a gentleman and a Christian, would never treat women this way. But soon enough, Koegel's side would win out. Floggings of twenty-five lashes and a sturdy prison block became the reality in Ravensbrück.

The nature of Ravensbrück evolved over time. Initially, survival rates at the camp were high. By the end of 1940, 84 prisoners had died out of a population of 3,500, a mortality rate considerably less than in the male camps at the time. In line with Nazi ideology, Himmler saw female prisoners as less dangerous and more able to be reformed with proper discipline and training.[6] Though some women were empowered by the Nazi regime and had chances to pursue careers, in Nazi mythology the ideal female should be fulfilled by motherhood, homemaking, and weekly worship. *"Kinder, Küche, Kirche"*—the three *K*'s of "children, kitchen, church"—was the traditional slogan used to describe a woman's role in society.

The camp might have opened with some lofty ideal of female re-education, but by the middle of the war, in 1942, conditions there bore no resemblance to the early reform fantasy. Strict rations, freezing temperatures, widespread illnesses, overcrowding, beatings, sexual violence, and executions were the norm. The SS doctors had begun a systematic program of selecting prisoners for murder by injection and gassing. So-called medical experiments used the prisoners as guinea pigs. Seeing the opportunity to use prisoner labor to enrich SS coffers and to help the war effort, Himmler converted the camp into a lucrative slave labor camp. Prisoners were worked to death, or once they became useless for labor, they were murdered. From 1941 onward, there was also a small men's camp attached to the main camp.

By the end of the war, Ravensbrück—one of the last camps to finally be liberated, in April 1945—had become a death camp with gas chambers, executions, and a crematorium that was burning up to the day before liberation. Initially built to hold 3,000 women, by February 1944, the camp held over 46,000, in the most inhuman, overcrowded conditions. Over 130,000 women passed through the camp during the war.

Even at the height of their power and hubris, the SS were worried that the truth about Ravensbrück would leak out to the German population. Ordinary Germans might balk at such cold-blooded violence inflicted on women, on German soil, just as they had done at the early programs of gassing the disabled and mentally ill. The SS worked hard to keep what happened in Ravensbrück secret. More than in any other camp, almost all the records at Ravensbrück were burned before the Soviet Red Army arrived.

After the war, there were other obstacles to learning the truth about Ravensbrück. The camp would become part of East Germany and served as a Soviet military prison camp before most of the structures were torn down. Later, when it was designated as a memorial, only loyal Stalinists were commemorated. The specific program of genocide for Jews and other populations was omitted from the official narrative. The fact that most of the prisoners were women meant their history was considered less important. They weren't seen as heroic, and the survivors themselves kept silent. If a woman survived such a place, especially a young woman, she was thought to have been a prostitute, a slur on her character implying that she had collaborated with the Nazis. Ravensbrück was falsely remembered as "just a labor camp." The so-called *Asoziale* and habitual criminals were completely ignored until only recently, when brave survivors fought to reclaim their history. No one will ever know the exact death toll. Estimates range between thirty thousand and ninety thousand killed.

IN THE SPRING of 1940—before the arrival of both Grete and Milena—the first major shift in the power hierarchy among prisoners occurred. The red triangles, political prisoners, wrested away the privileged functionary positions from the green triangles, the so-called habitual criminals. Assigning some prisoners special jobs saved the SS both staff and money. Without these co-opted prisoners, the SS would not have been able to maintain control over their vast empire of enslaved people.

Before the power struggle, the green triangle prisoners were the block elders, and they held the coveted positions in the kitchen and the *Effektenkammer*, the storage block where prisoners handed over their personal possessions upon entering the camp. Many from this group had been in prison before the war. They knew each other and had formed solid social networks. The green triangles looked down on the politicals as weak intellectuals.

All groups in the camp's caste system, like the green triangles, used their social networks to maintain positions of privilege in order to help each other survive. The SS, by co-opting them, often transformed someone who had been nonviolent into a brutal helper. Margot Kaiser, the first appointed *Lagerälteste*, the highest-ranked prisoner or camp senior, earned the nickname "*Lagerschreck*," "camp terror," from the other prisoners. Before the camp, Kaiser had been a petty nonviolent criminal, but Ravensbrück would transform her into a murderer. She would admit at the postwar trials that she had beaten at least ten prisoners to death during her time there.[7]

The brutality of Kaiser and other green triangles pushed the communist prisoners to act. As party members, they came to the camp with experience in clandestine organizing and a sense of party discipline.

They knew they couldn't get rid of Langefeld or Koegel or the SS, but the red triangle prisoners felt that they could surely outmaneuver Kaiser and others like her. Langefeld and Koegel were battling each other, and the red triangles used that rift to their advantage. Koegel liked the green triangles, but Langefeld found the criminal class abhorrent. The political prisoners were better educated and less coarse. Despite her antisemitism, she had already taken the surprising step of appointing the Jewish communist Olga Benario to be block elder for the Jewish block.

The red triangle prisoners came up with a plot to steal food and plant it on the criminal gang leaders in charge of the food storage. It worked perfectly. Langefeld took the opportunity to kick the green leaders off their positions and put the communist politicals in charge. From then on, when a German-speaking political prisoner arrived in the camp, Langefeld was alerted, and she would interview them to see if she could place them in a camp functionary job.

ON AUGUST 2, 1940, on the train to the town of Fürstenberg, Grete remembered seeing for the first time a "Bible Student," or "Witness for Jehovah." There were also prostitutes on the train who calmly told her they were going to a camp for three months of "reeducation." On arrival, they tumbled out of the train car while guards shouted for them to line up in rows of five, and growling dogs lunged at their heels. Grete thought to herself, *So the reeducation has started.*

But Grete had several advantages. She spoke German, so she understood the guards' orders. She was also hardened by the previous two years she had spent in a Soviet Gulag, and almost a year before that in the horrifying Soviet prisons. The obligatory bullying of the guards did not shock her, and she was not especially frightened by them. The actual appearance of the camp pleased her. Once they were inside the gates, she saw newly built wooden buildings in orderly rows. Along the central road were freshly planted trees. Each wooden block had a flower bed with red salvia blooming in the front. The gravel had been neatly raked. Off to one side were larger fir trees, and behind them the only stone building. This building, Grete would learn later, was the *Strafblock*, Koegel's punishment block. To the left was a watchtower and a large aviary, like in a zoological garden. Inside, peacocks strutted and bright parrots flew from branch to branch, calling out something that sounded to Grete like the word for "mother." It all seemed calm and clean. Ravensbrück was nothing like the hellish chaos and filth of the Gulag.

A group of prisoners in rows of five marched by the new arrivals. They wore matching white headscarves fastened at the back of their necks, and broad striped dresses with dark blue aprons. Their feet were bare. Their faces were blank, impassive. Next to them marched a woman in clogs who barked orders: "Left, right, left, right, heads up, arms by your side."

Grete's heart sank. She had gone from one extreme to another, from the lawless bedlam of the Soviet Gulag to the maniacal order of the German camp. This would be her life now; in rows of five, she would be regimented, drilled, shouted at. The noon siren howled. The startled new arrivals immediately covered their ears. The siren brought movement. Columns of marching women in rows of five came from all directions. Parading in order, singing songs, some of them carrying shovels. None of the prisoners gave any sign that they had seen the new arrivals.

Grete and her group were marched to the administration offices to be registered. Each woman was called out by name, and a card was made with her photograph, all her details carefully noted and put into her prisoner file. Next they were marched to the *Effekten-kammer*, where they stripped and handed over all their clothes and possessions. Again, every detail was noted on a card. It was all done, Grete would later write, with unsparing Prussian thoroughness. In the showers, they were inspected first for head lice by a Jehovah's Witness prisoner. Grete, to her surprise considering her years in the lice-infested Gulag, was found to be lice-free and allowed to keep her hair. Then another Jehovah's Witness, with the same penchant for thoroughness, inspected the pubic hair of each prisoner. Those found with lice were shaved there as well.

After Grete's group showered, they sat shivering on benches along the walls of the shower room until they were called for the next step in the procedure, the medical exam. Grete saw Dr. Sonntag for the first time. He was a towering man who tensely flicked his riding crop against his shiny black jackboots. Formerly a dentist, he had been given a new position, thanks to the war, as a doctor for the SS. Before coming to Ravensbrück, he had worked at Sachsenhausen, where he had performed human experiments involving mustard gas.

The fifty new women, some of them now completely bald, stood in a line trying to cover their private parts for modesty until Sonntag shouted, "Stand at attention. Hands to the side."

Sonntag called one after the other to step forward for their examination, then he peered into their open mouths. When it was Grete's turn, he asked her, "Why are you here?"

"Political," she answered.

"Typical Bolshevik shrew," he responded and flicked her on the legs with his crop to get her to move back into the lineup.[8]

They were given their prison clothes and marched off to Block 16, where new arrivals were kept in quarantine. Lined up outside the entrance to the block, Grete's feet hurt. She wasn't used to standing in one place a long time, and certainly not used to walking with bare feet on the flinty gravel. She had broken her foot in an accident at the Gulag, and the old injury constantly throbbed.

The elder of Block 16 was Minna Rupp, one of the German communists who had benefited from the earlier coup d'état replacing the green triangle with the red triangle prisoners. The coup had benefited Langefeld's power hold in the camp, but Koegel had won a different battle. Siding with Koegel against Langefeld, Himmler granted him permission in 1940 to administer corporeal punishment. The first person to receive the twenty-five lashes was Minna Rupp, for stealing a turnip. Despite her experience of SS brutality, once in power, Rupp did not hesitate to beat or report on prisoners to keep her fellow comrades on top. She was hated and feared by the prisoners in her block.

Reading from a list, Rupp called out the names of the new arrivals, one by one. They were given their mess kit: an aluminum cup and bowl, spoon, fork, knife, and towel. These felt like absolute treasures to Grete. In the Gulag, there were no bowls or cutlery provided to the prisoners. When she first arrived in Siberia, she had to figure out how to get such basic utensils. A young barber, in the first subcamp of the Gulag, had flirted with Grete, hoping she would become his "camp wife." Trying to win her over, he had given her a precious tin can that she used as her bowl.

Grete's group was ushered into the central dayroom in the middle of the two wings of tiered bunks of the block. The room smelled of wet wood and damp wool. At the central tables, Polish prisoners— also new arrivals, though after just a few days, they were now the old hands—were knitting gray socks for the German soldiers. The low hum of their conversation died when the new arrivals filed in. After a moment of looking each other over, the hum began again, only to be interrupted by Minna Rupp's booming voice, "Silence!"

Each block was divided in two, sides A and B, with two room elders in charge of keeping each side clean. The room elder showed the new arrivals the small lockers where they were to keep their treasures in a specific way. The towel had to hang on the little hook and be folded to look like a man's tie. The cup and bowl and utensils also had to be placed in exactly a certain order. Grete wondered at this new place; in the Gulag, if you didn't sleep with all your possessions tightly bundled under your head, they would be stolen. And even then, she had been robbed several times.

The new arrivals were told to sit at the tables. Grete noticed how frightened some of the others were. Before long, their meal arrived. "Silence! Line up for food." They rushed to get their bowls and utensils and find a place in the line.

Grete was astonished by this first meal. There was a sweet porridge with stewed dried fruit, white bread and butter, lard, and some sausage. She turned to the Polish women next to her and asked, "Is something special happening today? An inspection?"

The woman shook her head and looked strangely at Grete.

"Do we always get this much to eat, then?"

"But it's not that much," the woman answered, confused.

"Yes, but I mean . . ." Grete's voice trailed off. How could she explain that this was a feast by Gulag standards? But soon enough, as the war progressed and conditions at Ravensbrück degenerated, this type of "feast" would disappear.

After the meal, Grete experienced her first roll call. Twice a day, these would punctuate the next four years of her life. During the first quarantine period, she was less traumatized than many of the other new arrivals. Despite the draconian discipline, Grete found this new camp rather palatial compared to what she had recently been through. In Russia, in the Gulag, there had been absolutely no plumbing, no lavatories or showers or running water. There had been no tables or stools for prisoners, and barely any food. You had to fight for everything and form alliances to survive. In Ravensbrück, she used the same methods, and soon became friendly with many of the Polish women in the quarantine block.

But even if this was a nicer prison, it was still a prison. The barbed wire around the perimeter was electrified. And Grete was told about Katharina Waitz's escape attempt. One way that women sometimes committed suicide was to run and throw themselves on the wire. A Romani mother had done this the day Grete arrived. Her fingers had remained attached when they ripped her body off the wire.

Grete discovered that the bed-making ritual was one of the most onerous tasks. Johanna Langefeld demanded that the beds were perfectly made, each exactly like the other. Luckily, an older Polish music teacher came to Grete's aid and showed her how to use two pieces of board to make the edges of the pillow perfectly square, and a large makeshift wooden knife to flatten the wood-chip mattress. If a prisoner failed at making a perfect bed, the whole thing would be torn apart by Rupp, and all the bedding thrown to the floor. If the prisoner failed again, there were escalating punishments: going without a meal, standing at attention for hours, being reported and sent to the *Strafblock*, and even being beaten.

Soon Grete was knitting like an old hand, and after a week in the quarantine block, a messenger arrived calling out her name. Minna Rupp and two other German political prisoners were summoning her. They pulled her aside into the bunk area, which was normally strictly off-limits during the day.

"Were you arrested in Moscow?" Rupp began the interrogation.

"Yes," Grete answered.

They had heard she had once been the companion of the traitor Heinz Neumann, who had been arrested under Stalin's orders for his "political deviations." But they wanted to know the "real" reason for her arrest. She tried to explain that everybody was getting arrested in Moscow. All the Comintern members. "Good communists. Bolshevik heroes, even Lenin's best friend. Stalin is getting rid of all of them," Grete answered emphatically.

"You're a lying bitch," one woman hissed at her.

"How do we know you weren't sent here to spread lies, to discourage us?" the third one called out.

Grete had been like them: For over a decade, she was a true believer in the revolution. When she met Heinz Neumann in 1929, she left everything to follow him. Heinz was a rising star in the party. He had taught himself Russian and met with Stalin. Dedicated and zealous, he would become the principal mouthpiece of the German Communist Party. At twenty-seven, he dazzled her with his intelligence and insights about politics.

She was also charmed by his awkwardness when he was not confidently lecturing on fine points of party ideology. On the night of their first meeting, Grete remembered, he invited her for a walk in the park. In the semi-dark of the evening, he asked her, "May I give you a rose?" He handed her a geranium that he had just plucked from a park flower bed.

In 1931, she had watched the May Day parade in Moscow's Red Square. She had marveled at the Five-Year Plan and the modern factories. True, she had seen starving beggars and destitute children in the streets. She had rationalized what she saw. The revolution would take time. They couldn't expect to change the world overnight.

She and Heinz had done whatever was asked of them. They had sacrificed everything to bring about the dream when the workers of the world would unite.

But you can lie to yourself for only so long. With growing alarm, the German communists watched the rise of Hitler and found Stalin's silence difficult to understand. There were already purges of loyal party members and whispered rumors about the direction of Stalin's brutality. Heinz had warned about the rise of Hitler. He would proclaim, "Oppose fascism wherever you face it." And perhaps that implicit contradiction of Stalin would be his fatal crime. By 1935, when Grete and Heinz were called back to Moscow, they had both seen too many cynical things done by Stalin's henchmen to completely trust him. Their close friend Beso Lominadze[9] had been arrested, accused of terrorist deviations, and he had shot himself, preferring suicide to what awaited him. Beso had warned Heinz to open his eyes and admit that their "stupid dream of a revolution" had failed. On the boat journey from Le Havre back to Moscow, Heinz and Grete feared what awaited them. Still, Heinz remained faithful. He was so good at inventing excuses for the party's obvious failures. It would take several great shocks for both of them to see what had been so clearly before their eyes.

During the two years the couple lived in Moscow, Grete's misgivings about Stalinism grew into complete disillusionment. Neighbors denounced each other to settle petty scores. Many perfectly innocent people were swept up and disappeared behind prison walls. No one was safe from the mass paranoia. Stalin would get rid of anyone to keep himself in power. They had arrested Heinz, and she had no idea where he was. Then they had come for her simply because she was his wife.

While Grete was explaining these events, Minna Rupp and the others were interjecting: "You're lying!" and "That's not true!"

But Grete continued. She began to recount the horrors of the Gulag in Kazakhstan. "Ravensbrück is a sanatorium compared to the Soviet camps, you should feel lucky not to be in one of Stalin's prisons," she said to the angry shouts of her interrogators. Grete described how they lived in clay huts with dirt floors. The camp was full of common criminals but also once-loyal communists who had been arrested for little or no reason. She told them about the stories she learned of terrible famine in Ukraine and the disasters of collectivization. A good hardworking farmer from the Volga wondered if Hitler could really be worse than Stalin. He asked her, "Does Hitler take away land from the peasants like they do here?"

That's when Grete went too far. Her interrogators erupted in anger, shouting her down.

"You're a Trotskyite," Minna Rupp announced. "That's what you are." She spat on the ground in front of Grete's feet and walked away. The pronouncement was made. Grete was a betrayer of the revolution spreading lies about the mother country. She hadn't been able to shed her bourgeois imperialism. She was probably a fascist, planted there to weaken them. They would have nothing to do with her.

She had only just arrived, and already she had enemies.

AFTER THIS INTERROGATION, the other German communist political prisoners shunned her. But Grete made friends with the Polish political prisoners. They had no illusions about Stalin.

Her new friends proposed that she become their block elder. They wanted to get rid of the tyrannical Minna Rupp. Grete was German, a red triangle, and she knew about camps. The idea horrified Grete. She could not imagine herself in the role of block elder, enforcing discipline and making demands for that wretched bed-making. She would be working with the SS and the camp administrators. Collaborating with them. She refused to do it, but they begged her: "You won't have to bully us. We will help you. You'd have no problem with us. We would get away from that terrible Rupp. And everyone would be better off."

Eventually, they convinced her. Johanna Langefeld had a soft spot for the Polish prisoners. Through some machinations and connections, her friends got Grete's name on a list. A few days later, six women were called to the head offices to meet Langefeld. After a short interview and a long wait, Grete was told that she would be the new room elder of Block 2.

Happy to return to her Polish friends with the good news, she imagined their plan had worked perfectly. But then she saw the horrified looks on their faces. "But this is terrible! You won't be our room elder, you are being sent to the *Asoziale* block!"

Grete was going to have to work with the bottom of the camp caste system, the shunned ones. She was sure this was the work of the German communists, who were determined to make her life difficult.

In the beginning, the Nazi camps had held mostly political prisoners. Filled with members of the opposition parties, the camps were initially set up to terrorize and break the will of German political opposition to National Socialism, the Nazi Party, and by the time Grete arrived, they had largely succeeded. Running his concentration camp system, Himmler now set his sights on "cleaning up" German society of all the people he deemed as undesirables.

The idea of locking up a certain class of the population in "preventative detention" had already been in effect, though with far less zeal, in the period between the wars. Famous for its great tolerance and sexual freedom, the Weimar period also originated policies that the Nazis would follow to their logical extreme.

Joining forces with the 1927 anti–venereal disease law, middle-class feminists pushed forward an effort to abolish prostitution after World War I. After soldiers returned from the front lines, there was a massive outbreak of venereal disease, touching all sectors of the population. It was widely believed that prostitutes were responsible for spreading the disease. The new law would suppress street prostitution and place the women in welfare homes for treatment and reeducation. The sex workers themselves were never consulted. Intransigent prostitutes who refused to be reformed would be imprisoned to protect the public. Experts on crime, welfare, and social policy largely believed that there was a certain class of people who were medically defined as "degenerate, feebleminded, with psychopathic inferiority." According to the abolitionist feminists, "such individuals were born to be institutionalized."[10]

The women Grete would be working with, the *Asoziale* group, had been arrested for prostitution, vagrancy, begging, "moral inferiority," and "deviant" behavior such as "lesbianism" or having an abortion. In the surviving camp files, some prisoners are noted as coming from "genetically worthless" families. As the German authorities were trying to "clean up" the streets and protect good "Aryan" blood and morals, they sent these women to Ravensbrück in a steady stream.

When Grete arrived, the *Asoziale* blocks were overcrowded compared to the other blocks, and as conditions deteriorated, squalor and disease followed. Many of the women had venereal diseases and tuberculosis. Many were orphans or widows left homeless by the war. Some were young women who had fled the brutality in their homes and were trying to find their way in a fanatically patriarchal society. They were often sent to the *Strafblock*, where they were beaten. If food went missing in the SS canteen stores, the *Asoziale* were blamed as a group, though they had little or no access to the storage rooms. They were forced to stand out in the cold with no food, collapsing in place. They had the highest mortality rate of any group in the camp.

Grete's initial impression of their block was of utter chaos. The din was overwhelming, and "it smelled like a monkey's cage." For Grete, these women were barely human. "I felt as though I were naked in a cage of wild animals."[11] Like most of the other political prisoners, Grete pitied and disdained the *Asoziale*. They were seen as lost souls, devoid of higher moral values.

The language that we have today to identify queer, nonbinary, trans, and other gender-nonconforming individuals did not exist. Without words or language, there was only one term—"lesbian"—and it was a derogatory term for most. It is unclear if there were more queer women among the black triangle prisoners than in other prisoner groups, but clearly, the other groups believed so. The *Asoziale* lesbians were seen as "other" by the "normal" prisoners. Known lesbians were often arrested on some charge of deviancy and then placed in this disfavored group. The politicals would remember the *Asoziale* block for its "rampant lesbianism," but in the immediate postwar context, these witnesses were signaling that the *Asoziale* was the degenerate group.

The description of their existence was meant to emphasize the terrible suffering of the other "morally superior" prisoners. The majority of survivor accounts are profoundly homophobic, and the sight of lesbian couples is described as horrific, sickening, and deeply shocking.

Grete's account is no different. She saw lesbians as deviant, immoral, and degenerate. "Lesbian" and "prostitute" were almost interchangeable terms. She thought the women became lesbians in the camp because, as prostitutes, they suffered from a lack of a male clientele. She wrongly believed there was no "lesbianism" in the Gulags. There she had seen plenty of prostitutes who fared relatively well because they had a way to survive and make money. But in Ravensbrück, Grete felt, since there were no men available, the prostitutes fell into lesbianism. This was a common idea at the time: Women became lesbians because they had not yet found the right man. Lesbianism could be cured with a penis. They were at the bottom of the heap, not because the society had degraded them and consigned them there, but because they had some innate moral or medical problem.

Grete was horrified that she would be working with the *Asoziale*, but she was pleased that her new job came with wooden clogs for her sore feet; a better outfit, one that fit; and a green armband that allowed her some freedom of movement. Still, as well-dressed as she felt, confronted by this "other" population, she was overwhelmed and frightened. She recalls her first task of trying to distribute the meal. She asked for absolute silence during the serving of food, as was stated in the camp regulations, but realized that no one except perhaps someone standing right next to her could have even heard her in all that noise. Around her, the prisoners pushed and pulled. The women shouted orders at her: "It's table three's turn to go first." "No! Start here with table five." "It's our turn to scrub the pots." "Hurry up! The siren will sound, and we will have not gotten to eat anything." "What's wrong with you!" "Get on with it!"

No one listened to her. Immobilized by panic, Grete held the ladle over the large pot of soup. She had no idea what to do or how to get control over the situation, which threatened to dissolve into a full-scale brawl. Then, Grete recalled, "a powerful woman with lively brown eyes and a determined chin jumped onto a stool and bellowed in a voice worthy of a sergeant-major: 'If you don't line up in an orderly manner at once and stop mobbing the new room elder, the tubs will go back to the kitchen and then no one will get anything.'"[12]

The prisoners fell into place. From then on, the meal distribution went smoothly. The prisoner who had brought order to the chaos was Else Krug, a former prostitute and brothel madame from Düsseldorf. It is telling that in the history of Ravensbrück, Else is one of the rare black triangle prisoners whom we know by name. The *Asoziale* group was ignored after the war. They wrote no memoirs and received no compensation. We know a little about Else Krug because she became Grete's friend, and because after the war, her mother searched for her.

Else had arrived with the camp's first group of prisoners and gotten the job running a work gang in the kitchen supplies cellar. She held on to this job despite the communist coup d'état because she ran her gang efficiently. It was a great position with many opportunities for theft, but Else was careful not to be so excessive as to be caught. Whatever extra food the gang was able to get, they distributed fairly. Else had won the loyalty of the block; people wanted to work with her.

Else was sanguine about the world and human nature. She told Grete stories about her trade and her specialty in sadomasochism. "How about a little nature study?" she asked Grete before delving into another client story. Talking with Else was a real education. Grete had thought that after the time she'd spent in the Gulag, hearing the stories and sexual innuendo and vulgar curses, stumbling across couples making love and prostitutes offering their bodies, nothing could shock her. But Else's stories "made my hair stand on end."

With Else's help, Grete worked in the *Asoziale* block for two months. Grete assumed that the women in her block, if they showed good behavior, could be released from the camp. There were occasional releases of prisoners. Grete tried to appeal to them to at the very least make their beds properly. When they wouldn't, she created a work gang that would make the worst beds. But this backfired.

Women bribed her gang to do their beds, and others assumed Grete would do theirs. She comments that "a prostitute, often suffering from venereal disease, and often something of a cretin, her health undermined, used to late hours and no regular work" lacked discipline, but Grete acknowledges "the talk of re-education was hypocrisy. Society now brutalized them in a different fashion."[13] She never once considers that their apathy for the ridiculous bed-making could have been a form of agency and resistance.

Grete would write, "The asocials were naturally treacherous; they had no sense of loyalty."[14] And yet Else's ability to maintain her effective kitchen gang, show leadership with the *Asoziale*, and help Grete with her job demonstrated that this group had solidarity and loyalty. Grete could not see it. Instead, she remembered brawls between prostitutes; the worst insult one could sling was to comment on another's low rates and low clientele: "took two drunks in a doorway for a sixpence a time." Grete is condescending: "They were like naughty school children and took delight in dodging their obligations whenever they got the chance." But there is also compassion in her recollections. Once a month, prisoners were allowed to write and receive one letter. The letter had to be to a person whom they had designated when they arrived in the camp. As room elder, Grete was tasked with reading the letters to be sure they complied with camp regulations. In effect, Grete was responsible for the first round of censorship. To Grete, the letters were heart-wrenching. "Dear Mother, —I know I've been a great shame to you, but do write me just a word. I'm so unhappy. When I come out, I will make a fresh start; really I will. I will make up for everything."[15] Most in her block never received a letter in response. They had been thrown out of their families. Or they had no one to write to.

Still, Grete acknowledges that Else Krug was able to keep her work gang of twenty or so without a report or a denunciation for a year and a half. This was quite a feat in the constantly shifting power dynamics of the camp. Else led by sheer force of personality, and Grete admired her. Ultimately, Else was denounced and sent to the *Strafblock*. Though it was strictly forbidden to speak to prisoners there, Grete was able from time to time to see her, and they had whispered exchanges. "Grete," Else whispered to her, "they think they can get me down with work, but they're wrong; I'm tough. I can get through it better than any of them."

By 1941, Max Koegel, the camp commandant, had gotten his way, and there were often beatings of twenty-five lashes in the *Strafblock*. As much as he appeared to take pleasure in administering the beatings himself, there were too many for him to carry out alone. He delegated the task to his two *Strafblock* guards, but even they grew tired of it. He landed on the idea of having fellow prisoners do the beatings. Those who agreed to beat the others would get extra rations. In the winter of 1941–42, around the same time that the gassing transports began at Ravensbrück, Else Krug was taken from the punishment block to Koegel's office. He thought he had found the perfect collaborator to carry out his beatings.

"You are to be released from the Punishment Block to carry out floggings."

Else looked at him implacably. "No, Herr Camp Commandant; that's one thing I will not do."

"You dirty whore! You think you can pick and choose. That's a refusal to obey an order."

Else shrugged her shoulders. "If you put it that way . . ."

Koegel was enraged; he was not used to insubordination, except from his hated Jehovah's Witness prisoners. "Take the whore away. You will remember this moment, I promise."[16] A few weeks later, Else, having risked everything because she refused to turn on her fellow prisoners, was taken in one of the first transports for the gas chamber in Bernburg.

BY THE TIME of Else's transport, Grete was no longer room elder of Block 2. She had never really been able to control the women on her side of the block. And the guard who oversaw the block, named Margot Drechsel, did not like her.

As disdainful as Grete might have been of the *Asoziale*, Drechsel felt that Grete was too kind to them. A large portion of the *Asoziale* suffered from mental illnesses. The trauma of their situation led to all kinds of reactions. There were quite a few women who wet their beds. They were badly treated by the other prisoners for this, beaten and yelled at constantly. This only made their anxiety worse, and the problem increased. Similarly, the stress made those with conditions like epilepsy more prone to seizures.

One day, Drechsel was going to write up a report about a prisoner named Lina, who everyone knew was mentally deranged. Lina, an elderly woman with a perpetually worried face and the high voice of child, would be sent to the *Strafblock* and given twenty-five lashes. Grete knew that it would probably kill her.

"Frau SS Leader, you're dealing with a mentally defective. Lina's not responsible for her actions. Everybody knows she's not all there," Grete pleaded.

Drechsel looked up from the report she was writing. This was the last straw. She screamed at Grete, "Your mouth's too big; that's what is the matter with you. Such insolence! And an idiot such as you as room elder—no wonder your side is a pigsty. You've been room elder for too long. I'll report you. Understand? You're dismissed."[17]

The following day, Grete was told to report to Johanna Langefeld's office. Grete did not know at the time that Langefeld and Koegel were battling over control of the camp through the assignment of block elders. Ever since their resistance at Lichtenburg Castle, Koegel had hated the Jehovah's Witnesses. Nothing he did—not beatings, not threats, not starvation—could get them to budge. He had placed one of his favorite prisoners, Käthe Knoll, as elder over the Jehovah's Witness block, hoping she could brutalize them into submission. One of the most vicious and cruel prisoners, she had become infamous for her brutality. And she had succeeded in making the life of the Jehovah's Witnesses a hell.

Langefeld had no problem with the Jehovah's Witnesses. She saw them as model prisoners; they were clean and orderly. She admired their religious conviction. Langefeld's personal secretary, Marianne Korn, was a Jehovah's Witness. From Marianne, Langefeld heard daily reports about the tyrannical Käthe Knoll. Eventually, Marianne was able to bring Langefeld evidence of Knoll's theft—a report that even Koegel could not put aside. Now Langefeld had the opportunity to put in place her own block elder, someone she could trust. Grete's timing could not have been better. Her supposed crime of defending a simpleminded prisoner appealed to Langefeld's sense of her own Christian charity. Plus, Grete fulfilled the requirements: She was a German-speaking political.

When Grete entered the office, Langefeld was staring out the window at the dusty central camp square. She appeared distracted and didn't look at Grete right away. "You are room elder for the *Asoziale*?" she asked, her back to Grete.

"Yes."

Langefeld turned around. "Do you think you are capable of being a block elder?"

Grete was taken aback by the unexpected question. She did not know how to answer. "I don't think so," she stumbled. "I don't think I am suitable. I am already in trouble as a room elder."

Langefeld looked at Grete for a long moment in silence. Perhaps Grete's deep blue eyes and "Aryan beauty" had an effect on her as well. She brushed her forehead several times with her hands, as if pushing hair out of her face, a nervous tic that Grete would later remark became worse over time. "Very well, you will be the block elder for the Bible Students, Block 3."

Then Langefeld, remembering her authority, rapped her desk emphatically with her right palm as she spoke to underline her points. "Now, you must remember Block 3 is the inspection block. And you must pay constant attention to the neatness and orderliness. You never know when there will be an inspection. Everything must be perfect at all times. You are being given an important assignment. Go get your things and take them straightaway to Block 3."[18]

Grete, who had expected punishment, stumbled in bewilderment out of the office and to her promotion.

The Jehovah's Witness Block 3 was on the right-hand side of the camp street, opposite Block 1, the block with all the privileged political prisoners. When Grete entered Block 3, it was silent. She was struck by the smell of cleaning powder, disinfectant, and cabbage soup. The block housed 275 women, and they all sat in rows silently eating their soup. They had placed little cardboard papers beneath their bowls so they wouldn't leave a mark on the table. They had brown paper on the corridor between the tables, and scrapers by the door, where they would scrape off their shoes so that the floor stayed clean. If they entered the dormitory section of the block, they took off their shoes. They all wore their hair pinned back in tight buns. It was worlds from the *Asoziale* block, where Grete had been, and it took a while for her to feel comfortable.

Everything ran smoothly. The prisoners kept the block spotlessly clean. They worked together to fend off any charge of misbehavior from Koegel and his inspections. They were indeed "model prisoners."

Their religious fervor astonished Grete. They tried to convert her, but it was soon clear she was not interested. Perhaps she had had enough of following utopian visions after her experience with communism. And yet she quickly won their confidence. The Jehovah's Witness prisoners understood that with Grete, they had found someone they could trust, and their relationship could be mutually beneficial. Grete allowed them to have Bibles and even helped them find good hiding places for the forbidden books in the block.

Grete remained cynical about their obedience. In some ways, the Jehovah's Witnesses were perfect servants for the Nazis. Though they refused to do any work that was war-related, they were excellent housekeepers for the SS families; they looked after their children; they served as maids; they tended the SS bloodhounds, pigs, chickens, and rabbits. They were industrious, clean, and obedient. But they were also stubborn. All they had to do to gain freedom was sign a piece of paper that said, "I declare herewith that from this day on I no longer consider myself a Bible Student and that I will do nothing to further the interests of the International Association of Bible Students."

Grete couldn't understand why they wouldn't just sign. After all, she reasoned, to them, anything signed under duress had no meaning. But to them, signing the form would be making a pact with the devil. They were willing to die, and indeed, an estimated one thousand would die during the Nazi era for their beliefs.

A recurring theme in Grete's journey through the Gulag and Nazi concentration camp was her lucky timing. Earlier, Grete was sent to the Karaganda Gulag just after the Great Terror: a period of mass shootings among all of Stalin's camps. During the period she was there, the killings had stopped. Grete was handed over to Hitler right before those death rates would rise sharply again, turning the Gulags into gigantic mass graves rivaling those in Nazi-controlled territories. With her lucky new position as block elder for the Bible Students, Grete's life improved, as did her chances of survival. And Milena, the woman whom Grete would later describe as "the content of my life,"[19] would arrive soon.

ON ENTERING RAVENSBRÜCK, Milena Jesenská was put in Block 16, the quarantine block. This group was allowed a few moments of exercise every day at the "Wailing Wall." Grete knew she could find "Milena from Prague" again during the period of quarantine exercise. Grete's green armband allowed her some freedom of movement around the grounds. She began to risk going there to meet with Milena. It was the very beginning of their friendship, and Grete woke each day looking forward to that sliver of time together.

The other moment of the day when Grete could glimpse Milena was at morning roll call. Grete scanned the lineup of prisoners and felt her heart quicken when she saw her. They made direct eye contact across the central square. Without moving their heads or making any sign, they communicated their morning greeting to each other. Soon Grete could spot Milena in any crowd. Without her being conscious of it, her eyes were constantly searching for her. That head of hair, that regal gait, that profile that would turn into the full face of Milena. Grete also, without being fully conscious of it, kept track of where

Milena would be, mentally following the routines of her constrained day. And so Grete lived each day to get to the ultimate moment, when they could talk at the Wailing Wall.

Grete had survived the Gulag and the months in the camp by making friends and alliances. She would always remember Boris, the Lithuanian communist who had helped her get her quota done in Karaganda. He made her laugh and rolled cigarettes for her, but gallantly held the cigarette up for her to lick. They had been good friends for two months, before he was sent to Eastern Siberia. And there had been others all along the way. She had to say goodbye so many times. At parting, knowing they would almost certainly not live to see each other again, the prisoners' farewell was "Remember me."

But this new friendship was different. The sight of Milena seemed to focus the world. It was electric to meet someone who understood her so fully. Grete was entranced by Milena's voice. They could talk forever, if only they were allowed to. There was always more to say, more to share. What was most mysterious about this new friendship was that Milena seemed to feel the same way. She wanted to know everything about Grete. When Grete found her way to the Wailing Wall for a few stolen minutes, Milena's face would light up, and she would begin peppering Grete with questions.

"Tell it to me in order. Let's start where you left off," Milena said. Despite the gray pallor of her skin and her swollen hands and ankles, she smiled at Grete as if they were carefree and had all the time in the world.

How was it possible, Grete wondered, that Milena, who had just arrived to this horror, could maintain her cheerfulness and curiosity? The first month was the hardest. Grete had seen it many times. Most people cracked during the initial period of imprisonment. The change in their lives was so abrupt and rude. It took time to find equilibrium and adjust to the horror. Milena, though ill on arrival, appeared unruffled. She could be anywhere and she would remain herself.

Grete felt the pleasure of Milena's intense focus. And she admired the journalist in her, the way she listened and prodded Grete for details. Milena seemed to pull out of Grete long-forgotten memories with just a few chosen words.

"So tell me, how long did you believe in the Communist Party? The Comintern and all that? How long did the dream last that the Soviet Union was the model for a better world?"

The way Milena put it, parroting the party rhetoric, Grete knew she understood, that Milena had once believed the same thing. Grete remembered the exhilaration of believing in a greater purpose. Right after the Great War, when she was only nineteen, she had started teaching at a kindergarten for working-class children. Her father owned a brasserie in Berlin, and they were relatively well-off. Her mother was from a small village in Bavaria, but her father had done well in imperial Germany. "We had nice clothes and plenty of food," she told Milena. "We were petty bourgeois." She admitted this like a confession, still feeling the sting of the communist snub. And feeling the relief of being vulnerable to Milena.

At the end of the First World War, after years of bloodshed and destruction, the German Empire had sued for peace. This sparked a revolution among Germany's soldiers and workers, snowballing into mass demonstrations that toppled Germany's kaiser. Suddenly, seemingly overnight, the empire was no longer; Germany was a republic. The old order was gone and new possibilities were emerging. There was wild hope alongside severe economic hardship, with dizzying levels of rising inflation. Grete's family, though affected, maintained a relatively stable financial position. But she witnessed real poverty for the first time in the faces of the starving children in the kindergarten where she worked. "I felt guilty for my wealth, for the inequality," she told Milena.

Grete had grown up in Potsdam, which had been the sumptuous residence of Prussian royalty and the emperor. More than Berlin, "the second capital" symbolized the greatness of the Germanic civilization. Over a thousand years old, Potsdam was known for its palaces, wide tree-lined boulevards, lakes, and sublime views. Meant to glorify the Age of Enlightenment with the ideal balance between nature and reason, it had been created by the best of German thought and talent.

It lost a little of its special status at the end of the First World War when the emperor abdicated and Germany became a republic. But it still held symbolic importance. In 1933, when the Nazis seized power, the ceremonial handshake between Hitler and Hindenburg, which sealed the deal, putting the military firmly in the hands of the Nazis, took place in Potsdam's Garrison Church.

Grete grew up in this milieu, and she witnessed Potsdam's fall from grace. Her father was authoritarian and severe, which awakened in her a longing for freedom and a sympathy for the oppressed. Her mother, on the other hand, was liberal and well-read. Grete felt supported by her mother's gentleness. Her childhood in these perfect tree-lined streets and manicured gardens must have felt like a farce once she was captivated by revolutionary fervor. This perfection of Germanic ideals was fatally flawed, hypocritical. She rejected her father's life and his admiration for all things Prussian. She was ashamed of his nostalgia for the old empire. All those old pompous noblemen had led thousands of the young men to slaughter in the trenches and then the rest of the population into abject poverty. Her father's idea of Prussian superiority was sanctimonious and dishonest.

She and her sister Babette joined the *Wandervogel*, youth groups that were formed in the early twentieth century by high schoolers. They were not overtly political, rather focused on sports, spending time outdoors in nature, and romantic humanitarianism. Grete, who had moved to Berlin as a young woman, witnessed this new democracy as it was ceaselessly challenged. Germany was on its knees and forced to pay to the rest of Europe impossible sums for war damages. Grete admitted to Milena that she was never really interested in the Communist Party ideology, but she was drawn to the fervor and passion of the people around her. She was inspired by the example and writing of the revolutionary socialist and humanist Rosa Luxemburg.

"I translated Rosa Luxemburg," Milena told her, "into Czech." And then Milena quoted Rosa to Grete, "'Freedom is always and exclusively freedom for the one who thinks differently.'"

Grete felt a thrill of recognition. The two new friends shared this, their great admiration for Rosa Luxemburg for her bravery and insight.

To be a woman when there were only men in power all round her. And Rosa had criticized the Bolsheviks.

"Stalin hated her," Grete whispered.

"Which I take as an endorsement." Milena smiled.

They were sickened by the massacre and waste of young men's lives in the First World War.

Rosa had railed against the Great War, calling all workers to strike instead of going to war for their imperial masters. They had not followed Rosa's call to refuse conscription, and they had been butchered by the hundreds of thousands, used as cannon fodder. An entire generation of young men wasted, and a country destroyed. Inspired by Rosa, Grete joined the Communist Youth League in 1921, where she met her first husband, Rafael Buber, the son of the famous Jewish humanist philosopher Martin Buber. Rafael was as idealistic as Grete.

Martin Buber, the father, had formed the Socialist League in 1908, and like Rosa Luxemburg, he had called for a general strike before the Great War. In 1923, he had written his most famous work, *I and Thou*, which describes a relational dynamic that allows each to be their authentic self without objectification. For Buber, the "I-Thou" relationship was the only way to experience God and was an antidote to the isolation and materiality of modernity. Buber would later flee the Nazis to Palestine. After the war, he advocated for an open state of Israel, criticizing the Israeli treatment of Arabs. Buber's engagement with the political reality was always focused on the religious relationship of the self to God and the community. This would not be the direction of Grete's political engagement, which, with the fervor of youth, would draw her to more concrete action and doctrine.

Despite their revolutionary yearnings, Grete and her sister were following the traditional path laid out for them. Babette was also married. They were allowed a suitable amount of studies and a few years of an acceptable job, such as kindergarten teacher, and then they were to have children and be satisfied housewives. Grete gave birth to her first daughter, Barbara, soon after her marriage and a second daughter, Judith, in 1924. Judith was born in Heppenheim at the home of Grete's in-laws, Martin and Paula Buber. Grete and Rafael lived there for a year, but she chafed in her in-laws' home. Amid her political awakening, her marriage faltered. In 1926, she joined the KPD, the Communist Party of Germany, and worked in the office of a paper of the Communist International, or Comintern.

The winds of revolution were in the air. The sisters were enraged by the brutal murder of Rosa Luxemburg, and inspired by the hope that out of such misery and humiliation, Germany's workers would finally unite and rise up. Lenin, Trotsky, and the other leaders of the Russian Revolution believed that the true world revolution would come only when industrial countries, like Germany, had their own revolutions. Both sisters were captivated by utopian visions of the future, and drawn to more radical men than their husbands. Babette would soon become the companion of Willi Münzenberg, a young leader in the German Communist Party.

In a bitter divorce, Grete lost the custody of her two daughters to her husband's parents. Grete did not leave much of a record of what she felt about her divorce and the loss of her girls, but in an interview many years later, when asked why she kept the name Buber all her life, she responded that she had divorced her mother-in-law, not really her husband.[20]

In 1929, Grete met Heinz Neumann at Willi's apartment. He was brilliant, handsome, and radical. Grete thought his blue eyes and brown hair contradicted everything most Germans thought about the "Jewish type." For German communists like them, nothing less than dedicating their entire life to the cause was acceptable. Both sisters would leave their traditional paths and follow these men into more strident politics.

Grete described to Milena how swept up she was by Heinz's charm. Before she met him, he had been sent by Stalin on an ill-fated mission to China to begin the revolution there. Ill-prepared and ill-conceived, the mission ended with a bloodbath. Heinz barely escaped with his life. On his return to Berlin, he was denounced as the "butcher of Canton" by fellow communists. The central committee investigated him, and in the end, the blame was put on the Chinese Communist

Party members. With his customary flare for warping language, Stalin proclaimed that Heinz's survival was a "victorious retreat."

For a brief period, Heinz was elected to the Reichstag in Germany, before the Communist Party was outlawed and driven underground. During this time, Heinz felt Stalin was underestimating the danger of the rising Nazi Party. He would write letters to Moscow begging Stalin to pay closer attention to Hitler's rise. "Heinz said, 'Beat the fascists wherever you meet them,'" Grete whispered to Milena. "He knew what was coming."

Heinz was reprimanded and scapegoated, blamed for the failure of the German Communist Party. He was sent on another hopeless mission to Spain. Meanwhile, Grete worked as a courier for the party. And she was pleased when the party sent her to Spain so she and Heinz could see each other. She would always recall the sunny Mediterranean sky, her first discovery of the scent of orange blossoms, and the sight of branches laden with citrus fruit. They had a brief happy interlude together.

The Spanish Civil War, with all its factions and strange alliances, was where idealists lost their innocence. As W. H. Auden would later write, "Nobody I know who went to Spain during the Civil War who was not a dyed-in-the-wool Stalinist came back with his illusions intact." Heinz was the exception that proved Auden's rule: As a staunch Stalinist, he managed to remain a loyal believer in the party. Grete and Milena agreed, it took several shocks for staunch communists to see what was so painfully obvious: that Stalin was a despot and a dictator who had hijacked the revolution.

Heinz had been sent to Spain to repair his standing among his comrades. It was another disastrous mission. Grete explained to Milena how this was done. Loyal party members were sent to execute impossible orders. If you refused, you would be labeled a traitor, and when you failed, you had to submit yourself to central committee investigation, a self-inventory of guilt. You were always to blame.

From the lengthy self-examination and interrogations, you were forced to promise to accept the next task in order to redeem yourself. You had to admit your bourgeois tendencies hadn't been completely expunged from your character. Never was the mission itself questioned. Everything that came from Moscow was without fault.

With Milena's questioning, Grete was reminded of her early creeping doubts. Decisions were made far away, with little understanding of the situation on the ground. Doubting Moscow was the same as doubting Stalin himself. And so the party members fumbled from one horrific mission to the next while their comrades were called back to Moscow and disappeared.

Heinz's mission in Spain was a farce, and he begged the central party to allow him some independence to achieve at least minimal results. By the end of November 1933, he and Grete received a telegram to leave Madrid via Zurich. From there, they would wait for their opportunity to return to Moscow. The Nazis were now in control of Germany. And Heinz was wanted by the Gestapo. Heinz and Grete convinced themselves that the Soviet Union was the only anti-fascist power able to stand up and fight Hitler. They felt they had no choice but to continue faithfully following Stalin's orders.

On their way to Zurich, they passed through Paris and visited Grete's sister Babette. Willi and Babette had barely escaped arrest in Berlin when the Nazis came to power. In March 1933, ten thousand communists had been arrested and sent to the first concentration camps. Willi and Babette had fled to Paris, where Willi was gathering evidence that the Nazis were behind the burning of the Reichstag and publishing anti-Nazi articles. Grete learned that in March, her ex-father-in-law's apartment, where her two daughters now lived, had been raided by the Nazis.

Willi was no longer blindly following orders from Moscow. He told Heinz that there were rumors about him. Party members were calling him a "moral deviationist." Willi warned the two that arrest awaited if they returned to Moscow. He begged them to stay in Paris. They could work with Willi clandestinely fighting the Nazis in Germany. But for Heinz, to live outside of the party was unthinkable. As Arthur Koestler wrote, "Political neurosis carries its own Iron Curtain."

For a time while Heinz was in Zurich, the Gestapo tried to have him extradited to Germany. No other European country would have him, and the Swiss said his visa would soon expire. The Soviets magnanimously offered to take him. While these negotiations were happening, Grete spent several weeks with her sister in Paris. By the time she met up with Heinz in transit toward Moscow on a boat leaving from Le Havre, she dreaded their arrival in Russia.

Grete recounted to Milena how she and Heinz talked during the ten days of the sea crossing. Grete told Heinz the stories she had heard from other exiles in Paris. There was so much evidence, they couldn't all be lying. "They will probably arrest us when we land," he said, resigned to his fate. She had believed so fervently in the revolution. She had even sacrificed her children for the party. Or she told herself she was doing it *for* them, to make the world a better place for *them*. She was heartbroken.

Willi was also being called to return to Moscow. But he chose to ignore the orders, and with his impressive network of exiled German communists, he would put in place some of the early resistance groups against Hitler. Willi's network arranged for the first clandestine photographs of concentration camps to be taken and published.

GRETE TOLD MILENA her story in installments because she could not stay too long at the Wailing Wall. She tried to keep their time together short so that it would not be noticed. Ever since the interview with Minna Rupp and the other communists, she knew that it was dangerous for Milena to be too closely associated with her. But Milena ignored Grete's warnings with a little laugh and shrug of her shoulders.

Grete worried about Milena. She was too nonchalant, and furthermore, Grete was horrified by her pallor and her swollen hands. It was getting worse as she endured the cold and the long roll calls. Grete wanted to help her new friend. She needed to express her gratitude, her feelings. Knowing how much Milena must be suffering, Grete tried to slip her a roll of bread. Milena pushed her hand away. "No!" There was real disdain and shock in Milena's voice. "We are here to talk about you."

"But I just want to help." Grete was startled by Milena's vehemence.

"No!" Milena said forcefully. As if to say, *This is not what I want at all, not your token of friendship.* Grete felt a sting of shame, her face flushed. Why did Milena refuse her bread? Worried she had offended her, Grete tried to apologize and stumbled over her words. Her whole body prickled with panic. She did not want to lose her new friend.

"I meant no harm," she whispered, desperate to be back on good terms. "I didn't mean to insult you."

Later she would understand that for Milena, friendship meant complete sacrifice. She wanted to be the more giving, not the needy weaker one in the relationship. Milena was jealous of anyone else around Grete. And soon enough, Grete would be jealous of Milena's other camp friends. From the beginning, both wanted to exist solely for the other, to be the one the other needed.

Milena saw the look of fear in Grete's face and regretted her reaction. "Don't fret, Gretuška. I know you didn't mean it as an insult. It's just that . . . Let's keep talking. Tell me about Heinz. Did you love him very much?"

Grete began to speak but then stopped. She couldn't open her mouth. She fingered the bread in her pocket that she had hoped would make Milena so happy. Grete felt tears stinging her eyes. They were her first tears in many years. She shook her head. She didn't want to allow the tears, but they had broken through uninvited. They were tears of relief that Milena had forgiven her. But they were mixed with the memories of what Milena had asked: Heinz. Did she love him?

It had been three and a half years since that April night in their Moscow hotel room when the NKVD police, forerunners of the KGB, banged on the door. She and Heinz had waited for that fatal knock since their arrival in Russia months earlier.

They were surprised it had not come sooner. Instead of being arrested when they first got off the boat, they were housed in Hotel Lux with all the expatriate communists who had been called back to Moscow. In 1936, they were assigned jobs as translators of the transcripts of the first show trial of a Comintern publisher. They didn't comment on the absurdity of those transcripts. They kept their heads down. All around them in the Hotel Lux, among the expats, the atmosphere was thick with fear and paranoia.

Heinz was called in to report to the NKVD office several times to do a self-inventory and list his crimes against the revolution. He was asked to denounce others. He would be taken away and then return to their small room in the Hotel Lux shaken and distraught. Soviet records, released only after the fall of the Soviet Union, reveal what Grete never knew: Heinz did confess and did denounce other people in the hotel. He was desperate to get back into the good graces of the party. Besides these sessions with the secret police, during this time, Heinz rarely left their room. They spent all their time together. Grete remembered this as when their bond was the strongest. She had shifted her betrayed love for the party to loving Heinz. For that small time in Moscow, he was almost all the human contact she had. She didn't speak Russian yet, though she would learn it quickly out of necessity in the year to come. She needed Heinz to translate for her. Since they were regarded as "politically unreliable," they had very few friends. And so it was the two of them in that tiny room waiting for the knock.

Marriages made you vulnerable. Grete did not tell Milena how she too was taken from time to time and asked to denounce her own husband. She and Heinz had whispered about it, knowing their rooms were bugged. Since Heinz had already "confessed" to his earlier sins and "false views," she signed a paper saying that, in 1933, she had tried "to persuade him to correct his deviations and return completely to the party line." Everybody, even husbands and wives, was denouncing each other.

Stalin loved the concept of the self-inventory and the confession. It became the signature measuring stick of each successive secret police organization: the GPU, the NKVD, and the KGB. The truth didn't matter; the number of confessions did. The confession was a marker of success, no matter what methods were used to get it. Conspiracy theories were whispered when people dared speak. Good friends disappeared suddenly, and afterward, no one mentioned their names.

The pervasive fear of saying the wrong thing, slipping up, suddenly being in the crosshairs of the secret police, was similar to the atmosphere the Nazis had created in Germany among its citizens. In the Gulag, Grete would meet a woman whose only crime appeared to be that she had used a newspaper with a photograph of Stalin to light a fire.

The Hotel Lux was packed with foreign Comintern members. Many were German KPD members who had successfully fled the Nazis. More members of the German Communist Party leadership would be killed by Stalin than by Hitler. They were like trapped mice batted around by a fickle cat, and they turned on each other. Heinz and Grete had seen others hauled away in the middle of the night. They knew how people disappeared, and those who were left behind, their wives or family or friends, were outcasts. No one would speak to them for fear of further retribution by the Soviet police.

With the pounding on the door of their hotel room, Grete tried to shake Heinz awake. He could sleep through anything. She had marveled and then resented the way he slept hours and hours while she paced their small room. Now, with the police at the door, she could not rouse him. The police broke the latch on the door and were in their room. The head officer shook Heinz with much more insistence.

Heinz opened his eyes, startled to see the policeman. He looked at Grete absently, in a daze. It took him a few seconds to realize it was not a nightmare. Then, resigned, he slowly stood up and bowed to the officer.

As Heinz calmly dressed while the police ransacked their room, he admonished her, "Don't look so frightened."

The Soviet police interrupted them; it was forbidden to speak to each other in German. They sat facing each other across the small room. Grete felt stunned. The room had grown dusty with the overturning of all their things. It was April and still very cold in Moscow. Grete felt the draft through the hotel window. She had stuffed towels around the edge to block the cold, but the police had ripped them out too. Interspersed with Russian phrases, Heinz would say something to her in German: "Don't look so miserable and depressed. We shall see each other again, some way or another." He spoke to her with forced cheer, but also with that hardness that he had in him. He always criticized her sentimentality. It was, he said, due to her bourgeois upbringing. "This work," he had told her so many times, "means you must show no weakness. Remember the larger cause is all that matters."

The police stacked piles of papers and books, books by Trotsky, Zinoviev, Bukharin. They found a letter from Stalin to Heinz. "Ah, this makes it worse for him"—they were pleased with their discovery, as the letter proved how far Heinz had fallen from grace. Grete watched as they threw the letters from her children, who would soon flee to Palestine with their grandparents, into the jumble of objects they would confiscate, proof to be used against them.

Then it was time to part. Heinz put on his coat and hat. Grete leaned against the emptied bookshelf to steady herself. Her lips were tight and she clenched her fists, digging her fingernails into her skin, desperately trying to remain calm. When he embraced her, she felt a sob bursting through, choking her breath. "Don't cry," Heinz said. "Don't cry."

But in the last moment, just as he was being led out of the room, he turned back to Grete and strode toward her. She threw herself into his arms. His final words to her: "Cry then. There's everything to cry about."[21]

Grete, who had kept the pain of this memory so carefully locked up inside, felt the tears flow down her face. "Yes"—Milena nodded— "there is indeed everything to cry about."

It was a relief to be able to speak about this loss. After not saying anything more for a few minutes, Grete said, "I know he was killed. It's unconfirmed, but I know he's dead. That was the last time I saw him."

Milena brushed the back of Grete's hand with hers, and Grete felt the flush of contact. A shiver up her arm. They let their hands touch a few more times. Brush against each other softly. Milena sighed. Grete bit her lip. They walked in silence, alert to the guards and the other prisoners around them. And after one long brush when they let their hands linger touching for several steps, Milena shifted away slightly. After a moment, she asked, "What did you do next?"

Grete wanted to grab her hand, put it to her cheek. Instead, she stared at the ground. "I need to go. I've been here too long." And with that, Grete ran away, her heart pounding in her chest.

In the low hum of the Jehovah's Witnesses whispering their prayers that night, Grete felt her hand where they had touched. She tried to stop her heart racing. There was nothing in it, and there was everything in it. The gentle touch of a friend. These powerful feelings frightened her. She couldn't possibly be one of *those women*. They had to be careful that they wouldn't be mistaken—they must never be mistaken—for the other. Her enemies could not use it to report them. Because it was against the rules, the other thing: "Approaching another prisoner with lesbian intentions, engaging in lesbian debauchery, or failing to report such acts was punished" by flogging of twenty-five lashes.

She couldn't sleep. She felt exhilaration at the thought of Milena's touch, then dread at the thought of what it meant, and then fear if they were ever caught. Her dear Milena, she knew, would never survive a flogging.

THE NEXT DAY, when they met at the Wailing Wall, Grete continued the story. After Heinz was arrested, she lost her job and eventually the room where they lived. She had no way to make money. And they had taken her passport, so she couldn't leave the country. Her sister and Willi in Paris were able to get her a visa, but the Soviets refused to return her passport. She was trapped. She slowly sold off everything, bit by bit. With no way to work, nowhere to live, those were terrible days in Moscow. For almost a year, she survived like that. Most of their old friends did not dare to speak with her. She didn't blame them. But of course those friends also ended up being taken away in the middle of the night, just like Heinz.

Grete went from prison to prison, waiting in long lines, trying to find him, trying to give the allowed fifty rubles a month so that he could buy extra food and other necessities in prison. "They said without money, a prisoner in Lubyanka doesn't eat. There were so many others like me, in the same situation as me. Widows, even children who had both parents taken away. We were all standing in those endless lines. Frozen, starving, but begging to hand over our package and some rubles."

Heinz was arrested in April 1937. Records revealed after the dissolution of the USSR show that in November, he made a last desperate attempt to save himself, writing a note in his cell enthusiastically supporting Stalin's cleansing efforts against "all counter-revolutionary criminals and traitors." But the Great Terror was in full force. He couldn't "confess" his way to saving his life. Stalin's "cleansing" would eventually claim an estimated one million lives between 1937 and 1938.

On November 26, 1937, Heinz was put in front of a military tribunal, where he pleaded guilty of all the charges against him. Like a good Soviet, he confessed, and he was shot later that same day. Moscow would pass an order to liquidate Willi, Grete's brother in-law, that same month, but at the time, he was out of the Soviet reach. He was working from France, organizing and writing about the Nazis. The last article Willi was able to publish before going underground in 1939 was a warning to the French that Germany was going to invade. Willi would eventually be killed by Soviet spies during the war while he was working in the French Resistance.[22]

THERE WAS A spot along the path by the Wailing Wall where Grete and Milena were slightly sheltered from the direct sight of the guards. When they realized this, they would slow their steps at that moment. They did not have to say anything. They would just let the backs of their hands touch. Grete told herself they shouldn't risk it, but then, each day, she did. Once, Grete surprised herself by hooking her finger around one of Milena's fingers, and for a few moments, they walked slyly peeking at each other.

"Your finger is so cold," Grete whispered.

"Oh, Grete, I am always cold," Milena said, laughing. They were dizzying, these moments of risk and intimacy.

Then they dropped their hooked fingers, walked back to where they could be watched, and behaved as they had to, talking under their breath and carrying on with the story.

ALONG WITH THE political upheaval that Grete experienced during the Weimar period between the two world wars, there was a parallel sexual revolution in German society. From 1919 to 1933 was a time of unprecedented freedom for gender-nonconforming individuals. The poet W. H. Auden moved to Berlin in 1928 because there he had found a place where he could live openly, embracing his sexuality. There was a history of broad-mindedness about differences in sexuality. The term itself, "homosexual," or German "*homosexualität*," was first coined in an 1869 pamphlet arguing against the Prussian anti-sodomy laws.[23] The groundbreaking Institute for Sexual Science, led by Magnus Hirschfeld, was formed in June 1919, less than a year after the fall of the monarchy and the formation of a constitutional democracy. A core belief of Hirschfeld and other members of the institute was that scientific study, not religious morality, should dictate how society and the state dealt with sexuality. He believed that sexual anomalies were natural, "purely biological, not pathological." The institute was an important beacon for Auden of the promise of sexual freedom. He would bring visitors there and noted that on his friend Christopher Isherwood's first day in Berlin, Auden introduced him to the museum of sexual artifacts inside the Institute for Sexual Science. Berlin was the home of the first homosexual rights organization, the first gay journal, and the first sexual reassignment surgery.

A large number of gay and lesbian bars opened in Berlin during that twenty-year period. Ruth Margarete Roellig wrote a guidebook, *Berlin's Lesbian Women*, in 1928. A queer press emerged. Transvestite magazines, homosexual literature, and lesbian journals contributed to a thriving queer culture.

Two of the best-known publications for lesbians were *Freundin* and *Garçonne*. They passed on information about how to find and join a social club, and how to dress. They advertised parties. One prominent lesbian, Lotte Hahm, was often pictured in advertisements for her events on the back page of *Freundin* in a suit and tie, with her hair slicked back. She led the Violetta social club, and one of the most anticipated annual events was her summer moonlight cruise. The journals had political appeals, readers' letters, and debates on bisexuality, the nature of friendship, and other issues. Most important were the personal stories. Through reading the testimonials of other women who loved each other, lesbians could imagine their own lives and discover themselves. During this period, lesbians could and did create a community for themselves. But these new publications were sometimes banned due to the personal ads. It was feared that homosexuality could be contagious, and the personal ads were the method for the isolated to find a community.

The new openness and tolerance came with nebulous limitations. What would be allowed in one city at one time would be banned in another place for going too far. The boundaries of tolerance were constantly shifting. The queer culture thrived in this liminal space, at least relative to how they had been treated before and would be treated afterward by the Nazis. Hirschfeld's institute would be one of the first targets of the Nazi Party when, only a few months after Hitler became chancellor in 1933, it was ransacked, pillaged, and the institute's books and materials provided fuel for the book burning at the Opernplatz four days later.

The end of the war did not end the intolerance of queers. The perceived decadence in the historiography after the war blamed the sexual freedom of Weimar culture for the Nazi backlash. The narrative went that the perversion of the Nazis developed directly from Weimar Germany and the outrageous sexual liberty of the depraved queer community. One kind of behavior, seen as too morally free, would inevitably lead to another kind of moral decay. Movies like *Cabaret* are part of this imagining of history. The Nazi exploitation film genre emerged in the 1960s and '70s, with art house films like *The Night Porter* and *Ilsa: She Wolf of the SS*. Moviegoers could expect films featuring sexualized prison guards, a cruel lesbian commandant, and a sadistic doctor. The genre deliberately links political deviance with sexual deviance. In survivor accounts from this period, highly improbable stories of orgies among the *Asoziale* lesbians and SS guards are recounted. In the history of memory, it is disturbing to note the increase in sexualizing depictions of the Nazis came during the period of sexual liberation a generation later. Memory is always in dialogue with the present moment.

Another problem, which has repercussions to this day in the research and writing about women loving women in the camps, was the legal status of lesbians versus that of male homosexuals during the war. Male homosexuality was explicitly illegal in the German criminal code through the text known as Paragraph 175: "Unnatural sexual acts (*widernatürliche Unzucht*) committed between persons of the male sex, or by humans with animals, is punishable with imprisonment; a loss of civil rights may also be sentenced." Paragraph 175 was part of the code from 1871 until 1994, and only dropped after East and West Germany reunited as the Federal Republic of Germany.

Putting aside the conflation of homosexuality with bestiality, throughout the history of this law, legal experts had ongoing, confounding, and rather ridiculous discussions about what constituted fornication. Phallocentric and bewildered lawmakers firmly held that at the center of fornication, there had to be penetration. Then they tied themselves up in knots trying to decide what could be considered as penetrative sex. What about a penis between two thighs? What about masturbation between two men? What about oral sex?

Nazi authorities were baffled with what to do about female homosexuality, since in their minds there was no penetration. Thus, two women together could not be having "real" sex. Some argued that "Aryan" gay women could still be made to produce children for the nation. As long as they fulfilled their role in society, where was the problem?

Women were largely perceived as not having a sexuality—if their friendships were overly passionate, that could be cured simply by the introduction of a penis and heterosexual sex. Because women were not full citizens and not seen as sexual, gay women were not, at least legally, seen as posing a problem to the body politic.

Because lesbianism wasn't addressed explicitly in the legal code, some male gay activists after the war argued that lesbians were not persecuted by the Nazis. Since 2012, lesbian activists have tried to place a small commemorative orb, *"Gedenkkugel,"* at Ravensbrück with the inscription: "In memory of all lesbian women and girls in the Ravensbrück and Uckermark women's concentration camps. They were persecuted, imprisoned and even murdered. You are not forgotten." Until recently, their efforts to place the *Gedenkkugel* were met with controversy and their requests denied. A few male gay activists argued that a memorial for lesbian women would create the "myth of lesbian persecution."

Only in 2021 did the management of the Ravensbrück Memorial and the board of directors of the Brandenburg Memorials Foundation approve the installation. A ceramic ball was placed in the new memorial area on the former camp wall in spring 2022, as part of the observance of the seventy-seventh anniversary of the camp's liberation.

Officially, Nazi authorities did not recognize that female homosexuality could exist, but in reality, lesbians were persecuted. They were considered a corrupting influence on the wholesome "Aryan" nation. As with male homosexuality, there was a belief that the deviant behavior could spread like a virus. Youths could be seduced into the homosexual way of life. And lesbians had to navigate the deeply patriarchal society where women's roles were narrowly defined. In such a society, women were de facto oppressed. As Ruth Margarete Roellig wrote in her guidebook entry for the Violetta club, "Aside from the already terrible difficulties suffered by these women—who live more or less in economic dependence—because of estrangement from their parents, problems at work, and their being regarded as socially inferior, the worst forms of blackmail will thus be given free rein—and some would prefer death to life . . ."[24] Lesbians' invisibility in the German legal code mirrored an invisibility and isolation in society, which made them especially vulnerable.

German society under the National Socialist Party was oppressed and paranoid. People watched each other and turned on each other. Lesbians were denounced by neighbors. To argue that lesbians were not persecuted as lesbians is to ignore the fact that anyone who varied from normative behavior was suspect and vulnerable, and unmarried women were especially powerless. Women who ended up in the camp for their "deviant inhuman acts" were often arrested on other criminal charges, such as prostitution or vagrancy. The categories for marginal powerless women were almost interchangeable.

Being a lesbian might not have been explicitly illegal in the German criminal code, but it was explicitly illegal within the camps. Grete knew that the regulations in Ravensbrück stated "anyone who approaches other prisoners in a lesbian manner or who engages in lesbian obscenities, or who fails to report such activities" was to be punished.

Like in society at large during the Weimar era, homosexuality that was discreet and out of the public view was tolerated. Public appearances were what mattered to the Nazis, at least at first. It was an open secret that one of Hitler's closest early allies, Ernst Röhm, was a homosexual. Involved in the bungled Beer Hall Putsch in 1923, Röhm was a comrade of Hitler's from the beginning. In 1930, Hitler convinced him to lead the storm troopers, the SA or Brownshirts, and he rose with the party as a leading fascist, right-wing extreme antisemite. As long as Röhm did not "flaunt his sexuality in public," did not "corrupt youth," and did not "knowingly infect others with venereal disease," his private life was his own business. Röhm's demise came not for his homosexuality but due to infighting in the high ranks of the Nazi Party. Röhm and Himmler were rivals for Hitler's attention and control of the party. Himmler saw Röhm's SA Brownshirts as having too much power. During the Night of the Long Knives in 1934, Hitler, convinced by Röhm's rivals Himmler and Göring that the paramilitary SA had become too powerful, ordered Himmler's elite SS guards to murder SA leaders, including his old comrade Ernst Röhm. This was the beginning of Hitler's consolidation of all power into an absolute dictatorship that would go on to convict fifty thousand men of the "crime" of sodomy and send fifteen thousand alleged male homosexuals to concentration camps, where many were murdered.[25]

Precise numbers of how many women were deported or killed for their lesbianism, versus or along with other reasons, is impossible to calculate. Trying to compare the numbers and thus somehow calculate suffering is a useless endeavor. It does not get to the central truth about the intersectionality of persecution—that is the many ways women were controlled, oppressed, silenced, and made invisible. Isabel Meusen wrote, "The mechanisms of Nazi persecution directed at lesbians were mainly grounded in psychological terror and torment. Fear of attracting attention by falling outside the prescribed norm silenced lesbian women and drove them into invisibility . . . The repercussions of silencing through psychological pressures as exerted on lesbians by National Socialists lasted long into the 1970s, leaving a gap of apparent nonexistence."[26]

MILENA AWAITED GRETE each day at the Wailing Wall. And Grete continued her story, explaining when she knew Heinz had been killed or deported. It was in December 1937. Grete showed up at Lubyanka to pay the fifty rubles and give a package for her husband. She was told he was "no longer here." She wasn't told that he was already dead, but she suspected it. She was finally arrested in June 1938, seven months later.

She spent a year in various Moscow prisons awaiting her "trial" and eventual sentencing. She was interrogated four times, and each time there were outlandish accusations of her plotting against the Soviets, spying for the Nazis, working with all the foreign capitalists. She finally received her sentence along with a group of eight women whom she had befriended in the crowded prison cell. One by one, they were called out by name, and the judge announced their social status: Grete was a "socially dangerous element"—quite a similar term to "*Asoziale.*" It is unclear if she recognized the irony of this label later when in Ravensbrück the *Asoziale* were seen as less than political prisoners. The Soviet judge pronounced her sentence: Five years at a reformatory labor camp. The women were stunned; they had all received sentences of five, seven, even ten years of hard labor.

Their transport took two weeks on several overcrowded trains. They had almost no food or water. Sometimes the train stopped for a whole day in the sun and they sweltered inside. Once they were past the Urals, the guards finally told them they were being taken to KarLag, or the Karaganda Corrective Labor Camp, the largest camp complex at the time. When Grete arrived at Karaganda in 1939, she was one of thirty-five thousand prisoners there.

"When I learned I was going to Karaganda, I wept," Grete told Milena. "I couldn't believe I was going so far away from everyone I loved. I was sobbing and the guard took pity on me. He said, 'Don't cry. It won't be as bad as all that. You'll get home again.'" Telling this to Milena now made her and then Milena laugh.

"You had everything to cry about," Milena agreed, echoing Heinz's final words to Grete.

"In the main reception center at the Gulag, after the first few days, my friend Grete Sonntag and I found a place to sleep. A terribly cold hut with a miserable stove and frozen lump of coal. I went looking for wood to start a fire. And I found a crate. I almost got knocked out for taking that crate, but then as I was trying to chop up the frozen lump of coal the axe handle flew off. It almost hit me right in the head. Think of it. That would have saved me all of this trouble!"

Grete was laughing, but Milena shook her head. "No, it's not funny, Grete. Imagine if I got here and you weren't here for me. What would I do without you?"

The sincere way she said it made Grete blush.

"No more saying things like that, please," Milena admonished her.

"I just wanted you to know what an innocent I was in those early days in the Gulag. We needed to work. Because if we didn't work we had no money and there wasn't food really if you didn't have money. It wasn't like here, organized and orderly. You had to figure it all out yourself. My friend and I decided to try to work in the laundry because at least there we could wash ourselves and maybe get rid of the lice we had from the transport. The man running the laundry gave us two tiny slivers of soap, a pile of men's clothes, crawling with lice. We boiled them and then as we were washing them, scrubbing with our soap he stopped us. I think he felt sorry for us. He said, 'You obviously don't know. Keep the soap for yourself, it's worth money around here. Just boil the clothes, that's enough.' We agreed that we didn't need to bring innovations to the Gulag with the use of soap."

Grete told Milena about the flowers blooming on the steppes. Irises and red roses and other wildflowers in all kinds of colors. Milena loved flowers.

"I wish I could show you. If you could ignore the misery of the camp, it was beautiful. And at night! The dome of stars at night. The sky was so beautiful and vast there."

"I can imagine," Milena said. They both enjoyed the sky above Ravensbrück and the branches of the trees around the lake. "How they are like arms reaching up to heaven," Milena said with admiration.

Grete told her about the brief happy time she was put in charge of the care of the water oxen Vaisya and Mishka. "They liked me because I didn't beat them. And when we were out of sight of the guards I let them sit and graze while I gathered wild berries. But it was awful trying to get them to stand again." And she had to get to the water, fill up the pails, and return to where they were making clay bricks before the foreman noticed she had been gone too long.

She told Milena about the bedbugs and lice. They were everywhere in large swarming clumps under the boards of the bed, and crawling up the sides of the huts like ants scrambled from their nests. So many she could smell them. "They feasted on your body."

There was no water for washing yourself. Sometimes women would try to steal a small can of water and quickly wash themselves where it was most urgent. But there was dirt in all their pores and creases. People were covered in boils and infected bites.

They worked all the time. The mission of Karaganda was agricultural, established during Stalin's murderous collectivism campaign with the impossible and ill-conceived goal of turning the steppes into fertile fields of crops. They were trying to grow crops that could not survive the hot, dry summers. There were many peasant farmers in the camp who knew the whole mission was doomed, but they could say nothing. They had already lost their own farms due to collectivism.

"We had two days off a year, May Day and the November anniversary of the Revolution. The other days of relief came when Nature brought us a sandstorm or a snowstorm."

The world of the Gulag was vast and spread across the entire Soviet Union. The worst were the corrective labor camps that held roughly 1.3 million people during this period. The KarLag complex covered 17,600 square kilometers (6,800 square miles) and stretched across the Kazakhstan steppe. The Karaganda Gulag was established in 1931 and would operate until 1959. Over one million prisoners would pass through the gates. Many political prisoners ended up here, including author and Nobel Prize winner Aleksandr Solzhenitsyn, who wrote several works about daily life in the Gulag.

There was little need for barbed wire fences or enclosures; the sheer size and the barrenness of the landscape made surviving escape impossible—except once, Grete recalled to Milena: "There was a nomadic girl from one of the tribes that had roamed the steppes. A real beauty with black hair. She showed me a scar on her neck from where a stallion had bitten her while she was breaking him in. She loved horses and she managed to steal one. Somehow, she fell in love with a short thick communist bureaucrat from Moscow and they managed to run away together. Such an unlikely couple! She knew how to cross the steppes and where to find her nomadic family."

Milena loved this story. She marveled at how people found each other in such unexpected places.

MILENA LIKED TO compare where and what they were doing at different places during the same time. In 1937 and 1938, while Grete was in Moscow and Heinz was arrested, Milena had at last been offered her dream job by Ferdinand Peroutka, the editor of the weekly magazine *Přítomnost* (*The Present*), one of the most respected Czechoslovak newspapers at the time. He asked Milena to write about Czechoslovak national news. Up until then, in the 1920s and '30s, she had been constrained to write about "women's issues." She wrote about fashion and household questions, even cooking, though she was not really a good cook, according to her daughter. For a brief period in the early 1930s, she had flirted with communism and had written for communist magazines. She later claimed that the experience of parroting party propaganda had almost broken her ability to write at all.

With her new job at *Přítomnost*, Milena was able to express her political brilliance. These articles that bear witness to the coming storm show Milena's profound prescience on what the Nazis were planning. In March 1938, she wrote about how a pogrom happens, how ordinary people are exploited and their anger whipped up. She asked with great foresight, "What will we do ourselves," not just the great nations on "an international scale, but on our private scale?" When confronted by fascism, "it is more urgent that we know *how* we want to live and that we consider this *how* to be as important as life itself."[27]

While Grete sat in a Soviet prison awaiting her sentencing and deportation to the Gulag, Milena traveled in the Sudetenland, the northern area along the border with Germany that was the home to thousands of ethnic Germans, but also Jewish Germans and other Jewish émigrés. Milena wrote movingly about the plight of the Jewish immigrants desperate to cross borders and turned away by every country. She described what she called the "cold pogrom" then taking place in Austria, since the *Anschluss*, when German troops entered in March 1938. A cold pogrom was the "pragmatic, calm regulations introduced by the state that do not deprive the Jews of life, but deprive them of any possibility of living."[28] Milena chronicled the slow-moving disaster that was coming.

On September 30, 1938, the now infamous Munich accords were signed between Germany, France, the United Kingdom, and Italy, acquiescing to Hitler's demands and annexing to Germany Czechoslovakia's Sudetenland. Hitler claimed that this area of Czechoslovakia was always meant to be part of Germany and that the three million ethnic Germans who lived there longed to be part of the German fatherland.

For England and France, the agreement was seen as a way of

avoiding war with Germany—the policy known as appeasement. Prime Minister Chamberlain in England and Prime Minister Daladier in France were applauded as heroes who had saved Europe from another disastrous war. *The New York Times* reported that both Daladier and Chamberlain were greeted by cheering crowds when they returned to their home countries. Their actions were approved by the majority of the citizens of Europe. Though later he would be judged more harshly by history, immediately after the Munich accords, Chamberlain received thousands of letters and gifts expressing gratitude. He had preserved the peace of Europe.

Absorbing the blow of this betrayal by the other nations of Europe, Milena wrote in *Přítomnost*:

> When we open the newspapers, we read about the great recognition that Czechoslovakia has won for the sacrifice it has made for world peace. Wrong. We did no such thing because sacrifices are only made voluntarily. The truth is different: we were sacrificed and we have here among us several hundred thousand of the living fallen, together with thousands of German and Austrian refugees to whom we have granted asylum. The responsibility for these fallen does not rest with us but with the French and English governments who wanted this peace.[29]

By giving way to Hitler's demands, the leaders of France and England had removed the only real obstacle to Hitler invading the rest of Czechoslovakia. And they had put in the hands of the German Army a large stock of military armaments that the Czechs and Slovaks had built up to defend themselves. Those very weapons would be essential to Hitler's invasion of the rest of Czechoslovakia, Poland, and France a year later. The agreement also allowed Poland to take a chunk of Czechoslovak territory. The Czechoslovak nation, which had celebrated independence only a decade earlier, now was doomed. And Hitler's dream of controlling all of Europe was invigorated.

Stalin watched the failure of the other countries in Europe to stand together against Hitler, and it scared him. Once Hitler controlled

Europe, what would stop him from annexing parts of Russia? During the Russian Civil War, following the initial revolutionary uprising and assassination of the tsar, the Bolsheviks had somewhat surprisingly turned to the failing Imperial Army of Germany for help. Though sworn ideological enemies, they found a partnership that could be mutually beneficial. Once the German Empire had fallen and Germany lay in ruins, foreign troops occupied the industrial heartland, and Germany was forbidden by the Treaty of Versailles to rebuild their army.

Through the Treaty of Rapallo in 1922, the German aristocratic officer corps came to an agreement with the Soviet Union that allowed them to send soldiers, scientists, and engineers to secret military bases inside Russia.[30] Germany could rebuild in Russia, away from the view of Europe, and they could use the vast Russian resources to do so. The Bolsheviks needed the military knowledge of the old German Empire's army leaders, the Reichswehr. During the decade that followed, and especially during the peak period of cooperation between 1928 and 1932, Germany was able to reconstitute a large standing army and Russia learned how to make and use modern-day weaponry.

The relationship is hard to fathom as they were so ideologically opposed. The Bolsheviks felt that the world revolution would come and saw industrialized Germany, the home of Marx, as the epicenter of the industrialized capitalist world. Hitler's fascism was just the final groans of imperialist capitalism. And on the other side, Hitler saw Russia and the vast expanse of territory as the essential "living space" he needed for his thousand-year empire. The Russian hordes, formerly serfs of the tsars, would be the enslaved people he needed to build the new vast cities.

The German military elite, or the Reichswehr, accepted Hitler's rise to power. They had misgivings about the strange populist fanatic, but they shared his views on rearmament and felt they needed stability after the upheavals of the Weimar period. Hitler called off the agreement with the Soviets. He often ranted against the "Bolshevik Jews," but the years of preparation in Russia allowed him to rearm with surprising speed. He was able to march into the Rhineland, the border territory between France and Germany, occupied by French forces as part of the Versailles Treaty. Fifteen thousand storm troopers marched behind the army formations singing, "For today we own Germany and tomorrow we own the world." Neither France nor the other members of the treaty reacted in any meaningful way. And when it became clear that neither France nor Great Britain would assist the Spanish Republic against the fascist rise of Franco, an emboldened Hitler decided to use the Spanish Civil War as a testing ground for his new weaponry, deployed by the Condor Legion of the Luftwaffe, the German Air Force, whose pilots had been secretly training in the Soviet Union.

Stalin was busy purging and executing his top military leaders, many of whom had trained with the German military. The Soviets aided the Spanish Republicans, but with the chaos of Moscow, their aid was never all that effective. Heinz, Grete's husband, had probably witnessed this and other bewildering ironies while working in Spain.

The German Luftwaffe played a decisive role in Franco's victory, and over twenty thousand German airmen gained combat experience that would give the Luftwaffe an important advantage going into the Second World War.

From the ruins of the German Empire's army only two decades earlier, by 1939, Hitler had at his disposal an army of over three million men, armed with the most advanced weaponry.[31] An army that had been made possible largely because of the strategic partnership between these two ideological enemies.

Now Stalin saw how again and again leaders in Western Europe balked and refused to stand up to Hitler's aggressions. Germany had maintained important trade agreements with the Soviets. Germany imported key raw materials from the USSR, and they were among the most significant trading partners for the Soviets and their isolated fledgling economy. Inevitably, when Hitler moved into Czechoslovakia and then Lithuania and Romania, thus securing for his army a supply of oil, Stalin could see the writing on the wall. He decided to renew the earlier agreement between Russia and Germany. Together,

Molotov, the Soviet foreign minister, and Ribbentrop, the German foreign minister, created a treaty of nonaggression. Part of the pact included the carving up of Central Europe into "spheres of influence" and, most importantly, the partitioning of Poland. On September 1, 1939, now officially known as the start of the Second World War, Germany invaded Poland, and on September 17, Stalin ordered the Red Army to occupy the other half of Poland.

The agreement and the following cooperation sent shock waves through loyal communists around the world. How could Mother Russia ally herself with the fascist Third Reich? How could she allow the workers of Poland to be occupied by Hitler's army? The alliance between these two powers created an essential rift between political prisoners in the early days of the war.

Grete recalled when they heard about the pact in the Gulag. One of her friends declared very loudly, "The Russo-German Friendship pact is a work of a political genius, the greatest act of our great leader Stalin. My admiration for him is unbounded." Grete said that everyone felt embarrassed for him, but they also understood. He had spoken loudly to be heard by whatever spies were around listening.

GRETE'S LIFE WOULD be directly marked by this Faustian bargain.

After two years in the Gulag, she was taken from Karaganda back to Moscow. There followed a brief exhilarating period when she thought she would be freed. The train was a normal train this time: "It was an empty carriage with full-length places reserved for us . . . This time I was excited. I wanted to sing, laugh, whistle, do anything to express my feelings. The train was well-heated."[32] She was crestfallen when they arrived in Moscow and were immediately loaded onto police vans. She had felt almost free, but now she was being taken back to the prison where she had spent the year before she was deported to the Gulag, only this time, she found the prison transformed. It wasn't crowded and dirty. She was taken to a washroom and left alone with as much hot water as she wanted. She was given soap and disinfectant for her head lice. Months and months of Siberian dirt washed off her. She was given clean, lice-free clothes and then taken to a cell that was not crowded. She met other German nationals who had also returned from various places in the Gulag network. They were all curious about what was going to happen next. For a few months, they were fed well, allowed to rest, and began to return to relatively good health. Their skin and hair improved, and their cheeks filled out. It was no longer obvious that something terrible had happened to them.

Some of the women were Jewish and vehemently anti-Nazi. They had fled to the Soviet Union thinking they were coming to a safe harbor where they would be part of the revolution. Many of the women had been separated from their children, and this was a great concern. If they were going to be sent out of the Soviet Union, they didn't want to go without their children.

As part of the pact, the Soviets and the Germans traded prisoners, with the Soviets sending their German national prisoners back to Germany and vice versa. On a cold winter day in February 1940, Grete was marched across the bridge over the Bug River in Brest-Litovsk.

"When we were halfway across the bridge," she told Milena, "I looked back. The Soviet officials still stood there in a group watching us go. Behind them was Soviet Russia. Bitterly I recalled the communist litany: Fatherland of the Toilers, Bulwark of Socialism, Haven of the Persecuted . . ."[33]

That moment on the bridge, looking back, Grete left everything behind, all her youthful idealism, her love for Heinz, and her belief in the deliverance of the revolution. She did not know what awaited her in Germany. She knew she was wanted by the Gestapo and feared the Germans would simply execute her. Instead, Grete was sent to the Ravensbrück concentration camp.

"When I got here, I laughed. It was so much better than where I had been," Grete said emphatically to Milena.

A WEEK AFTER they started their daily interviews, Milena said, "When we are free again, let's write a book together."

"A book?" Grete was shocked. "Together?"

"About the concentration camps of both dictators, the roll calls, the marching column, the forced labor. Millions of human beings reduced to slaves."

"But I can't write," Grete said, shaking her head.

Milena was undaunted. "You will write the first part, everything you have been telling me; the second part we will write together about our life here in Ravensbrück. We will call it 'The Age of the Concentration Camp.'"

"But you aren't hearing me. I don't know how to write a book."

Milena quickly took hold of Grete's hand and squeezed it, then dropped it before the guard could see. "But Gretuška, anyone who can tell a story as well as you can, can write it . . . Your Prussian schooling has ruined you. Those essays they made you write." And she shook her head, laughing.

Grete felt the contrast between them. It was hard for her to speak easily of feelings, of love and grief and great happiness, the way Milena could. But it felt like a great unburdening, like exhaling finally after holding her breath for a long time.

By taking the stance of observers, Grete and Milena created a psychological protective shield. They were witnesses, watching and remembering. They had to survive so that one day they would tell the world what had happened. In answer to the parting prisoner, sure of their inevitable death, who asks the other to "remember me," they were answering, "We will remember."

That night in her bunk, Grete turned over those words: *When we are free* . . . They had future, a plan. She and Milena would write a book together.

WHEN MILENA SUGGESTED they write a book together about the concentration camps, it was prophetic. This was before the Nazis had settled on the Final Solution. Auschwitz had just opened a few months earlier, but the Nazis had not yet put in place their industrial-scale system of murder. And most people knew nothing yet about Stalin's mass arrests, purges, and the Gulag system.

Milena saw things others didn't.

In 1919, before most others, she recognized the brilliance of Kafka's writing and she was the first to translate his work into any language. The two had carried on a brief but intense epistolary love affair. Kafka seemed to understand the anxiety of the age, and Milena, a Cassandra figure, had a foreboding of the future, what she called "the tragedy of our generation." In 1921, she described a nightmare in an article she wrote for the journal *Tribuna*.

I was somewhere—infinitely far from home . . . Somewhere on the other side of the world, when the entire planet was at war. Or maybe it was the plague, or a flood. I wasn't precisely sure of the catastrophe. But like the others I was swept up by the panic. I didn't know where we were going . . .

Endless trains, one behind the other, left the station, completely full. Panic overtook everyone, no one wanted to be last. People fought for a seat with their life. Between me and the platform were vast crowds of people and there was no hope I would force my way through. Despair overtook me.

"I am young, I cannot die," I shouted . . .

It was as if I always knew something terrible would happen, and now it had arrived. I could breathe more easily because it was here at last . . .

As the train left, catastrophe began. The ground caved in, and the world changed into a network of train tracks. The trains carried away distraught people, people who had lost their homes and their homeland. The tracks overhung the abyss and the engines spun furiously. Finally, the train stopped at the edge of the void.

"Passport control! Everyone get off!" bellowed the desperate guard . . .

I was terrified. A customs officer approached me

demanding my papers. I extracted my ticket. It was
folded over twenty times. I unfolded it. The customs
officer, impatiently shifting from one foot to the
other, reached out his palm, having already decided
that he would not let me through. I looked at the
paper. I read in twenty different languages: "Sentenced to death."[34]

Milena's dream captured something that was true about her character. She always knew something terrible was going to happen, and
when it came, she, unlike others, could breathe more easily. Milena,
who led a chaotic and tumultuous life in normal times, was one of
those people who in times of crisis rose to the occasion.

FROM LATE 1940 to 1942, when Milena and Grete were first together
in the camp, it was not overcrowded. Though the rations were limited,
there was food; prisoners received half a loaf of bread a day. Indeed,
Grete would later write, "The first year and a half in Ravensbrück had
been almost idyllic."[35]

Both Milena and Grete had low camp numbers, indicating they were
early arrivals. And they were on the absolute other end of the status
hierarchy from the *Asoziale*. Grete was number 4208. Milena's number,
4714, was the source of one of many flattering nicknames she would be
given by other camp inmates. They called her "4711," after a famous
eau de cologne. Her married name was Krejcarová, and so her friends
in Block 1 called her "*carevna*," which means "empress"in Czech.

There was something astonishing about the way Milena refused
to submit to the camp authorities and how she got away with it. As a
rule, this type of rebel was avoided and ostracized by other prisoners.
You could get in trouble by association. But for some reason, this was
not the case with Milena. She had many friends from the Czechoslovak community, except some communist Czechs who found her lack
of discipline infuriating.

One spring evening in 1941, the trees behind the prison walls were just sprouting delicate green leaves. There was a soft breeze carrying the smell of early blossoms. Everyone was standing in silence, and Milena must have thought she was back in a park in Prague. She started to whistle a little tune. The communist prisoners all around were furious and exploded with insults at her to shut up.

Grete witnessed this from a distance. She worried about Milena's rash behavior, and warned her that the others would turn on her. But Milena shrugged. "It's easy for them. Those communists were born to be prisoners; they have discipline in their bones."

Milena was not born to be a prisoner, but she did have a few things going for her when she arrived at Ravensbrück in late 1940. Her father was a well-known doctor. She might have exaggerated her short stint in medical school, but she didn't need to exaggerate her German skills. By early 1941, camp administrators had been ordered to use political prisoners who spoke German in the camp offices as secretaries, or *Schreiberinnen*. After her period in quarantine, with the help of Grete's connections and some of her friends in the Czech community, Milena was given a good job as a *Schreiberin*, keeping records in the *revier*, the camp infirmary. This was lucky for her because with her bad leg, she would never have survived the hard work of the labor gangs. Because of their constant contact with the SS administrators, and the Nazi fear of contagion, those who worked in the infirmary or as *Schreiberinnen* had to be in good health. They were allowed to bathe. They received clean sheets once a month and generally were better off than the vast majority of the prisoners.

Schreiberinnen had access to more food and information. They typed inventory lists of supplies. They tracked and read the mail sent and received by the SS. They typed out lists of names of the convoys steadily arriving in the camp. They kept the records of the general camp population as well as daily mortalities from the *revier*—which together could be used to determine the number executed on a given day. They later typed the lists of names of people sent on "dark transports," no doubt to be executed. They were the primary source of information for the rest of the prisoners. In a world where survival was precarious, information about the future was essential.

Grete and Milena met whenever possible during Milena's quarantine period, and now they both had functionary jobs and were privileged prisoners. Their experience would never resemble what the *Asoziale*, or later hundreds of Jewish and Polish prisoners, would experience. As Germaine Tillion wrote, "There were a thousand camps in every camp."[36] Your experience was determined by so many things, including the languages you spoke, your education level, the friends you made, luck, and when you arrived in the camp.

Milena was put in Block 1, a special block where they had plenty of water, one bed per person (at least at first), clean clothes, no lice. They were allowed to receive regular packages from the outside world and to write one letter a month.

Milena's block elder, Rosa Jochmann, was a working-class feminist, a social democrat who had worked for the trade unions in Vienna before the war. Rosa's family had moved from Moravia to Vienna before she was born. Her parents spoke Czech at home, and her father had never really learned to speak German. Rosa and Milena spoke Czech together, and soon they were good friends. Rosa had reluctantly taken the job of block elder, having been convinced that she could make the life of her fellow prisoners a little better.

She took the job despite the complex and heartrending position it would put her in. A friend advised her, "Rosa, remember to always agree with the SS guards." She had to stand by and watch them beat a woman, even to death. "You are standing next to the scene and you are forced to pretend to be outraged by what the prisoner has done."

Rosa became a highly effective block elder. She was able to get and pass vital news to the prisoners. She could organize coal for their heating stove, and arrange for good jobs if a woman was sick or weak. Langefeld trusted her. Rosa could intercede on a prisoner's behalf, and Langefeld would listen to her. Rosa, who never self-identified as a lesbian, would meet her lifelong companion, Cäcilie "Cilly" Helton, in Ravensbrück. Cilly did call herself a lesbian. These were the privileges of being in Block 1.

Of course there were prisoners in the privileged Block 1 who used their power to enrich themselves and who ignored the suffering in the other blocks, or blamed the sufferers for their misery, buying into the racist Nazi ideas of their superiority. But Germaine Tillion in her account of Ravensbrück wrote, "In the privileged blocks we had our friends who never compromised, who took great risks, and who helped others. One of these people at Ravensbrück was Milena Jesenská."[37]

GRETE ADMIRED MILENA'S free spirit, but she would have liked her to keep her head down and not call so much attention to herself. Her heroics kept Grete in a constant state of anxiety. It was worry enough that Milena was ill. Grete noted each day the degree of Milena's swollen hands and shifts in her gray pallor. But Grete was more concerned about Milena's behavior. She was sure that eventually it would get her into trouble.

At morning roll call, Grete would immediately scan the area where Block 1 lined up and look for Milena. Grete needed to see her to begin the day. To make quick eye contact. They had agreed their day could not start without this moment, this stolen glance.

And then the day came. Milena was missing at roll call. Attuned to the slightest change, Grete saw the worry on the faces of Milena's blockmates. Where was Milena? Why wasn't she in her spot? The Block 1 prisoners were trying to cover the missing spot. Grete felt her throat tighten.

Had Milena been taken away in the night? Fallen ill? Was she in the *revier* now? Or had she been released? How would Grete find out? These and a thousand other questions tumbled through her panicked brain.

Then she saw Milena walking slowly toward her place in the line, as if nothing was wrong. To be late for roll call was a serious offense. Grete knew that Milena would most likely get twenty-five lashes. With her bad health, she might not survive them. She wanted to shout, *Hurry up!*

Normally a prisoner would hurry into place and try to show her sense of guilt, and hope for mercy from the SS guard. But there was Milena, sauntering along, blatantly taking her time to find her place. Everybody was watching her.

Almost in slow motion, Grete saw it, the infuriated elderly SS guard rushing toward Milena. The square was silent, as if the air had been sucked out. Grete couldn't breathe. How would she manage if she had to witness Milena getting beaten?

The SS guard lifted her arm to take a swing at Milena's face. Milena stood there with no fear, just looking at the guard straight in the eyes. The guard dropped her arm and stood open-mouthed, cowed. Grete exhaled. It was extraordinary.

Grete felt admiration for Milena, and fury. Later Grete rushed to her side to whisper fiercely, "You gave me such a fear this morning. I almost shouted out for you! Why do you push them?"

Milena was surprised and pleased. She beamed back at her friend's pleading gaze. "You were worried for me, Gretuška?"

"I was sick with worry. Why are you testing these brutes?" Grete said, her anger giving way to fear. How would she be able to protect Milena if she acted this way? "If you keep poking at them, they will snap."

"But if you show fear, you invite the blows. The funny thing about fear is that it won't let you stand still."

Then Milena told Grete a story about her father. The family lived on the sixth floor of a house in the center of Prague and from their windows they could see Wenceslas Square. There were centuries of tension between the Czechoslovaks and the German-speaking Bohemians, and one of the ways this played out was every Sunday, the German Bohemian students would do their customary stroll, or *corso*, on one side of the square with their red caps, and the Czechoslovak students would march on the opposite side. Sometimes the two sides would try to drown each other out with song. One Sunday, the German Bohemian students came right into the center, marching in formation and singing a German national song. They were not staying on their side. Then more Czechoslovaks appeared in the square. Milena and her mother watched this scene unfolding from their apartment window.

She held me by the hand, a little more tightly than necessary. My father was walking in the front row of the Czechs. I recognized him right away, and I was delighted to see him down there, but my mother was pale and tense. Suddenly a detachment of police came rushing out and placed themselves between the two hostile armies . . . Both sides continued to advance. The Czechs reached the police cordon and were ordered to halt; then a second time they were ordered to halt, then a third time . . . I don't remember exactly what happened then. I only know I heard shots and saw the peaceful crowd of Czechs transformed from a quiet to a shrieking crowd. Suddenly the square was deserted. Only one man stood facing the police rifles—my father. I remember clearly, absolutely clearly, how he stood. Calmly, with his hands at his sides. Next to him something terribly strange was lying on the ground—I do not know if you have seen what a person looks like when he is shot, when he falls to the ground. There is nothing human about him; he looks like a discarded rag. Father stood there for a minute—to mother and me it seemed like years. Then he bent down and began to bandage the human wreck that lay beside him on the pavement. Mother's eyes were half-closed and two big tears ran down her cheeks. I remember that she took me in her arms as if she wanted to smother me. Back then I did not know what happened. I only felt the great tension, the unbearable tension and mother's distress.[38]

Her father's bravery spoke to the very core of Milena's identity as "Milena from Prague." Part of her family's myth was that they were descended from Jan Jesenius, a Bohemian physician, politician, and philosopher, and an important Czechoslovak hero who was executed in 1621 along with twenty Bohemian nobles following the defeat of the anti-Habsburg rising at the Battle of White Mountain. After the defeat, Czech culture declined. Many were forced to convert to Catholicism, and German-speaking elites took the place left by the destroyed Czech aristocracy.

But several centuries later, by the end of the nineteenth century, there was a rising Czech nationalist movement. The First World War had added fuel to the divisions in Czechoslovak society. When a Bosnian Serb revolutionary assassinated Archduke Franz Ferdinand, heir to the imperial throne, Milena was eighteen and summering in

the mountains outside of Prague. Austria called for a general mobili-
zation of young Czechoslovak men, but many sympathized with their
Slav brothers in Serbia and resented the empire's rule over them.
The conscripted soldiers went to war singing Slavic songs in protest,
and Vienna responded by imposing martial law and censorship on
newspapers. The tension between Czechs and Germans in the city
worsened. Milena and her family were deeply influenced by this re-
vival of Czech culture. Perhaps to make up for his working-class
background, Milena's father, Jan Jesenský, claimed his lofty heritage
to Jesenius, which later was proven untrue. But Milena believed it
was true; she told Grete that he was her ancestor.

Despite the fact that the Czechoslovaks had been defeated, their
language and religion driven to the ground, they had survived. And
now Hitler was threatening to once again drive Czech culture to
the ground. "My Little Prussian," Milena chided Grete, "don't fear.
When I stand still, it means that I'm calmly anticipating the unknown, I'm prepared for it."[39]

But Grete could not stop worrying. Whenever she was away from
Milena, she feared for Milena. Milena seemed not to understand or
care about the danger of provoking the SS. Or there was something in
her nature that had to provoke. Grete would feel desperate to see her,
to check on her. Despite their privileged positions, it was still perilous
for them to meet too often. Prisoners' days were strictly proscribed,
and the order of the day was marked with a series of howling sirens.

Grete and Milena would soon call themselves "passionate friends."
Women from the political classes who had "passionate friendships"
described them as lifesaving. They acknowledged that they filled the
vital need for tenderness, for human touch. To ask how exactly sexual
they were is reminiscent of German lawmakers trying to figure out
what exactly constituted fornication. How Grete felt intimately about
her own sexuality remains unknown. Grete would write about the importance of touching Milena, of being close to her, of finding moments
to spend alone in each other's embrace. Grete's apparent homophobia, while loving Milena as her "passionate friend," can be understood in the context of the times. Much of society believed deviations

from "normal sexuality" would not exist except for the barbaric world of the camps. But even in the camps, as Milena marveled, love continued, despite all the ways it was forbidden and dangerous. And as Grete would write, "Milena and I succeeded in defeating the unbearable reality."[40]

BY LATE NOVEMBER 1940, the winter nights had grown long. It was bitterly cold. But one advantage was that the evening exercise period occurred under the cover of darkness. On a soupy moonless evening, there was a chill in the air and not a breath of wind. As they walked, they heard the sound of clogs dragging all around them and the low murmur of the others whispering. Grete felt the warmth of Milena next to her. She longed to touch her, take her hand. Almost as if Milena had read her thoughts, she slipped her arm underneath Grete's, hooked gently at the elbows. They didn't speak. They didn't need to. Grete felt at that moment that they understood each other completely. The sound of the others' footsteps crunching on the gravel grew distant. Grete later wrote, "For me nothing existed but Milena's hand on my arm and the wish that this walk might never end."[41]

Their waltzing strides were broken by the howl of the siren. Time to separate and return to their blocks. Everyone around them scrambled to get to their places, but Milena and Grete hesitated to drop their intertwined arms. A guard approached them, screaming orders. Milena tightened her hold and whispered, "Come to the Wailing Wall later. So we can be alone for just a few minutes." Then she let go and they pulled apart.

Grete heard someone shout, "Damn bitches."

She realized they were speaking about her and Milena. The slur implied *lesbians*.

LATER THAT EVENING, Grete slipped away from the bustling talk and evening prayers of her Jehovah's Witness women in Block 3. She was taking an enormous risk. If she was caught out at this hour, she would certainly receive a flogging and even perhaps solitary confinement in the punishment block. She ran past the lighted windows. To avoid making a sound on the gravel, she ran on the grassy edges. The night was pitch dark with no moon. She could hardly see a few feet in front of her. She was at the Wailing Wall but couldn't see where Milena might be waiting for her. She darted off to the far edge, tripped over a root, and fell forward right into Milena's arms.

They held each other for as long as they could risk it. They said very little, not wanting to break the spell of their first time alone together. "We need to go back to our blocks," Grete whispered. She felt almost drugged by this moment of closeness, and yet she was sick with fear.

"Yes, yes, but stay with me just one more moment," Milena pleaded. "Don't panic tomorrow when I am not at roll call. Sonntag has ordered some *revier* staff to be in the offices."

The next morning's roll call was endless. As she had warned, Milena was not in her place. And though Grete knew it was not cause for alarm, her heart ached. She needed to see her. To be sure Milena had made it safely back to the block after they parted.

Grete stood with the three hundred women from her block, all in rows, silent and motionless, facing the *revier*. The SS guard faced them with her back to the *revier*, going over the roll call. Behind the guard, Milena appeared in one of the *revier* windows in the corridor. She looked directly at Grete and placed her hand on the window. Slowly she waved. Grete felt a surge of joy, smiled and nodded back to her. She knew the gesture was for her alone, but all three hundred could see it. Suddenly she was gripped by fear. The long corridor of the *revier* had six windows, and Milena stopped at each one and repeated her gesture. Grete held her breath. She desperately wanted Milena to stop, and when she did, when Milena passed deeper into the *revier* out of sight, Grete ached to see her again.

PART TWO

1941

The List

On January 14, 1941, SS Reich Leader Heinrich Himmler
visits the Ravensbrück camp.

OBERAUFSEHERIN JOHANNA LANGEFELD HAD BEEN ISSUING ORDERS and shrieking commands for a week. Everyone was on edge. Something was about to happen. Langefeld wanted the blocks scrubbed and repaired. And it wasn't just the blocks; her anxiety ranged from the kitchen to the storerooms to the *revier*. The entire camp was on alert.

As *Schreiberin*, Milena soon learned the reason. Another secretary in the offices had read the memo: Himmler was coming to visit on January 14, 1941. Everything had to be perfect for Langefeld's adored *Reichsführer*. She wanted to show him that her methods of order and strict discipline were enough to keep the women in line. Koegel and his prisoner allies were savages. He had won out and gotten his *Strafblock*. Now he staffed it with the worst of the green triangle prisoners. Langefeld had heard of the harsh beatings that happened there, but she had no control over Koegel's punishment block. That was his realm.

Her realm was exemplified by Block 3, where Himmler would inspect Grete's Jehovah's Witness prisoners. The SS carefully curated the "model prison" version of Ravensbrück. Langefeld made doubly sure that all the beds had crisply folded blankets and smoothed out wood-chip mattresses. She wanted to show off her battalion of well-trained female guards. There is a photo of them all lined up as Himmler, entering the camp, walks by Langefeld, who stands at attention a little apart on the end, eager to meet his eye.

Koegel and Langefeld were vying for Himmler's attention and praise, but Himmler had other priorities. He wanted to discuss with the SS doctor in charge, Walter Sonntag, the progress of the experiments he had ordered to find a cure for gonorrhea. Himmler believed that German soldiers should regularly visit prostitutes; it was good for their fighting spirit. He had created brothels near the front lines. But there must be a way to stop the prostitutes from infecting his soldiers. He wanted Sonntag to experiment on infected prostitute prisoners in the camp to find a cure. Himmler loved the idea of human guinea pigs and was angered to discover that Sonntag had not even started the experiments.

Sonntag, an ambitious man, was tall and very strong. Survivors remembered that when he struck a woman, she always fell to the ground. Erika Buchmann, his personal secretary, testified after the war about his behavior. When a woman came to the *revier* complaining of a toothache, he was known to extract a perfectly healthy tooth next to the rotting one, with no anesthetic. She remembered the screams of agony heard through the *revier*. He carried a bamboo stick either in his shiny black boot or tucked under his arm. Because he hated to get close to the prisoners, he would examine them with his bamboo stick. After tearing off their flimsy putrid bandages with his stick, he would then poke at the infected wound. He seemed to revel in the cries of pain caused by this rough prodding.

Floggings put him in a cheerful mood. SS rules stated that a doctor had to watch the floggings to make sure the prisoner could withstand the punishment. Sonntag would order the flogging stopped only if the woman passed out, and when her pulse revived, he would order the flogging to start again.

And Sonntag was a drunk. *Revier* staff were often treated to his inebriated antics; one time, he rode a bicycle around the surgery table. He stole food from the prisoners' packages and had a special animosity toward Jews, refusing to treat them. Jewish work gang leaders learned to signal to *revier* staff when they walked by, returning from their work shifts of throwing bricks, to find out if Sonntag was there. If he was absent, they would ask for bandages.

Milena worked in the *revier* records office, with Doris Maase, a prisoner doctor, and Buchmann as allies. They wore yellow armbands, which allowed them to move more freely around the camp. On the face of it, the *revier* looked like a normal army sick bay. There was a ward of sixty beds. There were a fully equipped operating room, X-ray unit, pharmacy, and pathology lab. There were daily hours when prisoners could in theory see a doctor and get treatment. But neither the illnesses nor the treatments were normal. Women came to the *revier* with frostbite, dog bites, lacerations from beatings, hands blistered and infected from overwork, and severe malnutrition. To have any hope of treatment, the women had to be silent and obedient to please the whim of the gatekeeper nurse. Some days the

Nazi doctors just chatted and sipped coffee and never bothered to examine any of the patients lined up waiting to be seen.

Milena, Maase, and Buchmann witnessed Sonntag's daily savagery, and the windows of the *revier* looked out onto the central compound where they could witness the barbarity of the SS guards. From her desk, Milena glimpsed the freedom that lay just on the other side of the camp's iron entrance gate. Her corner of the *revier* stood out from the tension and despair of the office. Against camp regulations, she had decorated her space. She kept a flower in a container and a glass button on her desk. Once a day, the light would hit the glass in such a way as to make tiny rainbow reflections on the walls. On the wall behind her desk she had hung a color picture of a sunflower taken from an old SS calendar. And next to it was pinned a postcard print of her beloved city of Prague. How she got away with these infringements of the rules was something Grete could not quite understand. "Everything Milena did was a protest against the camp regime. She didn't march right in rows of five, she didn't stand right at roll call, she didn't hurry when ordered to, she didn't toady to those commands," Grete would later write.[1] And Milena was able to intimidate the SS.

Sonntag, perhaps knowing about her famous father, the renowned dental surgeon Professor Jesenský, was drawn to Milena and wanted her to like him. He treated her politely. He tried to get her attention when he spoke, but she ignored him. So great was his admiration that she could get away with snubbing him. When he offered her food from his breakfast, she turned it down without a word of thanks. He tried harder and harder to woo her until the clash came, as she recounted to Grete's horror.

"He tried to tickle me with his beloved stick. Under my chin. I grabbed it from him and pushed it away with all my force. He was like a boy, shocked that Mama was angry with him. I stared at him. He must have seen it in my face, I was hot with anger. He didn't say anything more."

"Oh, Milena," Grete said. "You have to be more careful."

"Ach! He's just a silly child," Milena said, shrugging her shoulders.

"A child maybe, but also a child who could throw a tantrum and . . ." Grete hated the sound of her own pleading pathetic voice.

"Gretuška, you are worried about me?" Milena was beaming with pride. The sun was shining through her curls and her smile lit up her face. Grete could not stay mad at Milena, nor would she ever get her to change. They were whispering this exchange in front of the office stairs, and Grete was aware that she should not linger or hold Milena too long from her post at the *revier*.

"He could still do something," Grete said. She was going to be worried about Sonntag's retribution for days now.

"He'll do nothing to me," Milena said. And it was true. After the incident with the stick, Sonntag gave up overtly trying to win Milena over, but surprisingly, he allowed her to continue at her job.

FOR SOME REASON, Sonntag had not received Himmler's order to experiment on the prostitutes. Himmler believed him because he knew Sonntag would not shrink from such a task. It was Sonntag who had carried out the mustard gas experiments on healthy prisoners in Sachsenhausen. He recorded that between October and December 1939, he had applied the lethal chemical directly to at least twenty-three prisoners and recorded with satisfaction when the prisoners' skin erupted in massive burning blisters. They suffered severe pain and many died.

Himmler may have also broached another more sensitive subject with Sonntag. The Nazi T4 gassing program of ten thousand mentally and physically disabled people at Grafeneck Castle had to be stopped because of a public outcry. The German population had gotten wind of the operation when so many of their loved ones had mysteriously died just after being transferred to Grafeneck. The families of the disabled had protested by posting identical obituaries in local newspapers across the country. Himmler believed the purge of these useless undesirable people was necessary to strengthen the "Aryan" race, but alas, the German population was too weak to stomach this necessary excision. It was clear that these types of programs needed to be carried out with much more discretion, away from the public eye.

As a Nazi doctor, Sonntag was trained in the ideology of public health that embraced racial cleansing, getting rid of such "defective people" along with Jews and *Asoziale*. In a thesis that Sonntag began in 1939, he wrote: "Reproduction by genetically ill and *Asoziale* elements of a people will inevitably lead to the deterioration of a whole nation. Sterilizing undesirables and eliminating them as far as possible is therefore a humanitarian project that offers protection to the more worthy parts of society."[2]

At the time of Himmler's visit, the Final Solution of mass murder had not yet been established. The plan was to force German Jews out of the fatherland, sending them to the very edges of Russia, or shipping them to Madagascar. But they had to be sterilized first, because otherwise the problem would persist. On that visit from Himmler, Sonntag learned of the efforts to explore methods of mass sterilization. Soon after, Sonntag began his own pilot experiment on Romani and Sinti children, including one nine-year-old girl.

Milena's job in the *revier* meant that she, more than most other prisoners, had a clear view of the sinister Nazi machinations. She was a fundamentally curious person, a born journalist. Her job in the *revier* put her in a position of privilege, but it came at a psychic cost. She heard the cries of the young girls whom Sonntag experimented on. She saw them stumbling back to their block. Part of Milena's job was to go every day to the morgue, which was behind the *revier*, and count the dead. In the early years of the camp, most of the women she found there had died by starvation, exhaustion, and infection. But now she found many of the same young girls she had seen walk into Sonntag's office, dead in the morgue a few days later. She saw the same results with the prostitutes whom Sonntag now started to "treat."

When she could, Milena would speak with patients waiting to be seen by the doctors, or with the newly arrived waiting for the intake medical examination. She asked their names and where they were from and engaged them in conversation. All of this was, of course, strictly forbidden. She didn't differentiate between the politicals and the *Asoziale*; she found them all equally interesting. They had such extraordinary stories of separation, loss, and even humor. They just wanted someone to listen to them. Milena would tell Grete that she was gathering material for their book, the one they planned to write when all of this was over.

Milena was in charge of the card catalogue in the *revier*, and it was her job to file the result of the swabs for venereal disease taken from the *Asoziale* prisoners. When a new prisoner arrived and was suspected of having VD, lab tests were sent off to Berlin. Milena was able to see when a positive result returned. She forged the results when possible, doing her best to save the woman. Milena made fake cards at her desk when no one was watching and kept them tucked away under a stack of papers.

When she saw that Sonntag was busy, she would go to the card catalogue and switch out the cards with her faked ones to save a patient from Sonntag's "barbarous cures." Once, Sonntag had surprised her, coming up behind her to comment on the newest transport, how they would have their hands full for a while with this useless bunch.

She quickly let the card drop and managed to step on it as she turned to face Sonntag. "Is it too much for you?" she asked archly.

"Nothing is too much for the purity of our nation," he snapped back. She knew he wanted her to agree, but she just stood there looking at him with no expression.

She boasted later to Grete how she had stood there until Sonntag, frustrated, walked away. Grete reminded her that Sonntag had once beat a prisoner nurse unconscious after he had caught her giving a piece of bread to a Jew. "Imagine if he had caught you?" Grete said.

"I'm the one who told you that story," Milena answered.

"I know, but do you remember?"

"I remember everything." Even some things that she was not ready to tell Grete.

Milena wasn't the only one working clandestinely in the *revier*. Maase smuggled out medicine and bandages to the prisoners; Buchmann, who typed up the daily lists of sick patients, could sometimes get a weaker person off a deadly work gang. But there were limits to what they could do.

Maase stayed in the *revier* overnight, and she witnessed when

Sonntag would enter, often drunk, with a syringe. The next morning, the person he injected would be dead. Milena did not tell this
to Grete, not yet. She did not want her to worry any more than she
already did.

GRETE AND MILENA developed a ritual of exchanging letters. It began
with Milena stealing a sheet of paper from the *revier*. She began each
letter with "my darling blue girl." Grete would respond "by return
mail," which was the following exercise period, when she could surreptitiously hand back the single sheet of paper. When there was no
more room for words, Milena instructed Grete to destroy it. Grete
hesitated. She cherished those letters.

Once, Milena wrote a draft of the preface for their future book. She
told Grete that after she read it, she must destroy it. Grete held on to
the paper for a few days. It was so precious, the beginning of their
book. But then she realized the huge danger if the paper were discovered. It was a risk not only to herself but also, more importantly, to
Milena. And so, heartbroken, Grete destroyed it. Grete confessed to
Milena how hard it was. Milena laughed. "I'll write it all over again
as soon as we get out. It will be as easy and natural as peeing."[3]

Soon after Milena arrived, the Czech communists confronted her.
There were clear lines of ideology in the camp that were fervently
discussed by the Czech prisoners, most of whom were well educated.
For the communists, Germany's fascism was the last stage of capitalism, part of the inevitable history of the decadent West. Only the
revolution could save them.

Milena was warned by the leader of the Czech communists, Jožka
Jabůrková, that she should have nothing to do with Grete, who was
a Trotskyite bourgeois. Milena had to make a choice between the
political communists, with their considerable power in the camp hierarchy, and Grete, the traitor. It astounded her that they thought
this kind of blackmail would work. When she told Grete about the
confrontation, she said, "They think it will work because that sort of
thing would work on them."

Milena simply shrugged her shoulders and continued her friendship with Grete. It might have cost her; perhaps some of her rations
and items were taken from her. But Milena had many friends, especially a group of Czechoslovaks from the arts community of Prague;
she had once been an important member of their circle. There were
communists who knew she had helped save some of their comrades
before she was arrested. And some communists found it hard to resist
her charm. Hanka Housková, a Czech nurse, who had been a member of the Communist Youth and knew Milena from before the camp
when they were in prison together, knew that she shouldn't be friends
with her, but she liked her. Jožka Jabůrková and Ilse Mochová had
called Hanka to task. "You know that Milena is a Trotskyist. And
that she's friends with Grete Buber. Her husband was executed as a
traitor to the Soviet Union. You already know that. That's not a good
friend for you."[4] The communists tried to keep strict party discipline,
going as far as forbidding smoking. But Hanka secretly continued to
be Milena's friend.

Grete was on the alert for snubs, for incidents when Milena was
hurt by their friendship. But Milena wasn't bothered. "There are
some people who love to talk about my bad reputation. They happen
to be communists now, but they would never have liked me no matter
what their politics."

"What bad reputation?" Grete asked.

"I was a wild young girl," Milena said, smiling. "You can ask
them. They'll have plenty of stories to tell about me." There always
were rumors about her decadence, even about her having had relations with women. She laughed and then listed all the good friends
she did have, writers and dancers and artists who knew her or her
writing from before the war. They had read her articles. They knew
she was anti-fascist. And they knew she had resisted the Nazis.

DURING 1940 AND the first half of 1941, the burning question for the
communist political prisoners was how long the Hitler-Stalin pact
would last. They tried desperately to understand why their great

leader had signed a treaty with the Nazis. When on June 22, 1941, Germany invaded Russia with Operation Barbarossa, the news came as a huge relief to many political prisoners. Loyal communists felt assuaged. Their cognitive dissonance and ideological contortions were over. At last things made sense.

The Soviet political prisoners were convinced this would end the war swiftly. The great Red Army would now swoop in and save them, and Germany would be crushed within a matter of months. Other political prisoners like Grete and Milena were not so sure. And if Russia won, what would be their fate? Grete had no illusions about what a Soviet government would do with her. And Milena wondered what the fate of her beloved Czechoslovakia's fledgling democracy would be. Grete later wrote that the Stalinists in the camp spread the word that when the Soviets came to Ravensbrück, she and Milena "would both be put up against the wall or sent to Siberia."

Hitler had planned on breaking his pact with Stalin after he had taken over Europe, but he was growing suspicious that Stalin was moving against him and planning to capture the Romanian oil fields Hitler needed to fuel his armies. The invasion along the 1,800-mile front took the Soviets by surprise and caught the Red Army unprepared. The Germans had allotted 150 divisions, about three million soldiers, including elite panzer divisions, 3,000 tanks, and 7,000 artillery pieces. It was, in effect, the largest invasion force in history. Despite getting bogged down by arguments over strategy in the German high command, and despite the Soviet scorched-earth policy, the rains, and supply line problems, the German Army had by mid-July advanced more than 400 miles into Russia and was only 200 miles away from Moscow. The news of the glorious and swift advance was blared over the loudspeakers along with deafening German military marching music.

The Soviets lost 250,000 men every week for the first six weeks. The Germans firmly believed that the Soviets would be beaten in a matter of months. The Wehrmacht's handbook concluded that the Red Army was "unsuited for modern warfare and incapable of decisive resistance against a well-commanded, well-equipped force."[5]

Milena, in her position in the *revier*, had a close-up view of the bravado among the SS. They were cocky and sure of themselves, and that much more vicious. Milena also had ample opportunity to observe Dr. Sonntag's behavior.

Sonntag had started an affair with one of the other Nazi doctors, Gerda Weyand, who had been at the camp since its opening. Gerda, with her youthful face, had a reputation as one of the rare decent doctors who treated patients with kindness, even if her medical treatment was perfunctory. But she had fallen under Sonntag's spell. Refusing to vouch for her in the war crimes trials after the war, Erika Buchmann wrote to Weyand saying, "Neither could I forget the times in the hospital, in Dr. Sonntag's room, when you were having fun for hours very noisily and regardless that on the other side of the wall were several ill people with fevers, pining for rest."[6]

In the summer of 1941, Sonntag and Weyand were married. Sonntag, who was very sensitive to issues of status, was allowed to move into one of the better homes for SS families. The SS officers with families lived a creepily idyllic life just outside the Ravensbrück walls. There on the hillside by the lake was a collection of pretty villas, Swiss-like chalets with steep-sloping roofs, flowers planted in front, and nicely kept gardens. The SS families had an endless supply of free labor to care for the gardens and clean their houses. There was a daycare center for the children run by the Jehovah's Witness prisoners. They were seen as perfect domestic servants. Nazi housewives praised their impeccable cleanliness. Like servants everywhere, they were able to witness darker intimate truths about these "perfect" Nazi families. Though Gerda Weyand would later write, "I have never been happier than I was at Ravensbrück," their servant witnessed violent outbursts and a drunken Sonntag beating his wife.

Sometime during the summer of 1941, Sonntag began administering lethal petrol or phenol injections to prisoners. Himmler had given orders to doctors at other camps, and probably to Sonntag as well, that they needed to kill off the "useless mouths."

Women who arrived pregnant were forced to have abortions or to give birth only to have their babies left in a bucket to bleed to death through their untied umbilical cords. Milena bore witness to these events during her daily job at the *revier*. Sometimes she risked speaking out.

According to Věra Picková, "I was walking down the corridor in the *revier* with Milena and the doctor came towards us. And Milena had found out how the babies were dying and said: 'Doctor, the children are being killed here. What are you doing about it?' She didn't get an answer. The doctor turned and walked away."[7]

ON A SUNDAY afternoon, during the "free" time allowed to certain prisoners—not Jews, or Jehovah's Witnesses, or prisoners in the *Strafblock*—Grete and Milena were walking together back and forth along the camp central ground. It was an unusually sunny day. The SS guard, apparently in a good mood, had turned up the radio to blare out Schubert through the loudspeakers. Surrounded by thousands of women also walking along the sandy ground, they felt glimmers of happiness. Because the music was so loud, they could risk talking. They chatted about concerts and operas they would one day attend together.

But the moment was ruined when one of the female guards pushed through the crowd and started to viciously beat two women with her whip. The guard shrieked insults: "You bitches! You whores!"

Once the women had fallen to the ground, the guard kicked them both furiously with her jackboots. Their crime was clear: lesbianism. These two inmates had been caught walking arm in arm.

Schubert was replaced with Nazi marching tunes. Grete's nerves were shot, and she wanted to head back to her block. But Milena had another idea. "Something forbidden, of course," Grete would recall.

Milena told Grete to follow her to the *revier* in a few minutes. In the *revier*, Milena took out the key to the consultation room that she knew Dr. Sonntag kept in his top desk drawer.

"No one will look in here on a Sunday," she assured Grete. "We will be perfectly safe."

They locked themselves in together. The sunny day rippled through the smoked-glass windowpanes like light reflecting off water. They were alone for the first time, in daylight, away from the eyes of others. There was never any privacy, but here, at last, they had this moment, sitting side by side on the examination table, in the sun-filled room, feeling each other's warmth. The barbaric world outside fell away.

In the quiet of the room, Grete felt shy. How to begin speaking, saying all the things she had been so careful not to say, not to be overheard?

Milena was gazing at her, smiling. Grete took up Milena's swollen hands. "Do they ache? Does it hurt you much?"

But Milena didn't like attention brought to her body, or her weaknesses. She had once been so strong. She wished Grete could have seen her then. "You are sweet," Milena answered, kissing Grete on both cheeks.

The dam broke, and they pulled each other into a tight embrace. Here, at last, was tenderness and human touch. Milena used a Czech endearment for Grete, calling her "člověk boží." It was close enough to the Russian term that Grete understood Milena was saying something like "my divine woman."

Grete, a straightforward girl from Potsdam who had followed her partner and the Communist Party like a good soldier until it had betrayed her, had never been adored. Heinz had rejected the idea of romantic love, calling it the vestiges of bourgeois elitism. He reminded her that what joined them was not love for each other but love for the party. Embarrassed by her middle-class status, she hadn't felt she deserved to be loved, much less adored.

Now the tenderness of Milena's words bewildered Grete. Milena was kissing her cheeks, her forehead, and Grete felt tears rising.

"But why? Why do you love me? I don't understand." Grete's voice hitched with a sob. "Why someone like you would love me?"

Milena pulled slightly away and took a deep breath. With her finger, she traced Grete's face. She loved her blue eyes, but it was more than that.

"You, my Gretuška," she said, solemnly, "you have the good fortune to love life without reserve. You are as strong and as good as the fruitful earth, a little blue village madonna . . ." She whispered endearments to Grete in her singular poetic voice as they kissed and touched each other. Grete wept. To be loved by Milena made everything—all the years of prison, all the fear, the hunger, and the suffering—worth it.

And what did Grete love about Milena? Milena had an aura, a regal presence. She stood out above the others. Grete was proud that Milena, with her penetrating intelligence, had chosen Grete to be her friend. But it was more than that. It was Milena's eyes. Even when Milena was happy, Grete could see bottomless grief there. Something about Milena was otherworldly and evasive. As close as Grete held her, Milena would slip through her fingers, just out of reach. Grete was captivated, and she ached with longing for more. She knew she would never be able to completely get through to her. She feared always that she would one day lose her. Grete wrote, "All my dreams of Milena are haunted by this feeling of hopelessness."[8]

ONE MORNING IN 1941, the camp siren sounded earlier than usual. It wasn't the standard drawn-out howl that called them to morning roll call, but a siren of shorter, more urgent bursts. It had a sinister feel to it. The block elders hurried everyone out onto the central camp square. The news traveled fast. They were scared and excited. "Hurry, hurry. Someone's escaped!"

The female guards wrangled their dogs. The commandant barked orders. Very quickly everyone lined up and the counting began. In the background, the prisoners could hear the gunning of motors, a kind of angry growl and hum. The SS were preparing for a manhunt. The count was done in record time: One person was missing from the *Strafblock*.

The trapeze artist Katharina Waitz had made a third escape, her most audacious. This time, she broke out of the *Strafblock*, where she had been since her previous attempt. It made an impression on the prisoners, and many recounted the incident after the war, including

Grete. In the night, somehow, Katharina had managed to crawl out of the *Strafblock* window, slipping past the guards and the dogs that roamed off leash. She crossed the whole yard to reach the SS canteen and climbed up onto the roof, even though the guardhouse was only meters away. From the roof of the SS canteen, she made her way to the high wall topped with electrified barbed wire. Once on the perimeter, she had to climb over five barbed wire fences and over a four-meter-high wall. She used all her high-wire skills to scale and leap. She used a pillow and blanket to protect herself from the electricity and barbs. At the final high barrier, Katharina leapt to freedom. In the morning, the SS found the blanket and pillow that she had left behind dangling on the wires.

The prisoners watched as the SS gathered and readied themselves for the hunt, the dogs straining at their leashes. Koegel announced that the *Strafblock* prisoners would be punished collectively for Katharina's crime. They would lose three days' rations of food. A wave of anger moved through the group. They were a hardened bunch ruled by a brutal block elder. Katharina, as a Romani woman, did not have many friends among them. They were made to stand at attention all day. Those who lost consciousness and collapsed were laid out in rows behind them.

Milena prayed that Katharina would make it to freedom.

Near evening, a group of female guards with their dogs and SS men and Koegel returned. In front of them was a miserable bundle of rags and blood, stumbling as they kicked her and pushed her forward. The dogs tore at Katherina's clothes and bit her legs. Koegel made her march through the lines of the standing *Strafblock* prisoners as she was led back to the block. The *Strafblock* prisoners followed.

"There she is," Koegel told them. "It's her fault that you'll get no food for three days. Do what you like with her."

The prisoners jumped on her and beat her to death with sticks and bars. They kicked her and bludgeoned her into a bloody heap. Later Koegel had her body dragged out of the punishment block into the central camp square so all the prisoners could see her.

"Take a good look. That's what will happen if any of you attempt escape."[9]

THE INCIDENT OF the escape and recapture weighed heavily on Milena and Grete. They could not speak about it, but the next time they were able to talk, they recognized the anguish in each other's eyes. "We should sing each other songs to cheer us," Milena suggested as they walked together by the Wailing Wall.

"I only know party anthems, and they depress me," Grete grumbled, looking down at her feet. She wanted to say to Milena, *It was so terrible what they did to the trapeze artist. How do people become like animals? You see what I say about the* Asoziale *is true.* But she kept quiet; she didn't want to upset Milena.

"Not even a Russian folk song someone taught you in the Gulag?" Milena asked.

The question reminded Grete of one Russian folk song she had heard often in the evenings when everyone was drunk and sad and homesick. The Russians loved this song; it made them weep. She was not sure of all the words, but she hummed what she couldn't remember and sang as much as she could before breaking off in embarrassed laughter. "Your turn now," she said to Milena.

Milena smiled. She loved to sing. And she loved Czech songs. There was a song that was popular in Europe before the war, but Grete had been isolated in the Gulag, so she heard it first that summer in 1941, when Milena sang it to her. "The wind sang me a song, a song of unspeakable happiness," Milena sang, and as she did, she risked giving Grete's hand a quick squeeze. Milena sang it in Czech and then sang it again more slowly as she translated it into German. She was teaching Grete Czech, so she used this and other song lyrics for their lessons. But this song, the one of unspeakable happiness, became "their song."

How could two prisoners feel this unspeakable happiness in that awful place? Even though they were kept apart by the strict rules of the camp, they lived in a rich world of their own creation, a world they alone shared. Grete would later write, "Every gesture, every word, every smile had its meaning. Constantly being separated and yet so close together, living always in anticipation of a brief encounter, even the bell of the little railway train running along the camp wall while we—Milena a few hundred yards away from me—were lined up for roll call, seemed like a loving message from one to the other. In that existence we lived without a future, we lived entirely for the present."[10]

IN AUGUST 1941, a sort of miracle occurred. It all started when one of the *Asoziale* began to drag a leg. She appeared to be paralyzed. Then more prisoners reported swelling and paralysis in their legs. Bertha Teege, then *Lagerälteste*, or chief prisoner kapo, reported the strange illness to Langefeld. Fearing that it was an outbreak of polio, the SS panicked. Koegel thought the strange epidemic had been brought on by one of Sonntag's experiments. Prisoners heard him shouting and swearing at Sonntag. Many prisoners thought the swelling was due to the new night shifts in the tailor's shop. But twinned with the Nazis' obsession with racial purity was their terror of epidemics and contagion.

The next morning, Teege was given the keys to the kitchen and the *Strafblock*. The camp was now in quarantine, and she was in charge. No SS personnel were allowed in the camp. The Nazis had left the prisoners in control. And perhaps because the recent harrowing scene of Katharina's capture was still so vividly on everyone's mind, no one attempted escape.

A wonderful peace descended. The sirens stopped. The infernal roll calls ended. Prisoners were ordered to their blocks, and there was no work done. There were no bellowing guards with their vicious barking dogs.

The paralyzed *Asoziale* were put together in a single block, the punishment barracks that had been evacuated and cordoned off with barbed wire. Everyone was warned to stay away from them. But

Milena, who counted many of the stricken women as her friends, ignored the warnings. She was going to help them, and no one dared to stop her.

Milena brought the quarantined prisoners food and bandages. She brought ointments for their swollen legs. And once they were all settled in their bunks, she would recite to them Kafka's *Metamorphosis*, in daily episodes. She had been one of the first people to recognize the brilliance of this little-known German Jewish writer and offered to translate his work into Czech. She knew Kafka's work mostly from memory, and when she didn't, she added her own touches. Kafka's words now seemed so prophetic. These women understood what Kafka's character Gregor Samsa felt like when he woke up one day suddenly transformed into a large insect.

Each afternoon, Grete met Milena at the "plague block." Milena would come outside and greet her. They sat on the ground with only the barbed wire fence between them. They soaked in the quiet and the August sunshine. They were blessed with perfect summer weather, cloudless blue skies. The camp seemed enchanted. You could hear birdsong and smell the hot earth. There was a breeze off the lake. Milena sang a sad nostalgic Czech folk song: "Oh, green hills that were mine. Oh, joy of my heart! It's a long time since I've heard birds sing. A time of sadness is rising over the horizon."[11]

They spoke of their childhoods. Milena asked, "Were you, too, as a child fascinated by glass marbles with colored veins? Weren't they absolutely magical?"

They talked about bright-colored bohemian glass, and then their summer vacations. They talked about mountain lakes. They remembered walking in meadows, the feel of a light summer dress on their legs. Milena remembered gathering flowers. She told Grete how she loved to walk with bare feet in the grass. Grete looked at Milena's swollen blistered feet on the dirt ground and she felt a pang of helplessness.

As Grete stood to leave, Milena handed her a folded paper. "Read this, then throw it away." Milena had written a fairy tale for Grete, "The Princess and the Inkblot." This fairy tale somehow survived and was found after the war, written on yellowed paper in Milena's desk in the *revier*. It begins: "The king had a daughter. She wrote poems all day long. The king was not happy and wanted his daughter to be like all the other children."[12] Writing is a curse, and Milena's tale poses a choice: Either be beautiful and find a husband—usually he is a silly fool—or be cursed and write.

The period of quarantine lasted for two glorious weeks. Bertha allowed the prisoners to take advantage of the rare freedom. They found each other and went for walks. They talked and shared stories. The Jehovah's Witnesses took out their clandestine Bibles. There was a huge outburst of creativity. Many women wrote poems on scraps of paper and made little booklets for each other. The *Asoziale* sang and danced. The Roma and Sinti showed off their acrobatic skills. You could even hear laughter from time to time.

Walking by the Romani and Sinti block, Grete wanted to stop to listen to the music. But Milena pulled on Grete's arm. "I hate Gypsy music," she cried. "I can't bear it. It reminds me of the worst thing that ever happened to me."[13]

"Worse than ending up here?" Grete asked.

"But this is where I found you," Milena answered. "Thank God I ended up here."

"Then tell me what was the worst thing?" Grete pleaded. "You make me tell you everything about myself. I want to know everything about you too."

"I will tell you, but you must promise to still love me after I tell you."

"Milena! Of course you know I will still love you."

"Don't judge me? I don't want those blue eyes to turn cold." Milena knew she was going to tell the whole story to Grete, but she hesitated.

They walked quietly and Grete whispered, "Please trust me."

"It was when I was a morphine addict and I would do anything to get my hands on drugs." Milena paused and felt Grete take in the information. "Yes, I was a drug addict, I was just like those poor girls in the *Asoziale* block."

Milena explained to Grete that she'd had a bad accident when she was pregnant with her daughter. And that was how she got this way, with the knee that would not bend. When her knee first became immobilized, she couldn't accept it. Never had she imagined that she, who so loved to hike and walk in the mountains, would become this way. Her father had heard about a cure in the miraculous waters at Piešťany. There were mud baths for the knee, but after every bath, they put her knee in an orthopedic contraption and tried to force it to bend. The pain was absolute torture, and it didn't go away after they stopped the sessions. It continued day and night.

She was given morphine, but it wasn't enough. She needed more and more, and her husband had to try desperately to find more than just what the doctors gave her. They were spending every penny on her morphine. She was in despair about who she had become. She couldn't control herself. She couldn't even find herself. What had become of her character? She tried to stop the drugs cold turkey. It was during this time, when she was going through the excruciating process of withdrawal, in her bed writhing with pain and sweats, hallucinations and madness, that downstairs from her hotel room, a Gypsy band in the bar played on and on endlessly this plaintive weeping music. It pushed her to over the edge, she told Grete, the cloying violin and the whirling frenzied music.

She woke one night and saw a revolver by her bed. Had her husband put it there to encourage her to take her own life? Or had she imagined the whole thing? She wasn't sure. "But it was that night," she told Grete, "I realized my marriage was over."

Grete wanted to know more about this marriage. She had told Milena all about her past, Heinz and the Gulag. It was Grete's turn to ask Milena about her childhood in Prague and everything that led to her being in the camp.

"Now, let's start at the beginning," Grete said. "What did you look like when you were three? Have you seen pictures of yourself at that age?"

"Very pale and delicate, with precocious, defiant eyes in a little round face and a tousled mop of hair." Milena told Grete that she was not a well-behaved child, and only her mother truly understood her.

LATER GRETE WOULD remember this period as their honeymoon.

Each block had an orderly room in the center for the SS guards during the day. With no guards, the little room was empty. It was a room with a door. Milena came to Grete's block when it was dark, and they spent entire nights together. Grete made a bed for them on the ground between the stove and the door. It was summer, so there was no fire and barely any light. They had to use their touch to see each other.

In the early morning of their first sleepless night together, with their bodies entangled, Grete was overwhelmed with a confusing mix of love and fear. She wondered if she should stop herself. "What would they think of us?" she asked Milena.

"It doesn't matter," Milena answered. She was straightforward. "This is love," she told Grete. "The great gift of love."

This is love, Grete heard in her heart when they moved together and responded to each other. *This is love*, she told herself, and finally there was time enough. Time to tease, to whisper poems, to talk. *This is love* felt deep in her body in ways Grete had never experienced. During the blissful period of camp quarantine, Milena told Grete the story of her life.

Milena Jesenská was born into a wealthy family in 1896. For the first five years of her life, they lived in a ground-floor flat next door to her father's dental office. But then, as his practice thrived, the family moved to the sixth floor of a baroque building right on Wenceslas Square in the center of Prague. This was the home she remembered most. Milena's father, Jan Jesenský, was a university professor of medicine specializing in dentistry. He was entirely self-made, one of eight children in a poor family. To pay his way through medical school, he had played violin outside cafés and worked as a porter—as Milena would later do in Vienna. Jan married Milena Hejzlarová, who came from a well-to-do Czech family; her dowry allowed him to set up a private dentistry practice.

According to his granddaughter, Jana Černá, or Honza, he resented his in-laws and the feeling that he owed them anything. With success came financial stability. Jan enjoyed dressing in the old-fashioned

Dr. Jan Jesenský, Milena's father

style of a provincial nobleman with a top hat and frock coats. He was also a gambler and could lose great sums in one night. His wife was beautiful and frail, with pernicious anemia. He had a series of affairs, one that ended in an actual duel that was, according to his granddaughter, one of the last duels fought in Prague. As a dentist, Jesenský was a leader in the field, pioneering what is now known as periodontal surgery. Many of his patients' faces had been severely damaged during the First World War, and he would attempt to reconstruct them.

Milena's mother was artistic. And the bedroom where she passed her time was decorated in the Czech fashion of the day with peasant-style wood carvings and rustic furniture. She loved bright peasant headscarves, which Milena would carry with her into adulthood as a keepsake of her mother. Mother and daughter were very close. Milena described her mother as having "green eyes with brown threads that traced a path to faraway impenetrable regions. Was she beautiful? She was, in every way, the most beautiful."[14]

When Milena was four, her mother, already ailing and anemic, gave birth to a baby boy. But she was too weak to feed the baby, and Milena's father, who was stubborn about weakness, refused to get a wet nurse. "If my wife can't nurse her babies, she shouldn't have them!" The baby died a few weeks later. But her brother's brief life left a mark on Milena. She wrote Kafka about her brother. In the exchange of letters between Milena and Kafka, only his half remains. Her letters were destroyed, perhaps by Kafka. But in Kafka's letters, he wrote that he had gone to visit her little brother's grave.

For most of Milena's childhood, her mother was bedridden or in a wheelchair. Jan believed that it was good for Milena's education to take care of her mother. It was also convenient for him to have her occupied at home and to leave him free to go out at night. She would sit in the stuffy room for hours, trying to keep herself awake and waiting for her father to come home from his parties.

One time, she snuck out while her mother was sleeping. She just needed some fresh air. She was gone for only half an hour. When she returned to the closed, dark room, her mother appeared to still be sleeping. After a few moments, she spoke without opening her eyes: "I quite understand, dear. I'd get away from here too, for a little while at least. If I had a chance."[15]

Another time, Milena's father, feeling sorry for his invalid wife, brought her some spring violets. The flowers cheered her. She had Milena move them several times that day so they were always in the sunlight, where she could admire and smell them. But that evening, the doctor received a visit from one of his charming female patients, and he rushed into his wife's room, apologized, and took the flowers from their vase to give to his visitor.

The last lingering years of her mother's life were difficult. She could no longer speak, but it was clear she suffered. Milena would turn her body over and treat the awful bedsores that festered and multiplied. When her mother slipped into a coma, the doctor wanted to give her some kind of injection to revive her. Milena grabbed the syringe from his hand and flung it to the ground, shattering the glass. She did not want her mother's suffering to be drawn out any longer. The doctor and her father acquiesced. Milena was sixteen when her mother passed away. She told Grete that all she really felt at the time was relief.

Milena was enrolled in the Minerva Academy for Girls, established in 1890 as the first *gymnasium*, or secondary school, for girls in Central Europe with the high educational standards of the old Austrian Empire. It was famous and still quite controversial when Milena attended in 1907. The graduates from Minerva were the first women in Czech society to go on to university. They had an aura of freedom and a desire to shock that made them easily recognizable to Prague citizens as "Minervans." The neoclassical building was decorated with sgraffito frescoes in red and white plaster, illustrating different ancient goddesses. The young girls studied Latin and Greek and other subjects usually reserved for boys only. Under pressure to prove that girls could do as well as boys intellectually, thirty out of forty of the first class of Minervans had obtained the highest possible score on the Ancient Greek exam. The school had a radical air of emancipation, and the girls considered themselves liberated women.

Milena's father would walk her to the door of the school each morning, proud that his daughter would be one of the country's most highly educated women. Both were remembered as very distinguished and smart dressers. Soon after Milena started school, her mother fell ill, and gradually Milena's relationship with her father deteriorated.

Once her mother had died, Milena was left very much on her own. The new freedom was exalting for someone with Milena's daring. She had read novels that elliptically hinted at unmarried couples checking into hotels, so she took a room in a dingy hotel and stayed there all night by herself.

"I wanted to know what sort of things happened in a hotel room that were so whispered about," she confided to Grete. "I lay awake with erotic tension, hearing the sounds along the corridor all night."

"And?" Grete asked.

Milena shook her head and laughed. "I longed for someone to open the door, but of course nothing happened."

Milena was also drawn to dark cemeteries. At night, she would sit on the walls around the graves and allow her emotions to run wild.

Her father eventually heard about her nocturnal ramblings and was furious. There were violent confrontations, but after her father cooled down, Milena was again left on her own to do as she willed.

Her two closest Minervan friends were Jarmila Ambrožová and Stanislava Procházková (later Jílovská), or, as Milena called her, "Staša." Jarmila was infatuated with Milena, and they resembled each other. They had the same long legs, slender build, and magnificent thick hair. Milena's was a deep reddish-chestnut color with extravagant curls. They wore pastel veils in the style of Isadora Duncan, and left their hair down in the style of the English Pre-Raphaelites. They wore sandals without socks, which was unthinkable at that time. Jarmila copied the way Milena dressed and tried to imitate her gestures and handwriting, but she remained the follower. Staša was more of an equal. Known as "the Siamese twins," she and Milena were rumored to be lovers.

Whether they were lovers or just experimenting teenagers, it was a deeply passionate friendship. Staša would remain a loyal friend to Milena for her entire life. It was the sort of friendship that can grow at that age, when one is still forming, trying on different styles and manners. They imitated each other, agreed together on what was good and bad about the world. They loved to shock and display their indifference to bourgeois morality. Milena rifled through her father's medicine cabinet, and they experimented with different pills together. They used cocaine, claiming they had a right to do with their bodies whatever they wanted. They shared a mutual desire to break from their families and the sense that it was wrong that they were being educated only to be offered to some man in marriage.

Milena had a deep sense of justice, and felt it was unfair that she should have so much when others around her were poor. She felt no qualms about stealing from her father to give to her less fortunate friends. During the First World War, when many of Milena's friends' houses had bare cupboards, Dr. Jesenský kept his home well stocked. Milena regularly hid soap and food in her skirt and passed out sacks of flour to friends. But she went further than simple redistribution of provisions. She stole money from her father, taking from his hoarded stock of gold coins. And one time, her father recognized that a young man, his student but also a friend of Milena's, was wearing his special expensive monogrammed socks that had gone missing.

She was never good with money and for most of her life she was in debt and in need of her father to rescue her financially. Whenever she had money, she spent it, often on lavish gifts for her friends, who regularly felt embarrassed by her exaggerated generosity.

For Dr. Jesenský, Milena had been a difficult child to manage, and as she grew into a young woman, she became impossible to restrain. They fought constantly, and yet they were irrevocably tied to and dependent on one another.

BY 1914, MILENA had graduated from Minerva Academy and her father decided that, since he did not have a son to follow in his footsteps, Milena would be enrolled in medical school. This brief period ended when she fainted at her first in-class autopsy. She hated blood and found the work her father did reconstructing the faces of soldiers both noble and grotesque.

Milena, once again, was free to fill her days. She and Staša drew the attention of onlookers when they strolled the Prague streets. They wore their hair cut short in the European style. They were modern, open to new ideas. They loved to read foreign writers such as Dostoevsky, Kierkegaard, Thomas Mann, and even Einstein. And at times Milena could be outrageous. A story everyone knew was how Milena once threw herself, fully clothed, in the Vltava River and swam across because she was late for a meeting.

With her new freedom and her intellectual curiosity, she discovered the creative and intellectual life of the Prague café scene: "In the café, one writes, makes corrections, converses. In the café, family scenes are played out; in the café, one cries and rails against life. In the café, one eats on credit, the most reckless financial transactions take place. In the café, one lives, one is lazy, and the hours pass."[16]

There were two cafés in Prague where writers and intellectuals gathered. Café Union had a predominantly Czech clientele, and Café

Arco was the central meeting place for the thriving German Jewish literati of Prague. The two cafés competed with each other to offer the most daily journals, European and Russian periodicals, international newspapers, and reviews. Decorated in the art deco style, the elegant Café Arco was one of the most important literary meeting places in the early twentieth century. Artists, writers, journalists, editors, and thinkers flocked there, including Franz Kafka, his friend and biographer Max Brod, screenwriter and film critic Willy Haas, and playwright and poet Franz Werfel. Young German-speaking students from mostly bourgeois Jewish families gathered here to meet and talk about German writers. But there was also an interest in Czech culture and language, and in Czech folk songs as poetry. The absurdity of the First World War had had a profound effect on the younger generation, who dreamed of a world without borders. And their cosmopolitan vision appealed to Milena, with her capacious curiosity.

There were heated debates and passionate meetings. Each group had their own table: the table of gentlemen poets, the table of gentlemen constructivists, the table of gentlemen pragmatists, and so on. The head waiter, Mr. Počta, would carefully guide clients to the correct table. The "Prague Circle," started in 1904, met regularly here. Their stated mission was to break from neoromanticism, and from the rigid class structures of the past. The members recited poems at night that had been written earlier in the day. They read and corrected each other's manuscripts, argued about painters, and fell in and out of love with each other. There were "open" relationships and same-sex couples.

Milena frequented both the Café Union and the Café Arco, one of the few brave enough to cross an invisible divide. Her reputation as a rebel preceded her. With her stunning head of golden-red curls, her flamboyant, colorful style of dress, and her lively intellect, she was a prominent personality. Soon enough, Milena had fallen in love with one of Café Arco's main characters, Ernst Polak. He was ten years older, highly cultivated, and charmed by Milena. He claimed to have noticed her at a concert, when Milena was sitting on the steps of the center aisle, immersed in the score. She was wearing a purple evening dress, as though she were at a royal reception.

Ernst was not Milena's first lover. She had an earlier boyfriend as well as a few erotic explorations with girlfriends and a memory that was traumatic for her: She had been sexually assaulted when she was modeling for an older artist, one of her father's friends.

But she considered Ernst as her first real passionate love. It was 1916. She was twenty, strong and vivacious. Ernst was thin, intense, and stooped, as if burdened by his thoughts. Milena loved his burning intellect and his dark, close-set eyes. She threw herself into being in love and overwhelmed him with her affections. After their first night together, she dragged him up Petřín Hill to watch the sunrise, and he grumbled the whole way. He was a city boy and teased her about her romantic sentimentality for nature. But he climbed the hill. Another time, she stripped a local park of flowers, snuck into his studio apartment while he was away, and filled every surface with blossoms. When she called him to see how he liked her gift, he claimed not to have noticed the flowers.

Ernst worked as a translator in a Prague bank, but his true love was literature. He was friends with and mentored many writers in both Prague and Vienna. Through Ernst, Milena would meet Kafka.

When word got to her father that Milena was galivanting around on the arm of the German Jewish Ernst Polak, Jesenský flew into a rage and forbade her from seeing him. It was unclear which her father hated more, that Polak was German or that he was Jewish.

Needless to say, Milena ignored her father. Still, he sent her and her friend Jarmila off to Hotel Prokop on Mount Špičák, a retreat where the family often vacationed, naively hoping he could put distance between his daughter and "that Jew." But Ernst rented a room in a nearby hotel. Wilma, a friend who was also at the mountain resort, recalled how Milena appeared in her bedroom in the early hours in a "heliotrope-colored dress holding a bunch of flowers. Her bare feet were wet with the dew from the meadows." She jumped into Wilma's bed, hugged her, and whispered, "'Ernst spent the night with me.' She was radiant, utterly exhausted and entrancingly beautiful."[17]

Milena's adoration for Ernst surpassed his feeling for her. He was used to having many liaisons, and he was not going to change his habits for her. Her identity as an emancipated woman meant she had to accept this. But Milena's moods were volatile. She tried to commit suicide at least once. A troubled letter from Ernst to their mutual friend states, "I have pulled her three times from suicide."[18]

She was desperate to keep Ernst's love and attention. And she was frustrated by his ambivalence toward the feverish pitch of her love. Meanwhile, Ernst suffered from the endless turmoil, drama, and the unsettling confrontations with her father.

In the spring of 1917, she became pregnant. Either she found a midwife or doctor to perform an abortion, or she tried to do it herself, but Dr. Jesenský discovered her situation and saved her from a terrible hemorrhage. All his rage about her relationship with Ernst shifted into care and attention for his daughter. He looked after her and gave her morphine to soothe her to sleep. Milena would remember his tender care in letters she wrote to him years later from Ravensbrück.

The truce did not last. Soon Milena was back to her old ways. Dr. Jesenský felt humiliated by his daughter's behavior—all of Prague talked about her—and she was constantly after him for more money. Milena blatantly shoplifted, and the shopkeepers would send the bill to her father. Besides her scandalous behavior, she left a trail of unpaid bills that would damage the family reputation.

By June 1917, Dr. Jesenský could take it no longer. Milena was practically living in Ernst's studio apartment. She owed a fortune in debts. There was yet another incident of shoplifting, and almost a duel with Polak. Ernst wrote to Willy Haas that he pulled out a pistol to stop Dr. Jesenský, but in the end, Milena was taken by force to the sanatorium Veleslavín. She was still under twenty-one and her father was her legal guardian. The head of the clinic was her friend Staša's father, who wanted desperately to get his own daughter away from the degenerate influence of Milena. Because of the rumors that Milena and Staša were lovers, Staša's father was eager to help Dr. Jesenský. She was admitted on grounds of "moral insanity."

Milena was not the only young, free-spirited woman, bristling against the restraints of patriarchal society, to be locked away in an asylum. It was a common recourse for fathers and husbands trying to control uncontrollable women. The clinic was an elegant villa, but Milena was often put into a small, dark cell for solitary confinement, with just a peephole of light. She would later write to her friend Max Brod, "You should know that psychiatry is a terrible thing when it is abused. Anything can become abnormal, and each word becomes another weapon in the hands of the torturer."

In Veleslavín, she remained defiant as ever. With her first experience of imprisonment, there were the hints of how Milena would behave later in Ravensbrück. She didn't conform, and she was able to charm the staff. She befriended a young nurse who was enthralled with Milena's romantic tale of thwarted love. The nurse eventually gave Milena a key to a gate through the high walls of the villa's large park. With the help of Staša, Milena was soon meeting up with Ernst again.

The ordeal was not easy for Ernst. Milena had left enormous debts that he couldn't repay. He needed her father's help. But Dr. Jesenský wanted to put Milena permanently under his own guardianship. This would mean she would be completely under his control and shut away indefinitely, perhaps her whole life, in the sanatorium. Ernst was desperate to stop her father. The drama with Milena had aged him. Though he was thirty-one, he wrote to his good friend Willy Haas, "All that I have learned these last days about reality, and psychiatry, the law, men, relationships, and last but not least, about myself, is frightening. I was forty years old, now I am sixty."[19]

Ernst offered to marry Milena to save her from guardianship. He genuinely cared about her, even though he was already involved with someone else, a calmer and less complicated woman. Perhaps Milena knew this about her future husband. He never had a shortage of lovers. Finally, Dr. Jesenský was mollified by an agreement that the two would marry and leave Prague. If Ernst would take Milena to Vienna, Dr. Jesenský would take care of Milena's Prague debts. Her father promised the couple a dowry to start their life in Vienna. Milena was released from the clinic on March 7, and on March 16, 1918, she and Ernst were married.

Whatever honeymoon phase she had with Ernst, it was far shorter than the "honeymoon" Grete would remember with Milena during the Ravensbrück quarantine. From the first day, Milena was miserable in Vienna. She later recalled in a letter to Willi Schlamm, "When I arrived in Vienna, I was a young girl. I couldn't even speak a word of German and I had nobody to help me. Ernst left me at the train station of the big city . . . and went to his lover . . . At that time I had nobody in the world."[20]

Ernst was not abandoning her completely; he was putting her on notice that, despite their marriage, nothing really had changed. Their new life in Vienna would be like their old life in Prague, each one free to go their own way. Milena exaggerated her situation. At the station, she was helped by a friend of Ernst's named Kalmer, who became her close friend. She would later save Kalmer from the Nazis. And Milena exaggerated her lack of German. But she was young, lonely in a strange city, and Ernst was not the doting husband she had longed for. She would later write, "Novels for girls end in a wedding. In life, the wedding is the beginning."[21]

Ernst was in his element in Vienna. His return to his native city was good for his career at the bank and for his position in the literary world. He had many friends, and Milena had none. She would soon feel isolated, awkward, and out of place. In Prague, she was known and admired. In Vienna, she was known only as Ernst's Czechoslovak bride, the daughter of a famous medical professor. In Prague, Ernst was proud to have the alluring, beautiful, and somewhat scandalous Milena on his arm. In Vienna, he appeared to be embarrassed by her. She seemed provincial, and since her German wasn't good enough to participate actively in the intellectual conversations at the cafés where Ernst spent most of his free time, her intelligence went unnoticed.

Milena would soon feel homesick for Prague. It was a strange time for Vienna. In the spring of 1918, the old Austro-Hungarian Empire was crumbling. Once a glorious capital of the empire, Vienna now faced a grim-looking future. Even so, the German-speaking Prague Jews Ernst introduced Milena to felt they were safer now in Vienna, and not really welcome in the increasingly nationalistic Czechoslovakia. Meanwhile, back in Milena's homeland, her friends were anticipating that Czechoslovakia would be its own country at last.

Furthermore, the reverberations of the Russian Revolution could be felt in the air. Just as Grete was being swept up by revolutionary fervor in Berlin, Milena was swept up by the promise of a world based on equality and workers' rights. She was naively hopeful about the winds of change, while Ernst's Viennese café buddies were skeptical about the future and the Bolsheviks. Milena missed her girlfriends back in Prague. And though she saw herself as cosmopolitan and sophisticated, she was fundamentally Czech. By the fall, Prague was celebrating its independence, and Vienna was humiliated in defeat.

With the loss of the empire, Austria's most pressing problem was food. Austrians could no longer count on the lands of Hungary and Bohemia to feed them. Ernst and Milena were quickly burning through her dowry money, and she would soon resort to selling off her trousseau.

Milena did have a few friends. But even they found her taxing. She was generous, but she expected the same limitless generosity in return. When her friend Willy Haas asked her to help him find a room where he could to take a new girlfriend, she found a room and filled it with flowers. He wrote, "As a friend, she was inexhaustible, inexhaustible in kindness, inexhaustible in resources, the source of which often remained a mystery, but also inexhaustible in the demands she made on her friends . . . out of place amid the erotic and intellectual promiscuity of Viennese café society during the wild years after 1918, she was very unhappy."[22]

Once, after she had joined Ernst and his friends at the Café Herrenhof, Franz Blei remarked, "Take a look at Milena; there she is again, looking like six volumes of Dostoevsky."[23] She had begun to take drugs. A friend of Ernst's supplied her with cocaine, which added to their financial problems. She resorted to theft, shoplifting, and stealing from friends. She taught Czech and worked as a translator. To make ends meet, she even started to work as a luggage handler at the train station. Ernst would not support her, not financially nor emotionally, and her father was not there to save her. Ernst was open about his other affairs, even bringing one of his mistresses home to live with them. Milena grudgingly accepted this ménage à trois. However, when she took a lover, Ernst was not so open-minded. He talked her new lover out of being with her. Milena took this as a sign that Ernst really did love her.

She wanted to be glamorous and beautiful like the women who attracted Ernst's attentions. She was arrested for the theft of some jewelry from an acquaintance, and this time she was brought to court. Her friends got her off on the grounds of "incapacity," noting her time in the asylum. She defended her actions, saying that she had stolen because of an "erotic crisis." She had pawned the stolen jewels to buy a new dress and hat because she was so desperate to attract her husband's attention.

At twenty-three, Milena was desperate. What was she doing with her life? She could sense that some of Ernst's friends avoided her and saw her as crazy. Around Christmas in 1919, she began to write her personal observations of Vienna from the perspective of an exile. She sent her work to journals in Prague. Her friend Staša was the editor of *Tribuna*, the journal that took her first article. Milena quickly found her unique journalistic voice and developed a following with a regular column. She wrote about fashion, about café life, about the cinema, but she also wrote about the poverty and food crisis in Vienna, the political tensions, and the life of ordinary Austrians. She had found an outlet for her curiosity and keen insights. Many of her articles appeared under the title "Letter from Vienna," but what Milena really longed for was someone to write back to her.

In Ravensbrück, Milena entertained her fellow prisoners by reciting Kafka's stories from memory. Milena's rendition of the grinding, absurd bureaucracy in *The Trial* made her audience laugh

Franz Kafka, 1923

with recognition. It was as if Kafka had seen their future, had known what was going to happen to them. Grete had never read Kafka. Milena explained that he was one of the truly great literary figures of their time. She was convinced that history would recognize him, even if he was barely noticed during his lifetime.

Milena had known Kafka in Prague, but only vaguely. He was a shy German Jewish writer who occasionally showed up in Café Arco. But unlike her husband, Kafka did not hang out in the café, because most nights he was writing and during the day he worked as an insurance agent. In Vienna, Milena read and was immediately taken with the few short stories that Kafka had published. In October 1919, on a visit to Prague, she spoke to him briefly, and the following April 1920, with the encouragement of Ernst, she wrote to him asking if she could be his translator into Czech. Kafka was flattered and found her interest "somehow moving and embarrassing."

He grew up in Prague speaking Czech, but his family and mother tongue were German. He wrote to her in German. He asked that

Milena write him in Czech. "I want to read you in Czech because, after all, you do belong to that language, because only there can Milena be found in her entirety, whereas here there is only the Milena from Vienna or the Milena preparing for Vienna. So Czech please."[24]

He was suffering from tuberculosis, hoping to be cured or at least to slow down the progress of the disease. They began tentatively sharing details of their lives. Both were lonely, and through letters they felt understood by the other in a way that was compelling. He understood her position as an exile in Vienna. She understood his anxieties and fear. Very quickly, they moved from a professional exchange about her translations to intimate details of their lives. The grammar of their letters switched to the familiar address, and she called him Franz. Milena asked him about other women. She confided to him about her marriage. We don't know exactly what she wrote because her letters are lost, but through his letters, we know that Milena told him that Ernst had other lovers, that she had no money, that Ernst no longer paid any attention to her. There was a long exchange when Franz wrote about the difficulties of being Jewish. He was also reading her articles published in Prague. Milena was exhilarated by his attention. He praised her column in *Tribuna*. He begged her to take better care of herself. From his letters, we can see that quickly she wanted them to meet in person, perhaps in Karlovy Levy in Czechoslovakia. This threw him into a panic. His anxiety wouldn't allow him to take such a step, not so quickly and impetuously.

Since Ernst clearly was not attentive, she poured her heart out to Franz, and he responded in kind. There were daily letters back and forth, sometimes several a day. Milena appeared to have been hurt by his refusal to meet. He begged forgiveness, and then there were urgent telegrams and further letters.

Franz wrote, "This crisscrossing of letters has got to stop, Milena, it's driving us crazy, one doesn't know what one has written, what has been answered, and in any case one is in constant trepidation."[25] He couldn't come see her, but he did go on to say that she must leave her husband. "You see, as far as I'm concerned what's happening is incredible—my world is collapsing, my world is rebuilding itself; wait and see how you (meaning me) survive it all . . . How will we go on living? If you say 'yes' to my letters then it is impossible for you to go on living in Vienna."[26] He meant living with Ernst.

This was not the first time Kafka had initiated a passionate epistolary relationship. With Felice Bauer several years earlier, he maintained a similar exchange that lasted for five years, from 1912 to 1917. They were engaged and un-engaged several times. Felice was a practical, straightforward woman whom Kafka admired for her good business sense. His relationship with her coincided with a great breakthrough in his creative work. He wrote "The Judgment" and *The Metamorphosis* during their romance. He hoped the relationship with Felice could bring him the family and social status he longed for. With her, through her, he could be a good upstanding Jew, father, and husband in society. But his letters to her were full of his self-loathing and his recognition of his inability to function as a normal person. Once again, her side of the correspondence has been lost. The final break with Felice came when Kafka contracted tuberculosis. He wrote to her, "To make it short: My health is only just good enough for myself alone, not good enough for marriage, let alone fatherhood. Yet when I read your letter, I feel I could overlook even what cannot possibly be overlooked."

Milena, ten years his junior, wanted to have children and a family. Once again, he was overlooking what could not be overlooked. Franz had warned Felice that the life she would have with him "is not that of the happy couples you see strolling along before you in Westerland, no lighthearted chatter arm in arm, but a monastic life at the side of a man who is peevish, miserable, silent, discontented and sickly." He should have repeated the same warnings to Milena.

During this heady time, neither of them was likely to heed warnings. Franz sent his letters to Milena with the address "General Delivery." The letters would be held at her local post office. It was Franz's effort to keep their correspondence secret from Ernst, though Ernst appears to have known about it and even read a few of the letters. Milena might have wanted him to read the letters. He had long ceased to pay attention to her, and here was the writer Kafka praising her brilliance.

Milena would rush to the post office each day, and Franz waited for her letters to be delivered to his office. Some days he was in despair because three or four days went by without a response from Milena. And then he would get a packet of her letters that had been blocked in the post. Several times, Franz gently, but with a hint of annoyance, admonished Milena to write more legibly: "Milena, the addresses are again unclear, the Post Office has written over them and filled them in . . . If the Post Office had my eyes it could probably read your addresses alone and no others. But since it's the Post Office—"[27]

When they began their correspondence, Franz was engaged to be married to Julie Wohryzek, whom he calls "the girl." Again, he had kept this engagement in limbo. Their relationship was faltering just as his engagement to Felice had faltered. Franz blamed himself for putting her through torment. He had pursued her and then he had grown cold. He knew he had to call it off. This was his pattern, he tried to warn Milena. But he had fallen in love with Milena through her words and words alone. If it could have stayed in that realm, that might have been enough for Kafka. But Milena wanted more than words. He made plans to visit her in Vienna and then changed them. He said he might collapse from the strain of seeing her. He would rather go to Vienna and just stand outside her house. He was terrified of disappointing her. He had an overwhelming anxiety about their meeting. He was haunted by what he called "the fear."

Then, finally, it happened. On June 29, 1920, only two months after they began their breathless letter writing, he wrote, "I am indeed in Vienna, sitting in a café . . . I'll wait for you Wednesday starting at 10AM in front of the hotel. Please, Milena don't surprise me by coming up from the side or from behind."[28]

The next letter is dated July 4—five days later. It starts, "Today Milena, Milena, Milena, I can't write anything else." According to Franz, their brief interlude together had been bliss. For him, this was a completely new, life-altering experience. Milena later would describe the visit in a letter to Max Brod: "Whenever he sensed his fear, he would look me in the eyes, and we would wait a while, as if our feet hurt or we had to catch our breath, and after a moment it would pass." She made him hike with her over the hills behind Vienna. She walked ahead with all her energy and zest for long walks, and he followed more slowly behind. She remembered his white shirt and sunburned neck. He didn't cough; he slept well each night; he was healthy, and the disease, the tuberculosis, was at bay. It was as if Milena had cured him.

Kafka immediately broke off the engagement with "the girl." But she did not take it well, and he was full of self-recrimination. Because of her despair, and because he was awkward, he allowed Julie to write a letter to Milena. And Milena had to answer her. It was a torturous, complicated exchange, which probably annoyed Milena and only heightened Franz's anxieties. He also sent a letter meant for his father to Milena for safekeeping. It is a brilliant letter, which in the end Kafka's father never read. His letter described how Franz, a quiet, introverted, sensitive child, had felt growing up with a tyrannical, narcissistic father. Kafka didn't use those terms. He anticipated Freud and schools of psychoanalysis. But for those four days with Milena, he had experienced relative calm in her gaze. An oasis in his tormented anxieties. In the margins of a letter dated July 5, he wrote, "And despite everything, I think if it is possible to die of happiness then I will certainly do so. And if someone destined to die can be kept alive by happiness, then I will stay alive."[29]

The four days in Vienna confirmed his strong feelings for Milena. Perhaps at last he had found the one companion he could share his life with. To him, it seemed absolutely clear what the next steps were. She had to leave her husband.

But this was not so clear to Milena. Ernst was, after all, her first great love. He had saved her from the asylum and several suicide attempts. It might no longer have been the case, but in the past, they had enjoyed a satisfying sexual life together. She was not ready to abandon her husband. At one crucial moment, she wrote to Franz (he quotes the line in his letter back to her), "I love him, but I also love you." It was the "also" that was a dagger in Franz's heart.

As he did with all women, Kafka held an idealized version of Milena, and one can imagine that she wanted to keep it that way. He didn't understand why she had no money. And all through their letter writing, he appears to be sending her money. He was appalled to learn she was working as a porter. He wrote that he could support her, modestly. But Milena knew she wasn't the type to live frugally. It is doubtful that she had shared with him the details of her past, the thefts, the drugs, her extravagance. Franz lived a very calm monk-like existence. There is no indication that they slept together during their first meeting.

As convinced as Franz was that Milena was the perfect woman for him, their four days together had stirred up doubts in her. There were a number of incidents that troubled Milena. She described them later to Max Brod. She observed how tortuous everyday acts were for him. How almost incapable he was of functioning.

On one day, they went to the post office in Vienna so that he could send a telegram. Milena watched with horror and compassion as he struggled to find the right window. He went from one line to the next, compulsively unable to choose. While he was consumed by his task, Milena observed the bemused expressions of onlookers. Finally, he made his choice, and Milena felt a moment of relief. He paid and received his change. They had turned at last to leave when he realized the clerk had given him too much change.

"I have to go back," he insisted to her shocked expression. "To return the extra krone."

But then, once again, as they were walking out together down the stairs of the post office, he realized he was wrong, and now he needed to go back to get the krone from the clerk.

It was one crown, a tiny amount of money. And he had made such a fuss, going up and down the stairs, back to the window. People were watching him. Exasperated, Milena said, "Can't we just forget it?"

Franz was horrified. It was not about the money. It was about being correct. He would continue to talk about the incident and the krone for a long time, unable to understand Milena's comment.

This type of scene played out before her everywhere, at every restaurant and shop. She felt embarrassed by him under the gaze of others. And at the same time, she felt great tenderness for the suffering and torment his anxiety caused him.

At one point, he gave a beggar woman a two-krone coin and he wanted her to give him one krone back. But she didn't have one krone. They spent a good two minutes talking about what to do about this. It must have driven Milena to exasperation. She could not be bothered with this kind of minute account keeping. But she understood him. Franz was not petty or greedy. She understood that if she asked him for twenty thousand kronen, he would give it to her.

With growing dread, Milena witnessed over those four days how all-consuming his compulsive anxiety really was. And she intuited that "his anxiety in the face of money is almost the same as his anxiety in the face of women." She could see that Franz was not someone who "chooses asceticism as a means to an end; here is a man forced to be ascetic because of his terrible clairvoyance, his purity and inability to compromise."[30] She saw that "life for him is something entirely different than for all other human beings."

Inexorably over the next few weeks after their meeting, Franz realized that Milena was not planning to leave Ernst. "I am not fighting your husband for you, this fight exists only within yourself." A few weeks later, he wrote, "For you see, Milena, if you had been completely convinced by me in Vienna . . . you would no longer be in Vienna . . . you'd simply be in Prague." She made excuses that are as ridiculous to us today as they were to Franz then. She wrote that she had to stay because Ernst needed her to polish his boots.

Milena was in turmoil. She begged Franz to meet her. She wrote telegrams and phoned him and even cursed him in letters. She needed to see him just for a day. He could not sleep thinking about this; he tormented himself; he wrote her letters full of self-hatred and self-loathing, but he did not go to her. And the reason was one that was so alien to Milena: He would not lie to his boss. He could not lie to anyone. And showing how little he understood Milena, he asked her, "By the way, since when are you capable of lying?"

When they finally met again in Gmünd for a day—it was doomed. Milena resentfully made it clear to him how much she had been forced to lie to Ernst in order to meet him there. The plan was that they would spend the night together. When he visited her on the first meeting in Vienna, she had returned home each night. Gmünd was supposed to be different. In preparation for this second visit, she had asked him to explain how his fear could cope with his "longing." Milena seems to have been trying to understand if they would be able to make love.

His letter to his father had addressed this issue obliquely. He wrote how his father left him with a feeling of shame about his physical weakness. But to Milena, Franz wrote clearly, or confessed for perhaps the only time, about his problems with sex. He explained his first sexual encounters left him with a feeling of disgust about his own body. He hated the sight of flesh. He had sexual encounters and desires, which he called trivial, embarrassing, and repulsive. But he said that with Milena he did not have this. She was too pure for him to feel sexual desire for her. This would not have reassured Milena.

He had once again misunderstood her. When they were lying in the fields in the hills on their first meeting in Vienna and he had his head "resting on your almost naked breast," she had said, in her poetic metaphorical way, they were already as one. He took this to mean that there was no need for sex. When she had written to him about the "half-hour in bed," he took her to mean it disdainfully and that this was only men's business. For Franz, this was fine because that "men's business" was "an abyss I cannot span, probably because I don't want to." He had been tempted in his past engagements with Felice and then "the girl" to get married because he wanted to have children. But the actual sex act was impossible to him. "Hastily, panting, helpless, demonically possessed . . ." he wrote, "maybe there isn't any other way to have children . . . let's skip the question for now."

All of this must have been terrible for Milena. "I was too much a woman to have the strength to subject myself to a life that I knew would demand the most rigorous asceticism, for the rest of my days,"[31] she wrote to Max Brod. In an article that she would later write for *Národní listy*, she expressed her belief that sex was important and necessary: "The erotic life of a person is something like the sun, like water, like air. Something joyful, vibrant, an elixir, something essential to life."[32]

Whatever did or did not happen when they met in Gmünd, it was clear that the relationship was not going to have a happy outcome. Franz wrote to Milena in September 1920, "I don't believe in letters anymore; even the most beautiful ones always contain a worm."[33]

They continued to correspond but with growing anguish and despair until Franz begged her to stop writing him altogether. He couldn't stand the strain of waiting for her letters and the pain of reading them. And she, though it broke her heart, complied with his wish. His health was faltering, and in two years he would be dead. She continued to translate his work. And she appeared to send him messages through her articles, quoting sections from his work that she was translating and making direct reference to things they had discussed in their letters.

In "Mysterious Redemption," published two months after their breakup, Milena, knowing that Franz read her articles, was clearly writing to him: "Pain shuts you up in a narrow cage, without doors or windows; there is no exit and no air. People walk by you, mute and blind; but all of a sudden some roof, cart or bit of sky seems to open wide the walls of pain, the invisible gates fly open and the lungs, liberated, exhale." The article is a longing plea to Kafka and an avowal that she understands his suffering. "I firmly believe the world helps. Somehow, some way, all of a sudden, unexpectedly, simply, compassionately. But sometimes this salvation is almost as painful as the pain itself . . . One has to press one's head between one's hands and ardently, ardently love life, so that it will be appeased by such a great love and redeemed from damnation."[34]

Though the relationship with Franz was tormented and painful, it had helped liberate her finally from Ernst. She was growing more confident about her own writing and career. Once Kafka and those daily letters of praise stopped coming, she looked around and wondered why she was staying in Vienna. She had her career, a readership following for her columns, and she wanted so much more from life.

WHEN MILENA RETURNED to Prague, she was no longer the young, emotionally volatile girl she had been when she first married. She was divorced from Ernst and now the editor of the women's section of the Czech newspaper *Národní listy*. She brought together a circle of creative female friends, many of them fellow Minervans. There was a strong sense of feminism in this group. They were forging a new world for women. They talked about the new fashion, which was simple and unencumbered, without all the old-fashioned laces, buttons, girdles, and constraints. She was a principal player in the Czech avant-garde of the 1920s and a group called Devětsil. Inspired by Le Corbusier and Bauhaus, she wrote about design and fashion that favored air, movement, natural light, and functionality. She also wrote about cinema, taking this newest art form seriously. She praised sports and exercise for the body, fresh air and freedom. She and her circle of friends were enthusiastic about the future and all the new technologies like the airplane and the skyscraper.

She did see Franz again a few times, and she might have been at his bedside right before his death, but she was at peace with their relationship. Milena would always love and admire him and hold him high above others. But she was wise about her choices. When she left Ernst, it was on her own terms, as a woman in command of her world. Ernst had made her lose her self-confidence. She had forgotten how brave she could be. Being with Franz would have entailed another kind of effacement.

In her obituary for Kafka, published in June 1924, she wrote, "His knowledge of the world was extraordinary and deep; he was himself an extraordinary and deep world. He has written the most significant books of Modern German literature . . . He was a man and a writer with such a fearful conscience that he heard things where others were deaf and felt safe."[35]

Around 1926, she met her future husband, the architect Jaromír Krejcar, on a daylong boat cruise organized by an art club on the Vltava River. As a wonderful raconteur who loved to dance and sing, Milena attracted attention. Jaromír spotted her and did not leave her side the entire day. It was love at first sight, and for once, it was mutual. He was the only child of a forester family. He had grown up in the woods and loved the outdoors, knew all the flowers, herbs, and animals. He could recognize the birds by their song and knew when and where Milena's favorite wildflowers bloomed in the mountains. They went on long hikes together. This was a refreshing change from the urban Franz and Ernst. After the torment of Franz and the ambivalence of Ernst, she finally had found someone with whom she could share her passion. Milena and Jaromír were very much alike in character. Both were capable of borrowing money to hire a taxi to drive them to the Bohemian forest or up to the high Tatra Mountains because they felt a need to be in nature.

In 1927, Jaromír's Olympic building created a sensation. One of the first structures in the country to use a concrete skeleton, it was called Olympic because it housed the Olympic movie theater along with various stores. Following this success, he won another commission to design a building that would include a new home for himself and Milena. He created a purely functionalist modern building with a flat facade and no frills. On the ground floor, there was a café and restaurant, and in the basement, there was a ballroom in the shape of an ellipse.

Jaromír's studio and the apartment he shared with Milena were on the top floor of the building with a wraparound terrace. Though it had an austere, functionalist exterior, large windows flooded the inside space with sunlight. From their apartment terrace, Milena could see the rooftops and church spires of her beloved Prague. Their apartment became a meeting place of the left-leaning avant-garde and intellectuals in Prague. Later Jiří Weil wrote, "In that time, when people gathered at Milena's for those Saturdays, it was beautiful, not the beauty of a picture magazine, but the beauty of life, bright and colorful."[36] Their apartment was very sparsely furnished. It had many modern innovations, including built-in bookcases and cupboards, a three-part couch with drawers for bedding, colored carpets, and up-holstery in a simple geometrical motif. Jaromír had designed the tables and armchairs in the large open living room around the fireplace. In Milena's room, there was only a wide chaise longue. A black cross hung over her bed, and a huge reproduction of Van Gogh's *Sunflowers* hung on one wall. Jaromír had his room on the other side of the hallway behind his office. He slept on a mattress that their maid, Marie, would lay on the floor in the evening and take away in the morning. The pared-down, sparse modernist feel was the opposite of Milena's father's baroque, darkly furnished, and overstuffed apartment.

Milena was at the height of her journalistic career. And by 1928, at the age of thirty-two, she was pregnant. She wrote in a letter to her good friend Staša that she was happy for the first time since her mother's death.

But something happened. During her final months of pregnancy, she hurt her knee. Septic arthritis turned her knee red and black, and terribly swollen. She could not bend it or walk. The pain was excruciating. Jaromír took her to a place known for its miraculous waters and mud baths. To try and mobilize the frozen knee, they used a torturous orthopedic device. The pain was overwhelming, and she was given injections of morphine.

To her daughter, she would tell a story of a skiing accident—she had wanted to prove to Jaromír that not even pregnancy could slow her down. To Grete in Ravensbrück, she told a story about how a swim in a freezing mountain lake had triggered a terrible bout of rheumatoid arthritis. From both, she hid the true origins of the rheumatoid arthritis that would plague her to the end of her life. The start in the long decline of her health was neither a frozen lake nor a skiing accident. The septic arthritis was venereal in origin. Penicillin was discovered in 1928, but it was only used as a cure for gonorrhea starting in 1943. Before then, treatments included intravenous mercurochrome injections, arsenic, silver nitrate tablets, and heat therapy. None of these treatments were truly effective, and some caused more harm, even death. After the First World War, sexually transmitted diseases had reached epidemic proportions in Europe. Prostitutes were blamed for the spread of the disease to soldiers who then brought it home to their wives. Modern epidemiologists believe that in the period between the wars, one in ten people had syphilis, and three to four in ten had gonorrhea. Though widespread and terrifying, it remained a taboo subject. Wives were not allowed to speak about it, and that powerlessness is believed to be one of the factors that inspired the suffragette movement. By the time Milena met Grete in Ravensbrück, her kidneys and bladder had been ravaged by the untreated venereal disease.

Because Milena was immobilized by her bad knee and possibly already addicted to morphine, the delivery of her baby daughter, Honza, was difficult. For thirty-two hours of labor, which ultimately ended in a Cesarean, Milena wished for a boy and gripped her thumbs, a Czech ritual when you are making a wish. Honza was born holding on to her thumbs. Milena would often ask her daughter, "What were you wishing for?"

Milena found her invalid situation almost too much to bear. She wondered if she would ever be happy again. She fell into a deep depression, not helped by the postpartum difficulties of being a new mother. Her father was attentive and consumed with helping her through the health crisis. He consulted other doctors. She was unable to care for her new baby, and he offered to take over caregiving, but Milena refused. She told her friend and colleague Jaroslava Vondráčková that she would rather drown her child than have it be raised by her father. There was a fragile peace between them, but she could not forgive him for shutting her away in the asylum.

She was taking more and more morphine, and in a letter to Jaroslava, she confided, "I live only for my injections of morphine, which almost no one knows and almost no one knows how many . . ."[37]

By the autumn of 1929, she was able to leave the hospital, but only with a permanent limp and a strong addiction to morphine. Soon she was out of work. Her contract with the *Národní listy* newspaper was canceled. Many biographical accounts of Milena, in fact almost all of them, remark that she had gained weight and lost her beauty.

She was part of a milieu and an era when her changed appearance would be remarked upon. She often talked about it with Grete, saying that at least in Ravensbrück she was able to lose weight and be her old size again. The dramatic change in her appearance added to her plummeting sense of self-worth.

She tried writing a column in another newspaper under the "baby" section, but when she wrote under a pseudonym about drug addiction, they fired her. The financial difficulties, along with her addiction, took a toll on her marriage. She and Jaromír were no longer in love and they separated. She had several male and female lovers during this period.

MILENA'S OFFICIAL FLIRTATION with the Communist Party began in 1930. In Ravensbrück, she would tell Grete that before her physical problems, she had been a superficial person not really interested in social or political problems. Having her whole life upended, along with becoming a mother, had changed that. In its ideal version, communism aligned with her innate sense of justice. Why should so many suffer and only a few prosper? She threw herself into the work and the ideology. She wrote for the journal *Tvorba* and for the communist illustrated weekly *Svět práce* (*World of Work*). As was her way, Milena became passionate about the ideals of communist doctrine. But the writing she did during this period is not very good. She would admit to Grete that it was wearying to write the same hackneyed slogans and catchphrases and bend reality to fit the party line.

She and Jaromír had divorced, though they maintained a strong friendship for the rest of their lives. Milena remained close to all her former lovers and husbands, and even, at times, took in their girlfriends and wives.

She was forced to leave their beloved apartment and move to a smaller one with Honza; Marie, the maid and nanny; and their many cats. The contradiction in being a communist and having a maid seemed not to have been a problem for Milena, who ended up converting Marie into a staunch communist.

In 1934, Jaromír was invited to the Soviet Union. He left as an ambitious idealistic architect, and he returned disillusioned, and with a new wife. Jaromír told stories of arrests for no apparent reason, and about Stalin's weird cultlike following. He had a story about a new modern building that was lauded as the great glory of the Soviet Union with its central heating and flushing toilets. But with the first frost, it was clear the heating did not work, and so each apartment had an old-fashioned stove pipe coming out of a window belching black coal smoke. He said that people did not dare inquire if a friend had disappeared, and when he asked about someone he had not seen for a few days, the response would be "Who do you mean?" He talked about the show trials where Bolshevik heroes were condemned.

Milena was asked by the party to take care of an ill comrade, Evžen Klinger, who, much to her surprise, fell in love with her. Meanwhile, the contradictions were growing, with the rumors about purges in Moscow and the rhetoric that clashed with Milena's common sense. She was always a person who questioned authority. The final straw for Milena came when the editor of the paper where she worked told her she had to break off her relationship with her new lover, Evžen, who had been declared a Trotskyite. She slapped the editor and stormed out, slamming the door. The choice between loyalty to ideology and friendship would always be an easy one for her.

The break left her once again without work. What little income she got was from doing translations from Hungarian with Evžen. He was Jewish, something her father must have hated, but even though she and her father were not speaking, her father still subsidized their life. Every Sunday, Honza visited her grandfather, and he gave her a coin for herself and an envelope for her mother. He would ask how Milena was doing, and Honza would provide the anodyne answer "Mom is doing fine."

Honza did not tell him about the daily effort to keep Milena supplied with morphine. She had discovered cough tablets called Dicodit that contained high levels of morphine, and were normally only available by prescription. They kept a yellow jar full of these tablets next to the tea set in the kitchen. But they never lasted long.

Then Honza and Evžen would scour the pharmacies, begging the different pharmacists that "just this once," they needed more tablets. Honza remembered the transformation in her mother when they were out of tablets and she began withdrawal. It was as if her mother suddenly became an old woman, drawn and exhausted yet bristling with rage.

One time, Milena decided to try to kick the habit on her own at home. She locked herself into her room and gave firm instructions to both Evžen and Honza that they must under no circumstances open the door or provide her with morphine. The whole family was happy, almost euphoric about Milena's resolve.

But eventually, Milena was begging Honza, through the keyhole of the locked door, that if she didn't get tablets quickly, she would be forced to throw herself out the window. A terrified Honza promised her mother that she would do everything within her power to get the Dicodit. Milena told her to hurry, that she had to get the pills and get back before Evžen returned from wherever he was because he would not let Honza give them to her. Honza rushed out into the Prague night in search of an open pharmacy. She was only a child, but she was terrified she would return too late. That her mother would have thrown herself out of the window. When she found the only open pharmacy, at Strossmayer Square, she also found Evžen. He too was scouring the city in search of Dicodit for Milena.

There were good times as well. Honza and Milena often went to the cinema together. Milena did not care if the subject of the film was not meant for children. And she seemed to have no problem convincing the ushers to let Honza attend, even if the film was restricted to adults. Afterward, they would walk home slowly, talking about the ideas and questions that the film raised. Both mother and daughter loved to walk through the city at night. Milena was never impatient and always happy to talk and listen to Honza's ideas. After watching *La grande illusion*, Honza had so many questions. She asked her mother to explain war, and what did "grand illusion" mean. They walked for hours discussing ideas of honor and human decency.[38] Honza remembered walking from chestnut seller to chestnut seller

Milena, circa 1930

in the cold winter, using the roasted chestnuts to keep their fingers warm.

Milena was fastidious about the beauty of their home. Their apartment was full of flowers. In the window boxes, Milena grew flowers from seeds, but the flowers in the vases were often taken from Vyšehrad Cemetery and from Letná and Stromovka parks. Once, Milena was caught by the park gardener as she was clipping half-open rosebuds to add to the already full bouquet in her arms. Honza recalled how Milena was able to convince the gardener that she was helping him by pruning the overgrown buds that were sapping the strength of the bush. He went from being angry to thanking her for being such a good citizen. It was a pity that not all citizens took such care of their public gardens. Honza knew only too well about her mother's persuasive powers.

As Hitler annexed Austria and then took the Sudetenland, more and more refugees from Nazi Germany poured into Prague. Milena became a contributor for the monthly *Přítomnost*, working for the

excellent editor Ferdinand Peroutka, who would later survive Buchenwald to become a cofounder of Radio Free Europe. Milena was
given free rein to report on what concerned her. She described the
plight of the refugees and the dangers of fascism. Some of her best work
comes from this period. Her reports were closely observed, precise,
understated, and intense. She was working with the Czechoslovak
Refugees Committee, founded by Marie Schmolka, a Czechoslovak
Jewish activist and social worker. They helped political and Jewish refugees escape the Protectorate of Bohemia and Moravia in the
lead-up to the war.

Despite his misgivings, Peroutka allowed Milena to travel to the
Sudetenland to write about what was happening there. Her ability to
get the human-interest story made her an excellent reporter. Besides
the political facts, Milena was able to talk to mothers who admitted
that they lived in fear that their children would turn them in to the
Gestapo. The children had been brainwashed into believing that it
was both an honor and a duty to denounce an enemy of the Reich,
even if the enemy was their own mother.

By 1938, Milena had seen the effects of the Austrian *Anschluss*
and the occupation of the Sudetenland. With her singular clarity and
vision, she realized that she had to kick her morphine habit if she
was going to survive what was coming. She entered a hospital and
underwent a difficult and painful detox program. She returned emaciated and depressed but clean, to Honza's relief.

Her sobriety came just in time.

On the night of March 14, Milena could not sleep; she knew what
was coming. As she would write in an article published in *Přítomnost*:
"How do great events happen? Unexpectedly and all at once. But
when they are upon us, we always find that we are not surprised."[39]

As she and Honza sat looking out the window of their Prague apartment, slowly, in the early hours, around three A.M., one by one, lights
went on in the other apartments around them. People were receiving the news. At four A.M., the radio announced, "Attention. Attention. The German Army has crossed the border and is moving toward
Prague. Keep calm!" Hitler would take all of Czechoslovakia and

declare it the German-ruled "Protectorate Bohemia-Moravia" and a "Slovak Free State." As soon as Milena heard the announcement over the radio to "keep calm," she began burning all compromising documents, as well as Honza's red Pioneer scarf, a real Soviet one from the days when Milena took her to the May Day parades.

When dawn broke, Milena, weary and heartsick, called her Jewish friends. Her first question was "Have you heard?" And when they answered "Yes," she told them, "Count on me. I won't let you down."

One of the people she called that night was Willy Haas. He later recalled, "Milena seemed to have been made to deal with catastrophes. The more distraught her friends were, the more calm, the more steadfast, the greater she was."[40]

In the cold, gray early morning, Milena watched as people took their children to school and went to work. The streets were silent. "I have never heard so many people being so profoundly silent," she told Grete. "No crowds formed. No one looked up from their desk. At 9:30, the vanguard of Hitler's army reached the city center. German Army trucks rumbled down Národní Třída, the Main Street of Old Prague. As usual, the sidewalks were full of people, but no one turned to look." For Milena, this collective ignoring of the triumphant Nazi army was a form of silent resistance.

In an article that was published on March 22, entitled "Prague, the Morning of 15 March 1939," Milena wrote:

The Tomb of the Unknown Soldier is on the Staroměstské náměstí. On March 15 it was buried under a mass of snowdrops . . . That strange force, which in some mysterious way guides our steps, had led swarms of people to this place, and they had laid armfuls of flowers on that little grave recalling great memories. The people around were all in tears. Men, women and children. And once again their behavior was typically Czech: no loud sobs, no sign of fear, no violent outbursts. Only grief. Their grief had to find some outlet . . . I caught sight of a German soldier at the back of the crowd. He raised his hand to his cap. He realized that these people were in tears because he was in Prague. I recall our beautiful illusions and wonder if Germans and Czechs, Frenchmen and

Russians will ever be able to live together in peace, without harming, without hating, without wronging one another.[41]

Sometime during the day on March 15, Milena's father called her. He knew about her activities and about her articles in *Přítomnost*. Their conversation was brief and terse. Her father expressed concern for her safety, and she batted away his worries.

Honza went to visit him a few days after the invasion. She walked to his house. Everyone was boycotting the trams since the Germans had put up bilingual German-Czech signs on all the stations and in the trains. Her grandfather was reading the newspaper, his face hidden behind the large journal. Honza ate her lunch in silence with just the ticking of the grandfather clock in the dining room. When she was done, he lifted his head from his newspaper. "And what is going to happen to that Mr. Klinger who lives with you?"

"Evžen? He will have to leave the country." Honza had heard her mother and Evžen talking about it. They kept nothing hidden from her.

"Where do you suppose he will go?" her grandfather asked.

"England." Honza thought that England must be a wonderful place, and she was almost envious that Evžen got to go on such a journey.

Her grandfather shook his head and grunted dismissively, "Well, I'm sure they can't wait for him to get there!" He stood up abruptly and walked to his desk. He rummaged around and then gathered a roll of foreign money. He put it in an envelope and handed it to Honza.

"Give him that so at least he can get himself a meal there. You don't think they will be waiting for him on the platform with open arms, do you? It'll help him get started."[42]

Then he returned to his newspaper. He wanted to make it clear to Honza that this token of solidarity did not mean that he liked Evžen. She finally tucked the thick package away in her coat and said good-bye to her grandfather.

When she got home, she gave the envelope to her mother. Milena burst into tears. Not only did it contain the foreign money and some dental gold, but also a gold watch he cherished that he was awarded long ago for receiving his school certificate.

Milena's work moved underground, and she resisted the Nazi occupation in multiple ways. She helped many people emigrate, both strangers and close friends, including Ernst Polak and later Klement Gottwald, who would become president of Czechoslovakia following the communist takeover in 1948 and who was, for a time, one of Milena's lovers. She was in contact with Major Jaroslav Hájíček from the leadership of the illegal organization Defense of the Nation and helped organize border crossings. She sent letters abroad through emigrants and couriers in which she kept the exiled government informed about the situation in the protectorate. And she collaborated to write and distribute illegal anti-Nazi leaflets and a newspaper.

A German medical student, Count Joachim von Zedtwitz, had brought together a small group of friends to smuggle Jews out of the country. Handsome, with the carefree nature of someone who had grown up in wealth, Joachim cultivated the air of a dandy and pretended to be somewhat empty-headed. But Milena saw through his strategy and appreciated his tactics. Joachim had an Aero coupe that he used to drive people to the border and relative safety in Poland. But his group needed a safe house, a hiding place for refugees awaiting their chance of escape. The Gestapo was already offering rewards to anyone who provided information leading to the arrest of prominent Jews.

Someone in the small group thought of Milena, who immediately agreed to help. With this group, Evžen escaped to Poland. Her apartment became a hiding place for various people threatened by the Nazis: Jews, communists, anti-fascists, Czech nationalists. On her advice, the group extended its aid to rescue Czechoslovak officers and aviators.

The qualities in her character that had once been judged as immoral now served Milena and the rescue group. She was a master at camouflage, at using her charm and intelligence to elude the system, at inventing stories under pressure. She found hiding places and enlisted others. She was impassive and shrewd when questioned by police. She was acutely aware of the danger all around her and took risks to save others without calculation. Joachim, who now spent most of his time with her, was impressed by her skills and political wisdom. "At the time," he said, "Milena looked like Churchill. She had the same bulging forehead, the same prodigious intelligence in her eyes, the same asymmetrical mouth drawn in at the corners, the same look of determination. Her resemblance to Churchill is no accident; their looks reflect the same political genius."

For a while, before the journal *Přítomnost* was shut down, Milena continued to publish articles praising the Germans while dropping subtle hints to her Czech readers. She had a sly confidence in her Czech readers. They could read the irony in her words, but the ignorant Nazi censors accepted her words at face value. An article she wrote in June 1939 used as its title a line from "Cannon Song," an anti-war song from Bertolt Brecht's *Threepenny Opera*: "*Soldaten wohnen auf den Kanonen*," literally meaning "the soldiers live on the cannons." She begins, "This is a German song and one of the prettiest. As far as army songs are concerned, the German ones are always prettier—or more soldierly—than ours."[43] The Czechs sang about love and flowers, while the Germans sang of blood and heroism. Milena must have been holding back her laughter as she wrote these words. The article passed the ignorant Nazi censors. However, after publication, Wolfgang von Wolmar, the SS agent overseeing the Czechoslovak press, confronted Milena. Didn't she know that song was from Brecht? And Brecht was a communist, hated by the Nazis? Milena smiled and pleaded innocence. She had no idea. She had heard the song somewhere and thought it was just a typical German song because it was so German and so soldierly.

He flew into a rage. "Enough! There are limits to everything. Do you think I was born yesterday?"

For Milena, pushing this man into a rage was a victory. She enjoyed goading and poking at the limits, manipulating the Nazi thugs. Despite Evžen's repeated pleas, she and Honza never joined him in exile. She had promised him they would to get him to leave Prague, where he was in grave danger. After he had successfully reached England, he wrote many times, but Milena always had an excuse to put off their departure. There was plenty of time. She had so much work to do. But mainly Milena did not want to leave her beloved Prague again.

Milena's apartment was a not-so-secret meeting place and a refuge. Joachim recalled, "Milena who always wore a blue dress and welcomed every new arrival with a sweeping gesture of hospitality comforted them all." But she took great risks. She talked too openly about her hatred of the Nazis. She appeared with Jewish friends in the streets, and when she learned that Polish Jews were being forced to wear a yellow star, she sewed one on her clothes and displayed it with pride.

It wasn't long before she was called in for questioning by the Gestapo. When she was asked if she was associating with Jews, she responded, "Of course I am. Have you any objections?"

They asked about Evžen—where was he? She shrugged her shoulders. Evžen had already made his escape.

"Is the father of your child a Jew?"

"I regret to say he is not."

The Gestapo agent was enraged. "That will not do. We are not used to such answers here."

"And I am not used to such questions," she replied.

In August 1939, Milena penned an introductory call to arms for the journal *V Boj*, which would soon become the most widespread underground journal of resistance. She appealed to Czechoslovak women to help their men and resist the Germans. The journal had a circulation of over a thousand, and the article was read by many more.

As brave as she was, Milena was aware of the growing danger. Honza remembers the last summer they spent together. The spring had been full of leave-taking, people escaping and people being arrested. Everyone prayed for the war and dreaded it. Milena sent Honza to a resort in western Moravia called Medlov, a collection of wooden huts around a beautiful lake. Milena joined her there in August, along with artists and intellectuals from Prague, all seeking a moment of reprieve from the tension of the looming war. Milena and Honza shared a hut with Jaromír and his new wife, Riva. There was a carnival atmosphere, a kind of frenzied hysteria. Everyone was slightly drunk, pushing away their fears for one last moment. Honza remembers that people gathered around the campfire at night. There was singing, the making of sudden friendships, and lovemaking all around. Nothing was secret. Milena took midnight swims in the lake floating on her back and looking at the stars. She was joyful, but then she could swerve into caustic sarcasm, followed by grief. Only eleven, Honza watched the adult world unravel around her.

Then came the news of the nonaggression pact between Soviet Russia and Germany, and the invasion of Poland. The escape route to the Polish border was no longer. They were trapped.

Honza and Milena returned to Prague. Milena helped as many people as she could. She went to police headquarters, asking after the disappeared. She delivered clothes to friends in prison. She had terrible insomnia and spent the nights listening to the radio, turning the dial in search of voices from cut-off countries. When she heard a familiar song, she would burst into tears.

Milena's principal concern was who would care for Honza if she was arrested. She regretted how much she had drawn her daughter into her work. But she also depended on her. The two were inseparable. Milena's parenting philosophy was to treat children like adults. An independent child, she had hated her father's attempts to restrain her. In an article titled "Children" for *Tribuna*, she wrote: "There are no children in the spiritual sense of the word. A child is a complete person; a child is a perfectly developed soul. There is nothing that a child cannot understand or sense."[44]

It was Honza's job to pick up the illegal newspaper *V Boj* when it was printed. With her short black hair cut like a boy's, Honza looked like the child she was and could pass by without calling attention to herself. She had become astute at hiding things from the Nazis. The day before Honza was supposed to go pick up the latest issue, Milena called the apartment to alert the person that Honza was coming. A strange voice answered the phone in Czech and said the owner of the apartment would be returning shortly. When Milena called the next day, she heard the same voice and the same story. But Milena still didn't believe it could be the Gestapo. Recklessly, Milena sent Honza to the apartment with instructions that she was to say she was coming to get her mother's books. If the Gestapo were there, she was to ask if she could call home to ask her mother which books.

The door was answered by a Czech-speaking police officer and behind him a German Gestapo officer. Honza tried the line about the books and said she needed to call her mommy to ask what books exactly and the officers started to laugh. They would take her to her mommy so she could ask in person. There was no way out. Eleven-year-old Honza tried to delay. She gave them the wrong directions to her house, but in the end, she had to lead them there.

In front of Honza, at the door to their apartment, Milena was arrested on November 11, 1939, along with Lumír Čivrný, a young student who was giving Honza private lessons. He was also part of the resistance organization and Milena's latest lover. At police headquarters, though the two were held separately, at one moment they were in the same waiting room. Milena had already been questioned, and Lumír, white with fear, was waiting his turn. Milena grabbed a wash pail and scrub brush that had been left in the corner. Pretending to be the cleaning lady, she scrubbed the floor, on her hands and knees, working her way over to Lumír, where she whispered, "I told them nothing. You were just a tutor who happened to be in the house." With this reassurance, Lumír maintained his innocence and was released. He would survive the war and become a well-known writer and, after 1968, a dissident.

Honza lived for a time with friends, then with her father, and finally with her grandfather. Milena was held at Pankrác in Prague and questioned many times, but she was skilled at these exchanges and often outmaneuvered the interrogators. She was sent to Benešov camp for people who had consorted with Jews, and then she was sent to Dresden prison. In the damp cold of her cell and with the

meager diet, her health deteriorated. The articular rheumatism
that had first destroyed her knee returned. Almost a year later, she
was informed that the charges of having collaborated in an illegal newspaper had been dropped because of lack of evidence. She
was returned to Prague to be released. She had a brief visit from
Honza and her father during this time. And then, instead of being
freed, she was handed over to the Gestapo for "protective custody,"
and in October 1940, at the age of forty-four, she was deported to
Ravensbrück.

BY LATE SUMMER of 1941, Grete and Milena's brief "honeymoon"
during the camp quarantine had come to an end, and Ravensbrück
began to slide inexorably into more sinister terrain. The sweet period
ended just as suddenly as it had started with the arrival of a specialist doctor. He quickly assessed the situation and declared the paralysis was just mass hysteria. Sonntag, disgraced, avenged himself by
applying electric shock to all the paralyzed women. Most recovered
quickly.

The food rations in the camp had been cut substantially. Since the
German invasion of the USSR in June, there was considerably less
food available in general, and every country in Europe was suffering
from serious food shortages. In the Third Reich, the minister for food,
Richard Darré, and his state secretary, Herbert Backe, developed
the "Hunger Plan," which allocated food stores to Germany away
from "inferior populations" in the occupied countries. The plan was
explicit about using starvation as a tool to eliminate unwanted people
and led to the deaths of at least seven million Soviets, European
Jews, and many others.[45]

In Ravensbrück, the black market for stolen food was thriving.
Grete had been able to organize regular food thefts through her connections to a Polish woman working in the kitchen. From time to
time, she could even get a few loaves of bread, which she shared with
the three hundred Jehovah's Witness women in her block. She had
managed to get Milena some bread and margarine too. But whatever

Grete risked, Milena outdid her in daring. And Milena could never leave a gift unanswered.

One morning during work hours, Milena managed to carry a tray with a bowl of precious coffee, milk, and sugar all the way from the *revier* across the yard to Grete's block "without spilling a drop," she exclaimed, brimming with joy as she handed it to Grete. If she had been caught, Milena would have been beaten and locked in the *Strafblock*.

"How did you get this?"

"Stole it from Sonntag. It's his bowl!"

Grete felt weak in the knees. She wanted to cry, to beg Milena not to take such risks. "Please, Milena. I couldn't bear it if something happened to you," she said.

"Take a sip," Milena urged her. She couldn't stop smiling. "Tell me it tastes good."

Grete took a sip. The taste filled her mouth. "Did you hear me?" Grete asked. It was hard for her to swallow. "I couldn't go on without you."

"I couldn't live without you either," Milena whispered. "My blue angel, don't cry."

"It tastes good," Grete agreed.

Milena kissed her on the lips. "Yes, it does." She winked, and then Milena was gone, rushing off before anyone noticed that she and Sonntag's bowl of coffee were missing.

BY LATE 1941, Milena, ringed with her head of memorable curls, was an important camp personality, probably known by almost everyone. They saw her when they arrived for their intake medical exam.

Anna "Anička" Kvapilová recalled her arrival at Ravensbrück in October 1941 and the moment she first saw Milena. Anička had read Milena's articles and knew of her from before the war.

I was standing outside the infirmary with a group of newly arrived Czechs. We had been sent there for our medical examinations. Depressed and

bewildered by our first terrible impressions of the camp, we were anxiously awaiting the next torment. And then Milena stopped on the
stairs, smiled at us, and called out with a friendly gesture, "Welcome,
girls!" It came from the heart, as if like a hostess receiving her friends,
she was inviting every single one of us into her home. I was flabber-
gasted. I looked up at her and saw her shimmering red hair that surrounded her head like a halo. I'll never forget that impression. It was
the first really human touch amid all the inhumanity.[46]

Milena had successfully saved many women, usually *Asoziale*
prostitutes, from Sonntag's experiments. Not only was she in charge
of the card file for VD patients, but she had access to medicine. After
she forged their results, she would smuggle medication to those with
bad cases. She befriended the sick in the *revier*, and before she left
each day, she would pass by their beds, with a kind word for the most
desperate. She told Grete this was part of being a journalist; Milena
was collecting testimonies. But her willingness to risk her life for
the *Asoziale* women impressed Grete. As she later wrote: "Not only
did she do her best to save these women's lives, she also befriended
the poor creatures, talked to them, and listened to their troubles. In
many of them she discovered sparks of humanity."[47]

The choreographer and dancer Nina Jirsíková remembers meeting Milena for the first time on a sunny Sunday during the weekly
"free" exercise period in the central camp square. Nina was walking with her face toward the sun, and she saw Milena ahead of her,
with her head of curls, now mostly gray, shimmering like tufts of
dandelion. Her eyes were particularly expressive. Nina had heard
about Milena before she met her. There was a group of women who
did not like her because of her politics. And there was a group who
condemned her for her risqué past life. But Nina discovered a person
who had an inner strength and force of will. Nina knew that Milena
had lived an extravagant and undisciplined life before the war, but
she was completely in control of herself, and through that inner force
she was able to overcome humiliation and suffering. "A part of her
brave heart has stayed in my memory and has made me stronger.

I will always be grateful to her. She was one of a few women who helped me survive during the first days of my arrival, the most difficult days."[48]

THERE WAS A tuberculosis ward in the *revier*. In the early years, prisoners with tuberculosis were relieved from the difficult work gangs, and often released to avoid the spread of the disease in the camp. This gave Milena an idea.

Lotte Henschel had shared a cell with Grete during the brief period when Grete was in the Alexanderplatz police prison in Berlin, awaiting her transfer to Ravensbrück. They had become friends. Lotte knew that Grete had come from the Soviet Union, and for Lotte, the Soviet Union was the land of hope. She was in the German prison for communist activities. Eagerly, she asked Grete about her experiences in Mother Russia. Lotte wanted to know all about the miracle utopia. Instead, as Grete recounted her tale, Lotte sat on the mattress next to her and wept. "All those years I was consoled and strengthened by what the communists told me about Soviet Russia. It was my only hope. What have we got to live for now?"[49]

In Ravensbrück, Lotte continued her friendship with Grete, and through her, Lotte also became friends with Milena. Lotte had already spent four years in German prisons, and Milena could see that her health was failing.

"We need to get Lotte released," Milena told Grete. "I already have Lotte's permission." It was a bold plot, another one of Milena's wild ideas, but Grete knew there was no stopping her. Milena explained how she had put Lotte's name on a positive sputum specimen, and soon Lotte was moved onto the tuberculosis ward.

Milena filled out a certificate of discharge and had Sonntag sign it. In the evenings, she and Grete sat by the window of the tuberculosis ward and talked to Lotte. They were in a celebratory mood. They talked about what she would do once she was out of the camp. In their minds, Lotte was already a free woman. It was just taking longer than usual for the Germans to process their endless paperwork.

But the slowness of Lotte's pending release was unsettling for Milena. Something was wrong. From her position in the *revier*, Milena learned that Sonntag was drawing up lists of prisoners. What exactly these lists were for was unclear. The number of women in Ravensbrück had grown to seven thousand, and it was beginning to feel crowded. This was nothing compared to the overcrowding that would occur later, but one rumor was the women on the list would be released to make room for others. They were mostly old or sick, with syphilis, gonorrhea, and tuberculosis. There were many *Asoziale* from the *Strafblock*. On Sonntag's early list, at first, there were only a few Jews.

The favored rumor was that they were being released to avoid another spread of illness like the "paralysis" plague. There were the occasional releases to buoy this hopeful rumor. The *revier* secretary Erika Buchmann and the prisoner doctor Doris Maase were released in the late summer. As *revier* secretary, Milena would have seen the list of 250 names, and she would have known most of them.

It would take a while, as the horror unfolded, to grasp what was happening. Indeed, for some, it would take years to understand the true evil of the Nazi murder plan. Milena was in the dark like everyone else about the meaning of Sonntag's lists. She had an innate capacity for optimism that kept her from succumbing to the crippling tension and depression all around her.

ROLLING IN LIKE a storm cloud, on November 19, 1941, a doctor named Friedrich Mennecke arrived at Ravensbrück to take over the compiling of the mysterious lists from Sonntag. Dr. Mennecke had been educated during the difficult economic period between the wars. His own father had succumbed to psychosis and died young at the age of fifty-one, leaving his sons penniless. Mennecke had to work in a mirror factory while his older brother went to law school. The factory was partially owned by Jews, and he lost his job when it was sold in 1928, no doubt adding to Mennecke's bitter antisemitism. He was foremost a National Socialist and then a doctor, choosing the specialty of psychiatry, perhaps because of his father. He rose in the ranks quickly because of his politics, not his skills as a physician. He was part of the T4 killing program, or the "euthanasia killings" at sanatoriums, where the mentally and physically disabled—according to Himmler, "lives not worth living"—were directed to be given "special treatment" in the form of murder by gassing. Mennecke was committed to "racial hygiene," though he would have preferred to use some of the patients as human guinea pigs. He wanted to study the brains of epileptic children, but his "medical" interests were overruled by the Nazi imperatives.

The earlier T4 program had run into trouble when the news of the gassings reached the families of the victims. By the summer of 1941, the T4 programs had killed eighty thousand Germans. Hitler, focused on his invasion of the USSR and ultimately the killing of three million Russian Jews, did not want a domestic scandal. The T4 program was momentarily halted.

But Himmler realized its potential to solve his own administrative problem. On a visit to his favorite camp, Dachau, Himmler saw that the camp was filling with sick and dying men, and seriously overcrowded, which could lead to contagion. Any prisoner who could not contribute to the war effort was a "useless mouth" and should be eliminated. Himmler wanted to adapt the halted T4 program and structure to his network of concentration camps.

The first such gassing experiment in the camps was started at Sachsenhausen and run by Dr. Mennecke under strict secrecy, because of the earlier scandals. Ravensbrück is not on the list of camps mentioned in surviving Nazi documents about the early gassing experiments, though we know through Mennecke's letters, testimonies in the postwar trials, and surviving witnesses that it did indeed occur here. Perhaps Himmler was worried that the gassing of women on German soil might be too much for the German public to accept. The news must never get out. It is also important to note that most Ravensbrück records were destroyed. And the Nazis tried to destroy as much evidence as possible about these formalized murder programs.

The Nazis developed a code for the different ways people would be murdered: "14f" denoted prisoners who died in the camp. "14f14" was for executions, "14f8" was for suicide, and "14f13" would now denote death by gassing.

The *Schreiberinnen* at Ravensbrück quickly learned that Dr. Mennecke was a psychiatrist and that he was staying at a hotel in Fürstenberg. Mennecke was soon joined by two other doctors at Ravensbrück to select the aged and ill women who were unfit for work. Dr. Mennecke's meticulous letters to his wife, Eva, sometimes two a day, recounting his daily work creating lists of women to be murdered, have survived. He detailed what he ate each day, at each meal, by the kilo. He told her how wonderfully he was sleeping, and how he changed hotels when Sonntag warned him about bedbugs. He wrote about his walks, the fog around the lake, and the lovely visit to the stables with Koegel and Sonntag.

He missed his wife and so arranged for her to spend a few weeks with him at the next concentration camp where he would make further selections. He met Eva, whom he called "mommy" or his "mommy-child," early in his medical career. She was a nurse, eight years his junior. He was her "Fritz-Pa." The letters are full of endearments both tender and vulgar, and deeply shocking. He had no qualms about what he was doing and casually recounted his daily routine at Ravensbrück. "The work is going as smooth as butter, since the forms are already filled out and I just have to fill the bottom with my diagnosis, principal symptoms, etc. I would not want to write you about the patients; (I will tell you later) it would be better in person." He called the women "portions" or "pats." He described what he was doing as "mercy killings" and felt that he was in the greatest moment of history, the purification of the "Aryan" race. He wrote with pride to his wife, "Let the next happy hunt begin!"[50]

His letters reveal the improvised, makeshift way the program was carried out. Mennecke was initially irked to have to work with two other doctors. He wrote petulantly to his wife, "I can do it all by myself." He explained that it was much quicker to find "useless mouths" in the concentration camp than in the asylum and sanatorium where he had worked before. He bragged about how he worked much faster than the other doctors.

Milena must have felt a sickening dread when she was ordered to get out all the files for the green triangles, incurably ill, amputees, "mental defectives," and sufferers of asthma and tuberculosis. It no longer seemed possible that the people selected would be released. She could see they were calling up healthy Jewish women and Jehovah's Witness prisoners.

Mennecke had come to Ravensbrück thinking he needed to find 320 women for his lists, but when the two other doctors arrived, he learned of new orders from Berlin. He wrote to his wife, "We will have more to do here than foreseen: about 2000 forms!"

This was about a third of the total camp population at the time. When it came to Jews, Mennecke needn't trouble himself with writing down a diagnosis. The paperwork was meaningless; Berlin just wanted the numbers. He complained to his "mommy," "Who is in charge in Berlin?"

Nevertheless, always following orders, Mennecke started a competition with the other doctors of who could fill out the forms the fastest. He wrote to his wife, "He who works fast saves time!" The doctors first processed the women on Sonntag's list and then continued to expand the criteria.

To Milena's horror, Lotte was called up to be examined. The whole camp now knew that when your name was called, you went to the *revier*, where you stripped and paraded in front of Sonntag, who stood while Mennecke sat at a table piled with forms. He read from the Gestapo files and occasionally made notes on the forms of the prisoners he selected. There was no medical examination. Mennecke was ticking boxes.

A large number were selected from the *Asoziale* block. For Henny Schermann, these words appear on the back of her photo in the Nuremberg archives: "Jenny [sic] Sara Schermann, born February 19, 1912, Frankfurt am Main. Unmarried shopgirl in Frankfurt am Main. Licentious Lesbian, only visited such bars. Avoided the name 'Sara.' Stateless Jew." She had been arrested at an illegal lesbian club, and she wasn't using the name Sara that was required for all Jewish women. She had been in the *Asoziale* block in Ravensbrück, and now she was selected by Mennecke. Henny Schermann would be murdered by gas at the Berberg killing facility.

We know from Mennecke's letters to "mommy" that he had to go on to Buchenwald before completing the task at Ravensbrück. The three doctors had only completed 500 forms. The job of finding the 1,500 others was left to the camp doctor.

MILENA WAS FRANTIC. If she had any doubts, now she was sure that all the work she had done to save Lotte would instead get her killed. One evening, soon after she had realized the danger Lotte was in, during the exercise period, Milena whispered to Grete, "I have to see you tonight."

It was autumn and the evening was dark. A coming storm churned in the air and they could smell rain. The cool wind was a welcome relief as it blew away the stench of the camp. Milena told Grete that half an hour after the SS made their nightly rounds, she would climb out of her block window, cross the camp yard, pass the hounds that roamed at night off-leash, and come to Grete's block. "Keep the door open for me," she said.

The guard room was empty at night. This was the room where they had spent many a night during their quarantine honeymoon. Even now, if the guard wasn't there, they would slip into the room for a few intimate minutes alone together. It was dangerous during the day; the guard could turn up at any moment. But it was even more dangerous to try to slip out at night. Grete wanted to tell her it was too risky. But then she felt ashamed of her fear when Milena was always so determined.

Half an hour after the night round, Grete opened the block door and listened. It was so dark she couldn't see her hand in front of her face, and the storm had arrived. It was pouring rain. She listened for footsteps, or the SS boots crunching on the gravel, or gunshots, with her heart in her throat. There was still a lot of activity in the block, and every time one of the three hundred women went to the washroom, Grete had to rush away to avoid being seen. She felt she might collapse with the tension.

With a burst of wind, the door opened, and in walked Milena whistling softly, *It's a long way to Tipperary*. Grete seized Milena by the arm and pulled her into the guard room. She was dripping wet. The slippers she had put on to avoid making a sound were soaked through. They sat down by the little stove that Grete had lit earlier. Grete was relieved. Now that Milena had made it here, they could have a whole night together. Milena wrung out her hair, and Grete laughed, "Your hair smells like a baby's."

Grete had Milena take off her wet clothes, and she wrapped her in the old blanket from her bunk. It wasn't enough to really cover her, so Grete wrapped her arms around Milena and rubbed her shoulders. For a while, they stayed like that quietly in each other's arms. Grete felt that somehow in this room they were free, they had escaped, but it came with the acute ache of knowing it couldn't last, that all around them lurked terrible danger.

Milena shifted so she could look Grete in the eyes. She took Grete's hands in hers and squeezed them. "Gretuška, I have to get Lotte's name off the list." Milena's voice was somber.

"You don't think she will be released?"

Milena shook her head. It was abundantly clear to her that to have your name on the list was a death sentence. Her eyes filled with tears. "I have to get Lotte off that list. If I don't, I will never forgive myself. It was all my idea and now . . ."

Grete tried to comfort her that night. They spoke of what to do. Grete argued that maybe the people on the list would just be sent to another camp, maybe a sanatorium. Milena shook her head. Though she was an optimist, she was also incapable of lying to herself. The evidence was clear. She whispered to Grete, "Though it is unimaginable, we must imagine it." The quiet comforting night together that Grete had longed for was filled with grief. In the impending doom, they pulled tighter into each other's arms.

Milena sent another sample of Lotte's sputum to be analyzed. And then another. They were returned with a negative result, of course.

While Sonntag was having his morning coffee, and while long lines of sick prisoners waited to be seen and aided, Milena knocked on the door of his office. Dr. Gerda Weyand, his wife, was there. Since her marriage, she no longer worked as a doctor in the *revier*. She didn't like Milena or the influence she appeared to have over her husband.

"Why are you bothering us?" Gerda snapped.

But Sonntag lifted his hand. "What is it?" he asked.

"It's something rather miraculous, sir." Milena then explained Lotte's amazing recovery from tuberculosis.

"Why did you send more samples?" Gerda was annoyed and suspicious.

"Because Lotte seemed so healthy. Not at all sick. And I thought maybe there had been a mistake with the first sample. And there was."

"Yes, yes." Sonntag was distracted by this news. "I need the numbers," he said. "If I take her off the list, I need someone else to take her place."

Milena felt the jolt of dread. If she saved Lotte, she would be condemning someone else. "But she does not have tuberculosis," Milena insisted, almost crying out. "She is perfectly healthy. A good worker. Remember?"

Lotte had worked in the infirmary before when Gerda was still a decent doctor. They had worked together.

"Lotte Henschel?" Gerda asked.

"Yes, Lotte, she's not sick anymore. I mean, she never was," Milena pleaded. Gerda looked at her husband and then Sonntag stood.

"Calm down. And behave yourself. Get to work." Sonntag pushed Milena out of the office.

Milena had to reach to Sonntag somehow. And she couldn't think about what he said, how Lotte would have to be replaced by someone else. Desperate, a few days later, she cornered Sonntag when he was drunk. He said, "Ah, yes, the one my Gerda liked so much." So Gerda had spoken up for Lotte, and now Milena watched as Sonntag with his trembling hand scratched Lotte's name off the list.

Sonntag's behavior was more erratic than ever. He was drinking more heavily. Milena soon found out why. He had lost the battle with

Koegel. In December 1941, Walter Sonntag was sent to the Russian front, to Leningrad.

IN DECEMBER, NEWS reached the camp that Pearl Harbor had been attacked by the Japanese and the Americans were now joining in the war. This buoyed everyone's spirits. The Americans were coming, but when? How long would it take?

Many wondered if they could survive another winter. The gray sky was like a marble tombstone over the camp, and bitter icy winds tore through their clothes and the cracks in the wooden sides of their blocks. It was one of the coldest European winters of the twentieth century.

Sonntag was gone. He would later be replaced by Dr. Karl Gebhardt and by Dr. Herta Oberheuser, both sadistic Nazi doctors. But for a little while, nothing more was done about the selection list. The prisoners didn't know that the incomplete list was hanging over the SS commandant Koegel's head. He needed more names. A week before Christmas, Koegel abandoned the pretense that the selections were based on medical reasons, and therefore required a medical doctor. He announced a meeting with all the block elders.[51]

This kind of meeting was uncommon. No one was sure if it had ever happened before. The block elders were uneasy. They didn't like it. Their fear was well-founded and shifted to horror as they listened to Koegel. He wanted them to provide names for the list.

Rosa Jochmann, the block elder for Milena's block, remembered that Koegel said they were to give him names of all the cripples, bedwetters, amputees, "mental defectives," and sufferers from asthma and tuberculosis. He wanted the names of all the women who were too old or too sick to work so that they could be sent to a sanatorium. He pointed his head toward the *Strafblock* and said, "If you fail to do this you will end up there, and you know what that means."

How did Grete deal with this request? Did she and Milena talk about it? Their positions of power afforded them some safety, but also demanded of them a certain level of complicity with the Nazi crimes. It was a tenuous tightrope act. Sometimes it demanded they make trade-offs between the survival of their own group and that of the larger camp population. After the war, some block elders denied ever handing over names, claiming they refused on principle. It's hard to believe that they got away with refusing. Grete did not deny providing names. In the book she published in the first few years after the war, she wrote simply, "We were given to believe that they were to be transferred to another camp, where they would have only light work to do."[52] But she and Milena had worked frantically to get Lotte off the list, so they suspected the truth. Grete's omission about the details of this task perhaps speak to a sense of shame.

As usual, the *Schreiberinnen*, the prisoner secretaries, were the first to get clues to what was happening, as bits and pieces of evidence crossed their desks. There was a new word they began to see on the documents: "*Sondertransport*," "special transport."

One of the secretaries who had been responsible for recording all the deaths told them about a change in regulations. Up until December 1941, deaths were registered in the Fürstenberg town registry. But then, in December, the authorities created a special registry just for Ravensbrück deaths. Another secretary who worked in the section for correspondence with prisoners' families reported that new forms had been created. Rosa Jochmann remembered that "she told us that in the offices they had been told to make 1500 copies of a form with the following words: 'You are herewith informed that 'blank' has died at Ravensbrück as a result of a blood clot.'"[53]

In December, a new revolt broke out among an "extremist" group of the Jehovah's Witnesses. The women refused to do war work, which was any work at all. They also refused to come to the roll call, considering that this was a form of acquiescence to the Nazi war machine. Koegel was apoplectic with rage. The extremist group was first sent to the *Strafblock* with no straw, no blanket, and no clothes. They were fed soup only once every four days. After fifteen days, Koegel ordered twenty-five lashes for all of them, but he needed help. It was then that he pulled Grete's *Asoziale* friend Else Krug into his office, bargaining that if she helped administer the lashes, she would find her life improved. Else refused, and her name was added to the list.

SINCE THE EARLY days of the camp, some prisoners had been allowed to write letters. The writing paper, which could be purchased at the canteen, had the letterhead "Ravensbrück Concentration Camp," with the rules for correspondence printed beneath the heading. Each category of prisoner had different rules. The Jehovah's Witnesses were allowed only five lines, but the politicals like Grete and Milena were allowed sixteen lines twice a month.

They could also receive highly censored mail: 150 words a month, delivered on Saturdays. Milena exchanged letters mostly with her father, and occasionally one would come from Honza.

Grete had no contact with her daughters. But from time to time, she received a letter from her sister or her mother.

The letters were never enough. Milena and Grete would read them together, over and over, out loud, translating and parsing the German—all letters had to be written in German to pass the censors—searching for coded messages and sometimes finding them. Grete's mother wrote letters that were cool and straightforward. She explained that Babette, Grete's sister, was now in Mexico. At the start of the war, the French government decided to round up all German nationals living in France. Babette was sent to the Gurs camp. Then, in June 1940, with the approach of the German forces, the prisoners in Gurs were released. Grete knew that Babette and Willi's plan had been to immigrate to Mexico. But the letters made no mention of Willi. Grete was sure this meant he was fighting in the French Resistance. Milena and Grete put their heads together searching for clues about the progress of the war, about the actions of the resistance. Though it was satisfying to find a hidden message wormed inside the words, these letters left Grete with a feeling of emptiness because of their calculated aloofness. And because they were so different from the letters Milena received from her father.

With Milena's father, there was nothing calculated. Their complicated relationship and the desperate situation evoked an effusive emotional response each month. He helped Milena as much as he could, sending her food and medicine. Their exchanges were overtly tender. More so, perhaps, than they ever had been with each other before. It was astonishing to Grete. They spoke of their feelings in a way that Grete and her family could never speak to each other, openly writing about grief and love and longing. Grete wondered what it would be like to be on the receiving end of such a letter.

For Christmas in 1941, the camp administration, probably hoping the mail from the outside world would subsidize the dwindling prison resources, suddenly allowed prisoners to receive one package with food, and the package could also contain a coat. Grete opened her package from her mother and found a golden-yellow knitted jacket. She was thrilled. Milena would love the honey color. Grete ran to find Milena to show off her fabulous new warm coat.

"Look, look," Grete exclaimed, twirling around in front of Milena. "Isn't it wonderful?"

Milena smiled.

"Don't you love the color?" Milena nodded, but Grete could see she was holding herself back. "You got a package, didn't you? Show me what you got?"

Milena shook her head and tried to turn away.

"What is it?" Grete grabbed her hand. "What's wrong?"

Milena's eyes began to tear up.

"Didn't your father send you something? Anything?"

Milena nodded and wiped away her tears with the back of her swollen hands.

"Show me," Grete pleaded.

With a sigh, Milena pulled out the box from under her bed and opened it, revealing a Bavarian-style costume jacket. They both looked at it for a long time in silence. Grete felt a giggle rising. It was so strangely old-fashioned, like a costume for a play set in the last century, and so extremely out of place.

"It's meant to be patriotic?" Grete offered.

"He has such bad taste," Milena said in an embarrassed rush. "Can you believe it?" And then she wiped away another tear and laughed along with Grete.

But the laughter hid the hurt. Milena had been stunned by the coat. After all the tenderness she poured into her letters, and all the emotion she read in the letters she had received from him, she had thought finally they were close, but fundamentally they were worlds apart. Those letters had been a refuge, but the relationship was an illusion. He could not imagine what she was living through. He did not really know her, and he never would.

"Maybe it will warm you?" Grete offered, laughing louder.

"Your mother knows how to highlight your blue eyes. She sent the perfect jacket for you," Milena said, touching Grete's cheek.

Milena was disappointed—Grete could see it. Of all the things for her father to send, how could he choose this musty, ridiculous costume? Milena explained that when she got ill, she had gained weight and could no longer wear the fashionable clothes of her youth. But now she had lost all the weight. She described the gorgeous tailored suits she used to wear. He could have sent one of those. "I have a whole closet full of them still in my childhood room. At least I did. Who knows what he's done with them."

"It doesn't matter," Grete said, rubbing Milena's back.

"You're right." Milena brightened. "After this is over, we will have all the time in the world to get new outfits made. Now I see how the blue of your eyes has to be highlighted. I will have the best suits made for you from the best tailor in all of Prague."

"And I will get colorful dresses made for you," Grete added. "You will never wear gray or black again." She knew Milena missed color. Moaned about the drab, leaden, monotone hues of the camp.

"We will be so chic, walking arm in arm down the boulevard. We will turn heads," Milena said, remembering herself and Staša when they were young in Prague. "They will long to be us!"

"And we will be working together," Grete added.

"That's right, every day writing our book. But we must take breaks to go to the café in our nice outfits." Milena added, "We will have coffee and lovely pastries and wear gorgeous clothes."

Then Milena began to describe the apartment they would live in, the neighborhood in her beloved Prague. She imagined how they would decorate it, down to the two desks facing each other in a sunny room. "We will live together," Milena said, "in an apartment full of flowers."

PART THREE

1942

❧

The Siren

Roll Call, drawing by Nina Jirsíková

THE GOOD NEWS DURING THE WINTER OF 1941–42 CENTERED AROUND the Yankees. Since the Americans had entered the war, hopes were high they would bring a swift end to the Germans. But the extremely cold and harsh winter made the end feel a long way off. A heavy uncertainty hung over everyone.

Despite the near disaster with Lotte and the list, Milena continued to take risks and intervene to help her fellow prisoners, her protégées, as Grete called them. One such person was Maria Hiszpańska, a young Polish painter. She was a quiet, timid girl. The work outside—hauling, shoveling, tossing bricks—was ruining her health and her hands, Milena told Grete. Maria made realistic, brutal drawings of everyday life in Ravensbrück and signed them with a small mouse. And so prisoners affectionately called her "Myszka"—"little mouse." "Myszka must be helped so that her artistic talents are preserved," Milena insisted. Milena stole paper and pencils from the infirmary and forged an inside-duty card for her. Grete reluctantly hid Myszka every day in the Jehovah's Witnesses' block.

Grete found the young artist too sensitive, and worse, she was self-pitying. Couldn't she see that everyone was in the same miserable boat? Grete was a little jealous of Milena's praise for Myszka's artwork, and Grete worried about the danger should her drawings be discovered. She wondered if this risk was worth it, but every day, Grete hid the artist in the block because Milena asked her to. In the camp, Maria would make over four hundred drawings, but most were destroyed. After the war, she created expressive woodcuts of her traumatic memories and became known as the "Polish Käthe Kollwitz."

Milena did not limit her rule-breaking to acts of altruism. She took a sly pleasure in breaking the rules just to upset the careful camp order. One of the things they all collectively hated vehemently was the siren. They called it the "howler" because it startled them out of sleep in the morning, howled them to roll call, to work, to sleep; it bellowed at them throughout the day. It was operated by one of the SS guards; she was the only person allowed to push the button, which was just outside of the infirmary blocks. Each time it howled at them, breaking up a stolen moment of closeness and pulling them apart, Milena would say to Grete, "Just once, I would love to press that button, just to see what would happen."

"Would you want to be thrown in the bunker for something like that?" Grete asked, alarmed.

"Who says I will get caught?"

"Milena, you won't always get away with everything!"

ONE MORNING BEFORE dawn, Grete woke to the soft touch of Milena sliding into her bunk in the darkness. Grete startled awake.

"It's me," Milena whispered in her ear.

"What are you doing?"

Milena shushed her and kissed her on her cheeks, her neck, her lips. "You are beautiful when you sleep. Someday I will stay awake all night just to watch you sleeping peacefully," she whispered. Milena's hands sought out Grete's naked skin.

To Grete, the moment they spent was like a dream, half awake and flooded with pleasure. When she felt her body respond to Milena's touch, she wanted to cry out, but Milena put her hand on Grete's mouth.

Milena murmured, "One day, I will let you be as loud as a siren." And then she quietly slid out of Grete's bunk and whispered softly into her ear, "This time it's going to be me that makes everyone jump out of bed." Then she was gone.

A few minutes later, the siren howled. Grete pulled the blanket over her head to hide as she shook with laughter.

In the end, there were no consequences for Milena's action because no one believed that a prisoner would ever dare touch the button. The SS guard, the official button presser, said nothing, for fear that she had overslept and would get punished for it.

ON JANUARY 4, Dr. Mennecke, dressed in a black overcoat and carrying his briefcase, no doubt containing another letter for "mommy," returned to Ravensbrück. Himmler also made a visit in early January. The first gassing was about to take place. Himmler knew it was risky to use these "experimental" methods on women in Germany, and so the whole process was to be conducted with utmost secrecy.

The women in Ravensbrück, along with most of the world, had no way of knowing that on January 20, 1942, in a pretty villa in a leafy suburb of Berlin, called Wannsee, high-level Nazi officials and party leaders gathered to coordinate the "Final Solution" to the "Jewish problem." European Jews would be concentrated in the east, far into Russia. The Germans would either murder them straightaway or work them to death. At the meeting, there was no mention of the concentration camps, and no concentration camp officials were in attendance. At the time, the plan for the camps was to fill them with Soviet POWs and other political prisoners. They were to be used as slave workers to build the massive new expanse of German "living space."

The first month of Operation Barbarossa had been so successful that Hitler and Himmler were grandiose in their dreams. All those captured Soviets would form an army of slaves to build a new vast empire. They would begin across the border in Poland. And for that reason, they had decided to build a second camp, called Birkenau, next to the small camp of Auschwitz. This camp complex still had nothing to do with the Jewish Holocaust. Initially, it was a mass grave for Soviet POWs, who died in large numbers upon arrival.

But the planned influx of Soviets to labor in the camps for the Nazi war machine never materialized. Hitler's blitzkrieg stalled in the freezing winter of 1941–42. German soldiers did not have warm enough clothes. More than 130,000 cases of frostbite were reported. Frozen grease had to be removed from loaded shells; tanks froze and seized. The few Soviet POWs who arrived from the east were too sick and weak to work. The building of the new camp fell behind schedule.

To keep his empire of slave camps relevant, Himmler needed to revise the use of his network of *Konzentrationslager*, or KL, the German word for "concentration camp." Six days after the Wannsee Conference, he came up with a repurposed plan for his camps. After a lunch with Hitler where the Führer ranted about the Jews being just as bad as Russians, Himmler made a note in his diary after calling Reinhard Heydrich in Prague: "Jews into the KL."

Himmler then excitedly alerted his camp leaders, "Get ready to accommodate 100,000 male Jews and up to 50,000 Jewesses in the KL within the next four weeks."[1] He was a little optimistic about the timing, but he wanted to be sure the camps took care of the "useless mouths" to make room for the ones who could work hard. And perhaps he was already planning to expand the 14f13 program, the killing of "useless mouths," to a new larger mass-gassing program, the annihilation of the Jews.

MILENA WAS SURE that everyone in the *revier*, all the sick and disabled, were on the selection list. But names were constantly shifting. The first real information came from a Polish prisoner working in the staff canteen who had seen the list left on the table. On February 3, she had been ordered to give a larger portion of food to the SS drivers, "to reward them for their loathsome task." On the piece of paper left on the table, she hadn't seen any Polish names. Most of the names seemed to be from the *Strafblock*.

That same evening, the block elders were briefed that in the early-morning hours, those selected would be sent to the bathhouse for preparation for transport and that the Jewish block would be called. That night, after the guards had done their final rounds, no one slept. Women moved from block to block to pass the rumors, to confer about what was going to happen, and to say goodbye. Rosa Jochmann went to see her good friend Käthe Leichter in the Jewish block, to say her farewell. Käthe was an important Austrian labor organizer and feminist. The Jewish block was in a general panic. Some were sure this was the end, while others argued that since they were strong and healthy, they were being sent to another camp to work.

At two A.M. in the cold, dark morning, the order was given to prepare the women for transport. Names were called. A group of Jews, along with a large group from the *Strafblock*, joined another group of

Jehovah's Witnesses and *Asoziale* at the bathhouse. Langefeld was at the bathhouse, where she checked the names off the list and the women were ordered to strip and then given civilian clothes. Within a few minutes, the trucks drove up to the gates.

The rest of the prisoners had been ordered to stay in the bunks and were forbidden to look out the windows, but Milena watched the whole thing from the *revier* window. She would later tell Grete what she saw. There were screams and shouts in the *revier* as the sick and dying were dragged out to the bathhouse. Some limped on crude crutches; some were unable to walk. Those who couldn't walk were brutally dragged from their beds and dumped into the straw at the bottom of the trucks. The way they were treated left no doubt in Milena's mind about where they were headed.[2]

Rosa exchanged a few last words with Käthe. "If it really is that I never come home again, please look after my three boys," Käthe told her friend as she waved goodbye. Rosa later wrote, "Käthe Leichter wrote many wonderful poems, we had to destroy them all at her request because she always said: 'I have them in my head, and I know I'll definitely come home.' Unfortunately, all but one have now been lost."

The *Schreiberinnen* had been ordered to mark the files of the women who had been loaded onto the trucks with that word "*Sondertransport*," "special transport." It was important that the first mass gassing of women on German soil be kept secret. And three days later, when Koegel met with Himmler, he was able to report that all had gone off without a hitch. In Himmler's diary, he noted that also present at the meeting was Professor Max de Crinis, the leading T4 specialist. In this meeting, Himmler was making the link between the T4 program, the killing of the handicapped, and the 14f13 program, the killing of "lives not worth living." And just a few weeks after the Wannsee Conference, Himmler was hatching the plan to use his concentration camp network for the Nazis' evolving Final Solution. What all three murderous programs had in common was the use of gas for killing on a mass scale. Professor de Crinis's advice to Himmler on the use of gas at that stage was crucial.

Though Koegel was pleased that the fate of the *Sondertransport* had successfully been kept secret, it wasn't long before the prisoners knew the women on the transport had been killed. A few days later, the trucks returned and dumped the clothes of the women who had been on the transport at the *Effektenkammer*. Mixed in with the clothes that came back were the walking sticks, crutches, dentures, glasses, and other essential personal items that had belonged to their departed friends. If there was any doubt before, there was none now. Rosa Jochmann later recounted how the news was received: "Within half an hour of the lorry returning all the people in the camp knew about it and everyone knew the women were all dead. There was a cruel silence. The women didn't talk to each other—even the prostitutes . . . At roll call everyone was obedient. The block elders didn't need to shout."[3]

On the next transport, more Jewish women were taken, as well as most of the green and black triangles, except for those who had volunteered to help Koegel with the flogging. Else Krug was on this second transport. She was Grete's friend from the *Asoziale* block who had been in the *Strafblock*. She and another Jewish girl volunteered to try to hide some paper and pencils in the hem of their clothes. They would write messages and tuck them into their clothes so that when the lorries returned, the other prisoners could find the notes and learn where they had been taken. The clothes with the notes came back. One said, "Arrived at Dessau. Told we now bathe and will be given new clothes and assigned jobs." Though the notes were inconclusive, everyone felt it was certain they were murdered somewhere near Dessau.

The *Sondertransporte*, or special transports, continued through the end of March, by one estimate leaving every fourth day. There were around ten in total; roughly 1,600 women were killed in this way. Who was chosen to be on the list for each transport became less and less clear. Perfectly healthy and strong women were selected. When the command went out to get ready for a transport at two or three A.M., the wailing and grief could be heard across the camp.

Once again, it was the secretaries who had gotten further proof about the fate of the *Sondertransport*. They were told to fill out bogus death certificates for the women who had been selected. The place of death was Ravensbrück, the date was always in the future, after the transport, and they were to choose among a selection of three causes of death: heart failure, infected lungs, or poor circulation. They were told to prepare letters for the next of kin informing them that because of fear of contagion, their loved one had been cremated, and for a fee, they could recuperate the ashes. Letters went out to families all over Germany, but it was difficult for officials to inform the next of kin of *Asoziale* prisoners, and often the entire families of the Jewish prisoners were gone. In such cases, the letter was sent to the local police station. One such letter, signed by Koegel, has the code "14f13" marked in the corner next to the date, revealing that the enclosed death certificate was a sham and the death was by gassing.

After the war, it slowly began to emerge that the women had been sent to Bernburg, which was one stop after Dessau. At Bernburg, in a former sanatorium, a gassing center had been built disguised as a shower room; adjoining rooms were a crematorium, a dissecting room, and a mortuary. After death, gold teeth were extracted. These were sent in batches to T4 headquarters. In this way, the cost of the killing was self-financed, according to one official.[4] All the files from Ravensbrück were burned, but correspondence from Gross-Rosen and Buchenwald revealed details of the transports to Bernburg. After the war, the truth emerged through the tireless work of survivor groups who pieced together the evidence.

LANGEFELD WAS FEELING more and more sure of herself at Ravensbrück. She was proud of her female guard corps. She had trained them well, and their life at Ravensbrück was pleasant. They had decent living quarters, good meals, a nice uniform, and even a hair salon, where they were pampered by prisoner hairdressers. The style at the time was the Olympia roll, a single curl swept from the front. The salon was popular among the staff and the SS guards' wives.

The one hitch was Koegel and his awful SS men, and of course the green triangle prisoners he had recruited to do his bidding. Langefeld hoped she would eventually be able to appeal to Himmler, showing him how her methods worked far better than Koegel's.

Koegel had his protégées, and Langefeld had hers. She was often seen with her favorite prisoner, the Polish countess Helena Korewina, to whom Langefeld delegated more and more power. Through her influence, the political Poles took over many of the functionary positions in the camp. Langefeld, encouraged by Helena, had opened an arts-and-crafts shop where the artistically talented prisoners carved and painted gift items. The SS guards turned a blind eye to this, sometimes commissioning and purchasing items from the prisoners for their girlfriends or wives.

But Langefeld continued to battle with Koegel, who certainly felt her familiarity with some prisoners was dangerous and far too soft. Her kindness toward Polish prisoners had not been missed by the prisoners either. As one Polish prisoner later said, "We always knew she wasn't 100 percent SS."

But the pleasant life Langefeld had created for herself and her guard corps was upended in the spring of 1942.

With the development of gassing as a form of mass murder, it was decided to create death camps, not on German soil but just across the border in Poland, at Auschwitz, where Jews could be sent to be exterminated or worked to death. But Himmler had a problem. Up to this point, there were few women at Auschwitz, and so there were no female guards who could deal with this influx of women. He wanted Langefeld, his most experienced female guard, to run the new women's section there. She was to take with her one thousand prisoners who would work as kapos, or prisoner guards, and a small troop of her female guards. So little was known about Auschwitz at the time that a few prisoners volunteered to go, thinking that conditions would be better at this new camp.

BY THE SPRING of 1942, darker times had arrived. Grete remembered a moment that marked for her the shift toward the horrific.

There was a large influx of Polish prisoners—"It seemed almost as though Hitler had determined to wipe out the Polish people altogether." He certainly was determined to wipe out the Polish Jews. By the end of the war, three million Polish Jews, making up over half of all the Jews who would die in the Holocaust, would be murdered in the camps. That spring, ten Polish women were singled out and taken to the punishment block. Shortly before evening roll call, the camp streets were cleared and prisoners were ordered to their blocks. But Milena watched and took note from the *revier* window. She saw the ten women being marched across the camp square, barefoot and in long coats like penitents. They were led out of the camp gates. Milena told Grete that "they turned and waved goodbye," maybe hoping that some of their friends would see them.

A few moments later, the evening roll-call siren howled. The prisoners poured out of the blocks and lined up in rows. Then they stood in silence. From the other side of the wall, they heard a volley of gunshots. A second later, there were a few single shots. Grete flinched, and she saw the Polish prisoners mouthing prayers. Everyone knew they had just listened to the execution of those ten Polish women.

Grete wrote that the expressions on people's faces changed from that point on. Executions behind the wall during roll call became a regular occurrence. Their nerves were on edge as they listened for the volley of guns. Sometimes there were screams. It was almost worse, imagining the scene that they could hear but not see. "A new and terrible period had opened up for Camp Ravensbrück and our hearts were heavy with dread."[5]

The year 1942 marked a turning point in the war. Though the genesis of the Holocaust is long and complex and had begun decades earlier, this was the moment when the Nazis created the dedicated death camps of Treblinka, Sobibor, and Belzec in Poland. Most Jews deported to these camps would not survive more than a few hours; there were only three survivors to give testimony from Belzec. This was also when the Nazis decided to use the prisoners in the camps as labor for their faltering war effort. The lofty dreams to use Soviet POWs to build gleaming new Nazi cities in the east had been shelved. Now the most urgent need was to use slave labor to build weapons.

Ravensbrück, along with other camps, shifted from its earlier purpose of "reeducation" to a true slave labor camp, with its accompanying extermination and "annihilation through labor." Also striking was the huge influx of European Jews. Up until mid-1942, Jews were a minority in the camps. Now daily transports arrived with European Jews and no place to put them but the hastily built blocks and tents in the swampy grounds around the lake.

Himmler appointed his good friend Oswald Pohl to oversee the running of all the camps with the new mission of mass murder and mass slave labor. An added emphasis was on making prison labor more economically efficient and rooting out corruption in the leadership. In an act of political theater, Pohl orchestrated a reshuffle of camp leadership. Commandants were sacked or moved to other camps. Koegel was moved to Majdanek, and Ravensbrück got a new leader, Fritz Suhren.

Conditions in Ravensbrück quickly deteriorated. Grete recalled that in 1942, when Jewish mothers came from Holland, Belgium, and France, they brought their children with them. At the sight of the children, the prisoners were moved to tears. Grete remembered the first one, Angela, a little nine-year-old, "dirty and ragged, but pretty as a picture." But soon enough, the children became just another part of their camp life. Since they did not work, they were given minimal food, and so the children went from hut to hut, begging for scraps. Grete wrote that they were a nuisance, constantly begging at the block doors.

The population in the camp increased, and with it overcrowding. Now it was three people to a bunk. Lice became endemic. There were no more new prisoner clothes or footwear. Prisoners were given clothes from the *Effektenkammer* or old worn-out clothes from prisoners who had died.

General discipline deteriorated. The perfect green lawns that had so impressed Grete when she arrived were now trampled to dirt. Because of logjams at the doors, prisoners climbed out of windows to get to roll call in time. Marauding groups would raid the kitchen gangs bringing the food to the blocks and rob them of their bread. Suhren, the camp commander, created a camp police, putting some of the most violent prisoners in charge. And there was a parallel camp leader, a Gestapo agent named Ludwig Ramdohr, who organized a network of prisoner spies.

Because of the shortage of food and supplies, the Nazi officials began to allow some of the prisoners to receive parcels of food from outside year-round, not just at Christmas. This shifted some of the burden of feeding the prisoners to the German population. Since they were trying to create a more efficient labor force, prisoners were working twelve-hour shifts and needed more food. The parcel system brought a new social hierarchy into the camp. French and Soviet prisoners were not allowed parcels. *Asoziale*, Romani, and minor political prisoners received very few. In the camp underground economy, anything could be bought with food. Before long, those who received parcels were better dressed and had "servants" to wait on them. The SS were the first to profit from the parcels, stealing what they wanted upon arrival. The Red Cross was sending parcels that were systematically pillaged by the SS as well.

Despite the increased risks, with Ramdohr's spies and the overcrowding, Milena found ways to slip into Grete's block for short visits. She needed to recount all the information she was collecting, what she was witnessing in the *revier*. They had thought Sonntag was terrible, but the new SS doctors were much worse.

Grete herself had witnessed one of the new Nazi doctors refuse to treat the open wounds of a group of Jewish women who had been on the terrible brick-throwing gang. This was one of the worst work assignments. Barges loaded with bricks for the new buildings arrived at the shore of the lake, and the prisoners would form a human chain tossing the bricks from hand to hand to unload the barge. The job was dirty and dusty, and the bricks tore the skin from their hands. The blisters and wounds became infected, or in the winter frostbitten. When their block elders asked for bandages, they were thrown out by the doctor, saying, "Jewish cows outside." Later their wounds became infected with maggots, and many of them died.

Milena witnessed a daily reign of terror at the *revier*. With ten thousand in the camp, roughly one hundred a day needed medical treatment. They had to stand outside in all kinds of weather waiting to see a doctor. The SS matron decided who got to see the doctor and who didn't.

"She throws them out for anything," Milena told Grete. "If you lean against the wall or whisper you can be sent away. And God forbid if a woman was brought on a stretcher or happened to be Jewish or Gypsy. Then she just cries, 'Corridor case.'"

The "corridor cases" were set down on the floor along the corridor of the *revier*. They gave them some kind of narcotics for two days, and then, on the third day, one of the doctors injected them with Evipan in the heart muscle. Milena squeezed Grete's hands. "Do not go there if you are sick."

"I'm strong, Milena, I am not going to get sick. It's you that I worry about." Grete pulled Milena closer into her arms. What she was witnessing was taking a toll on Milena.

"It's a Death Chamber. That's all the doctors do." Milena whispered the words into Grete's shoulder, where she had laid her head. "All the other real medical care, the bandages, the ointments, the treatment for fevers, boils, sunburn, all that is done by prisoners."

In the early years at Ravensbrück, if a woman arrived pregnant, she was either released or sent away to have the baby and then returned to camp. But now, no matter how many months along they were, pregnant women were forced to have an abortion. The SS doctor Rolf Rosenthal, along with a prisoner midwife and nurse named Gerda Quernheim, performed these abortions. Many women died from the procedure. There is little or no record of who these women were or of their abortions. Many were Polish women who had slept with German soldiers. Like Jews arrested for having sex with Germans, they were accused of *Rassenschande*, or polluting the race. They were given red triangles, but they were known as "bed politicals" and not accepted by the other political prisoners. After the war, none volunteered to give testimony or record their story since being a "bed political" still carried a stigma of shame.

Gerda Quernheim was recruited by the SS doctors when her special midwife skills were noted. It was said that Quernheim sometimes induced labor and then strangled the baby upon birth. Milena would hear a baby cry, but only for a moment. Quernheim disposed of the dead babies in the camp boiler, sometimes carrying the bodies across the camp yard in buckets covered with a cloth. Her status grew when she began assisting with the lethal injections. Survivors recount that she helped give lethal injections to one young prisoner who was a bed-wetter, and to another who had a toothache. The relationship between Quernheim and Rosenthal became sexual, which was evident to anyone working in the *revier*. They could be heard carrying on inside Rosenthal's office.

Milena was especially horrified by the case of a young Ukrainian girl. When Rosenthal and Quernheim approached her bed, the sick girl tried to escape. She ran down the corridor and jumped out the window. She was caught and brought back, taken into the "death chamber," as Milena called it. Since it was Milena's job to count the corpses laid out in the *revier* bathroom each evening, she later saw the girl there. She told Grete, "Her face was badly bruised and beaten and there were injection marks in her chest."

LIKE MANY LARGE German industries, Siemens & Halske AG were profiting from the booming war economy of the National Socialists. Siemens was the first company to work in cooperation with the SS to move their factories close to concentration camps, avoiding the Allied bombardments in the Berlin area, and profiting from the free forced labor. Siemens used only female prisoners to do the delicate work of coiling spools and making other electrical instruments for the German Army. In June 1942, Siemens built twenty work blocks next to the Ravensbrück camp. Up to 2,300 prisoners worked there and were housed in the nearby blocks.

Siemens used the female prisoners to labor in their factory, but they used male prisoners to build it. A group of male prisoners was sent to Ravensbrück early in 1942 to build the Siemens factory in an inhumane period of ten weeks. Over three hundred male prisoners died, and another three hundred were so ruined by the hard labor they were transported to Dachau to be murdered in the gas chambers.

Grete's block of Jehovah's Witnesses had been moved to the newer blocks in the recent extension of the campgrounds. Their block was up against the wall, and the male prisoners working there were housed right on the other side. Male and female prisoners were kept strictly separated, but through the cracks in the boards, the women could see the men. They looked like skeletons. They were being brutally beaten and bullied by their kapo guard. The Jehovah's Witness women were touched. Grete noted, "What no longer moved them when it happened to their own sex seemed dreadful when it happened to the men."[6]

They were able to establish contact with the men, who pleaded over and over, "Give us bread."

The women found a space where the sand had blown away, leaving a small hollow beneath the fence. They smuggled bread, carrots, and margarine, slipping the items into the hollow. But it took only a few days for one of the men to denounce the smuggling.

Grete was called into the head office. The food smuggling had occurred in several of the blocks along the wall, so luckily, there was no proof pointing solely to her and her Jehovah's Witness women. She was not directly sent to the punishment block. Instead, she was told as punishment, she would become the block elder for the Jewish block.

Grete was horrified. Everyone knew what was happening to the Jews. At least once a month, the block elder had to produce names and accompany them to the gates for a *Sondertransport*, knowing full well they were going to their deaths. The last block elder had been shattered by the experience, and after a few *Sondertransporte*, having lost her mind, she herself was taken. Grete would rather do anything else. She begged to be relieved of the block elder's responsibilities.

"*Oberaufseherin*, please send me for outside work. I'll do anything rather than be block elder there."

"Are you refusing an order?" the head guard snapped.

"No, of course I'll go there if you order it, but please put me on outside work. I've been a block elder for long enough."

No one ever asked for outside work. Nor to lose the special privileges of a block elder. The guard was surprised, but in the end, she agreed. "Very well; outside work, then."[7]

Grete had been with her Jehovah's Witness prisoners for almost two years, but the bright side was that, as an old political, she was able to get into Block 1, Milena's block, where they shared a bunk and now could be together all night.

Their life took on an almost domestic hue, with their daily routines and private affections. They were each other's first sight when they opened their eyes. They shared the gossip picked up around the camp: who had gotten important news in a letter, hints about how the war was going and what the Americans were planning, and clandestine cultural events going on in the camp. They ate together. Sometimes Grete would try to slip an extra bit of turnip into Milena's bowl when her head was turned and Milena would do the same until it became a game they played, each one trying to give the other her food.

Everyone thought of them as a couple, as passionate friends. They no longer had to sneak away to try to steal a moment together. They knew that at the end of every day, they would have a chance to catch up. Each night, Milena fell exhausted into the bunk, and she would sigh, "Oh, if only I could sit by the side of the road again and not be a soldier anymore!"[8]

During the day, they were focused on the task of surviving and gathering evidence. It was all for their book, their project of bearing witness. It was also a necessary element of camp survival. You had to be ever on the alert to catch the slightest shift in the winds, to anticipate the next calamity, and to help those in need when possible. But at night, when at last they could hold each other, they could just be together as they drifted to sleep, each one thinking they were standing watch over the other, protected, protective, and beloved.

ROSA JOCHMANN HAD been at Ravensbrück since April 1940, and she had been an effective block elder for almost as long. Whenever a new political arrived in the camp, Rosa and the other "political elders" sought her out and quizzed her about what was going on in the outside world. If Rosa chose to do so, she might be able to get the new arrival moved into her privileged Block 1, where Rosa helped the new prisoner procure a good job. This was what Rosa had done for Milena when she arrived in 1940, and in the summer of 1942, she did the same for a communist prisoner, Cäcilie Helten, or Cilly.

Cilly had been in several prisons before arriving at Ravensbrück. In April 1934, she was arrested for distributing communist leaflets and sentenced to two years and ten months in prison for plotting to commit high treason. In January 1941, she joined an underground resistance group with Anneliese Hoevel, whom she had met in prison. Hoevel and her husband were arrested by the Gestapo. Under interrogation, Hoevel spoke about Cilly and about Cilly's homosexuality. The German authorities assumed the two women had had an affair, and they sentenced Hoevel to death. Cilly was arrested, but then acquitted for lack of evidence. However, in August 1942, as was the case for Milena, Cilly was not released. She was sent to Ravensbrück for "protective custody."

Soon after Cilly arrived, she became seriously ill with typhoid fever and pneumonia. Milena and Rosa made sure she was not declared a "corridor case." Whenever she could, Rosa went to the *revier*, probably snuck in with Milena's help, and she would wash Cilly, bring her a clean shirt and some food to eat. Cilly survived, and she and Rosa developed a close relationship. Soon they were inseparable. They were known as a camp couple, "passionate friends" like Milena and Grete.

How they self-identified during that time must be seen in the context of the camp and in the context of greater society's rejection of women loving women. As already stated, language about gender and sexuality was limited. In general, the term "lesbian" was considered a slur, and an insult. Memoirs and survivor accounts underline the problematic homophobic historiography of the Holocaust canon in the years following the war. Rosa and Cilly, like Grete and Milena, were of the political class. They called themselves "passionate friends," and I want to respect their choice of language and acknowledge that the specific nature of their most intimate moments remains private.

There is much we cannot know. But because of their place in the camp hierarchy, their love was tacitly normalized, whereas relationships among the "degenerate" lesbians of the *Asoziale* class were abhorred and disparaged. Grete in her writing used a classical hierarchy, placing her lofty "intellectual" love against the base "physical" love of the *Asoziale*. This framing aligned with the Nazi belief that "normal" women did not have sexual desire. Only degenerate women, prostitutes and lesbians, could not control their sexuality. The fact that these women had physical desires proved that they were genetically broken. Prisoners in the political class in functionary positions, like Rosa and Grete, maintained this clear class division between "pure" love that was possible in the "higher" political blocks and "degenerate" lesbian love in the *Asoziale* blocks.

This distinction was important because there was a lot at stake. Same-sex relations between both men and women were illegal in Vienna, where Rosa lived, until 1971.[9] Same-sex relations were illegal in all US states up until the early 1960s, and they were still illegal in four US states until the 2003 ruling of the Supreme Court in *Lawrence v. Texas*. Being called or known as a lesbian was such an abomination that Rosa's political enemies would use the accusation against her after the war, trying to discredit her and her political career.

Rosa and Cilly were remembered by survivors as helping the children in the camp whenever possible. Because being a lesbian and a pedophile were assumed to be twinned deviant behaviors, Rosa was also accused after the war of being a pedophile. Accusations of homosexuality were used against camp functionaries to settle old scores. And indeed, communists, postwar, wanting to discredit Grete's accounts of the Soviet Gulag and erase Milena's role from the camp history, accused them of being degenerate lesbians. The fact that long after the war these accusations could damage a person's career and memory illustrates the danger and the depth of society's homophobia both inside and outside the camp walls.

Both Cilly and Milena had female lovers before the war, though they would have been at risk if they publicly acknowledged it. Perhaps if they were alive today, they would identify as queer, or bisexual. As many queer historians have pointed out, the terms "lesbian" and "homosexual" stick to the heteronormative binary, which erases the many shades of human sexuality. And for Grete, who was protective of Milena's memory, she perhaps was more rigid about what she publicly considered normal gender behavior. In her eponymous book about Milena, she brushed aside Milena's earlier love affairs with women as youthful folly.

> While most of her girlfriends were unduly given to sensual pleasures, Milena, though quite capable of enjoying herself and often accused of amorality, was more intellectual in her ways . . . Milena, the most daring and most anarchistic, was almost the only one who was able, thanks to her energy and vitality, to fulfill the expectations justified by her great gifts. Thanks to some secret force within her, she was able, after sinking to the lowest depths, to rise again and find her way back to normal life and the pursuit of high ambition.[10]

What were "the lowest depths"? Was it her drug addiction, her experimentation with cocaine, or her homosexual adventures? It is unclear. And where Grete got this information is unclear. Was this what Milena told her? Or was this what other people who knew Milena in her youth told Grete later? Or was this Grete's interpretation?

A few pages after alluding to Milena's "lowest depths," Grete writes about lesbians in the camp: "Some of the women in Ravensbrück took refuge in passionate friendships, others eased their heartache by talking endlessly about love, and still others resorted to political or religious fanaticism. The passionate friendships of the politicals usually remained platonic, while the criminals and asocials often took a frankly lesbian character."[11]

The "usually" and "frankly" seem to be important qualifiers. Grete is indicating that by remaining "usually" platonic, these passionate friendships were good, whereas the criminals, of course, would fall into "frankly" sexual bad behavior. Grete's homophobic account aligns with many prisoner testimonies after the war. "Lesbian love spread like an epidemic. It was like a plague," wrote Polish survivor Wanda Półtawska.[12] French survivors claimed that it was "the Germans with their 'special morals'" in the *Strafblock* who corrupted the weaker women, and it was the "Julot," which was their term for butch lesbians, who ruled over them in debauched orgies.[13] Survivors describe rampant lesbianism in *other* groups, among *other* nationalities, or only with the criminal *Asoziale*, and, of course, within the ranks of the hated SS female guards.

Historian and former director of the Ravensbrück Memorial Insa Eschebach examines why this need for stigmatizing was so acute in the camps and concludes that "the socially traditional, homophobic stigmatization of the figure of the lesbian—as well as the prostitute—primarily serves to emphasize one's own moral superiority. Under the extreme conditions of prisoners' society in the concentration camps—that is also under the conditions of enforced uniformity—the desire for distinction, for the proof of one's own superiority, seems to be the most important thing."[14]

We know there were women loving women in the camps primarily because the other prisoners talked about them in such derogatory ways. We know very little about their experience from their own voices. In the postwar survivors' accounts, lesbians, trans men, and sex workers were common criminals, and as such not recognized as needing to be honored. Their suffering was not noble. They gave no testimonies in war trials; they wrote no memoirs; they gave no interviews. They are not part of the archive. They received no government benefits for survivors. In fact, a few male homosexual survivors from Auschwitz went on to be persecuted and imprisoned following liberation. Indeed, so thoroughly have they been erased from the historical record, we know very few of their names. Because they were despised and stigmatized by the other prisoners, these survivors were silent after the war.

Survivor accounts, full of homophobic and exaggerated accounts of homosexuality, are rarely compassionate or favorable toward women loving women. The kinder accounts argue that it was only because of the loneliness and extreme conditions of the camp that same-sex relations happened at all. They were just a byproduct of the prison environment. There are those who believed that women turned to loving other women out of a lack. "Many of the women became lesbians. Few were lesbians by nature . . . the nights were long, loneliness lay heavy on the hearts—thus woman was driven to woman," according to Erika Buchmann.[15] Buchmann later claimed there was a "lesbian circle" among certain camp functionaries. She was one of the political prisoners who accused Rosa Jochmann of homosexuality after the war.

Grete described a "lesbian prostitute" named Gerde who "serviced a number of women, but not for money." She explained women would pay Gerde with food. This was described as proof of Gerde's moral decline and not of her agency, using barter and sexual power for her survival.[16] By maintaining a clear sense of shock at this trade, Grete could keep her eyes closed to the complex trade-offs she was forced to make for her own survival.

The way Grete writes about Gerde and the "degenerate acts" of lesbian love reveals her to be very much in accord with her times. She was speaking from internalized moral codes that were widely held. And she felt that her strong moral code had been important to her survival in the camps. She might have been struggling to cope with feelings of shame, and inner conflict. What is more astonishing is Milena's apparent acceptance of love in all its forms.

Grete acknowledged that Milena didn't see these *Asoziale* woman the same way she did. When there was the epidemic scare and no one was supposed to go near the *Asoziale* prisoners in quarantine, Milena went there anyway. Grete registered her surprise when she wrote that Milena had actually befriended many of them, and found humanity in them. Milena took risks to try and save the prostitutes with gonorrhea from Sonntag's experimentation, perhaps because she understood their suffering. When Grete described a scene to Milena of "a degenerate *Asoziale* prostitute" wiggling her hips trying to get the attention of a male prisoner in the distance, "Milena didn't think it funny, but said with a sigh of relief, 'Thank God, love is indestructible. It's stronger than any barbarism.'"[17]

Grete admired Milena for this capacity to love beyond the societal norms. "To her, love was the one thing that really counted in life. She felt deeply and intensely and was not ashamed of it. To her love was something clear and self-evident."[18]

THE MORNING AFTER Grete's transfer to Block 1, she marched out with the other women in her work detail, passing through the gates of the camp. It was the first time in years that Grete had been outside of the walls. They walked down a sandy path that edged the Fürstenberg lake until they came to chicken runs, a pigsty, and a group of greenhouses. Through her friendships, including the help of Rosa Jochmann, Grete had been able to get a coveted job working in the kitchen garden gang.

The first day, she was set to work shoveling clay, dirt, and manure. This was hard labor, and it left her hands blistered. In the distance, she saw the flower beds full of blooms for the SS officers' homes. It filled her with delight to see such vitality and color. But after a few hours, the attractiveness of "outside work" wore off.

Still, her new job had special perks. The garden gang had an arrangement with the Jehovah's Witness prisoners who looked after the pigsties to set aside some of the slops, a pail of potatoes that they could eat. The SS officer in charge of the garden was not typical; he was quiet and did not bully the women. He did not threaten reports or punishments. They could count on him to turn a blind eye when they ate tomatoes or cucumbers from the vegetable garden.

A friend of Grete's, Eva Busch, who had been a well-known actress and cabaret singer, and after the war would be a gay icon, worked in the greenhouse. Eva convinced the SS officer that Grete had an unusually green thumb, and she was transferred off the shoveling duty into the greenhouse. Grete was then able to get Lotte brought into the greenhouse. Grete wrote, "The most important service anyone could render a prisoner . . . was to get her a job where she had an opportunity to supplement her rations. The garden gang was fortunate in that respect."[19]

In the greenhouse, the three women, Eva, Grete, and Lotte, felt the pressure ease. There was no imminent threat or danger. A sense of delight transformed them into children. They created an aquarium in a cement basin. They would bring frogs and salamanders that they found in the gardens back to their little aquarium and spend hours watching them, squealing with laughter at anything their aquatic pets did. They gave them playful names and made up stories about the animals. If someone in charge appeared at the greenhouse, the women would rush about with pots of dirt or watering cans, pretending to be extremely busy.

The kitchen gang supplemented their diet with food from the garden. It was harder to smuggle that food back into the camp and share with their friends, but they found ways. Tomatoes could be hidden in armpits. They hid vegetables in pots of dirt that they claimed were for some SS garden. It reminded Grete of when, during a particularly lucky time in the Gulag, she was sent to work in the root cellar. There she had access to carrots, onions, potatoes, and beets. To smuggle the food back to her group of camp friends, she had fastened a bag that hung from her waist and went between her legs.

During all her years as block elder, Grete had been in a constant state of suspense and tension. The Jehovah's Witness block was the show block, and they were submitted to a continual parade of VIP visitors. Everything always had to be perfect. Adding to the pressure, the extremist Jehovah's Witness prisoners were endlessly pushing the boundaries, and Grete was forever trying to keep them and the others safe. Now, as a member of the kitchen gang working in the greenhouse, she wasn't responsible for anyone except Milena.

She knew that other prisoners on other work gangs were being driven to their deaths. News about what was happening in Auschwitz was trickling back to them in whispered rumors. A dozen Jehovah's Witness prisoners had been sent back from Auschwitz for an unknown reason, perhaps a clerical error, and were being held in the prison block, where Grete had a chance to speak with one of them, Rosa Hahn, whom she knew well. "Terrible things happen in Auschwitz," Rosa whispered to Grete in a frantic rush. "You won't believe me, I know, but living human beings are thrown into the fire including little children. Jews chiefly. All day long the smell of burning flesh hangs over the camp. You can't believe me; I know it. But I'm speaking the truth . . ."[20]

Grete didn't believe her. Rosa Hahn had once been a pretty woman, but now her face and skin were sunken and skeletal. She had a crazed look in her eyes. Grete thought surely Rosa had gone mad. Grete planned on seeking her out later, thinking she would be transferred to her old block. But as Rosa Hahn had predicted, the whole group of Jehovah's Witness prisoners from Auschwitz were executed a day later. It shook Grete, and she tried to repress her dark thoughts about Rosa's haunting account.

For a while, the terrible things that were happening remained just on the edges of Grete and Milena's world. They were able to steal moments of happiness in their little oasis of love. Grete hesitated to tell Milena about Auschwitz, about what Rosa had said. But their project was to bear witness; they had to remember everything together.

Milena was not oblivious to what was happening just outside their bunk. She was tormented by what she was witnessing in the *revier*. Grete tried to soothe Milena with stolen food. Milena was losing her teeth, pulling them easily from her swollen gums. She would sigh and place the tooth in Grete's palm. "Oh, and I so liked this one," Milena lamented.

Grete had felt powerless watching Milena's health deteriorate. Now she could do something; at least she could bring her vitamins in the vegetables she smuggled from the garden. Milena laughed when Grete held up a red tomato, like a magician had pulled a rabbit out of a hat.

"You can't share this with anyone," Grete admonished before handing it to Milena, knowing that she was just as likely to give it to some sick person dying in the *revier* as eat it herself. "In fact, I want you to eat it right here, right now, in front of me."

"The whole tomato?" Milena asked.

"The whole thing. I won't give you your treat if you don't finish your supper."

"I love your treats," Milena said playfully.

When Milena bit into the tomato, it burst, and some juice and seeds ran down her chin. They laughed at the messy abundance of a tomato. For a moment, Grete could see the younger Milena, the playful, wild girl. She was still in there somewhere. And after this was all over, Grete would feed Milena, bring her back to health and take care of her. They would reach the end of this hell together.

IN THE FEW moments before sleep, as they lay in their bunk together, they would talk about their lives from before and outside the walls of the camp. In those gentle conversations, they made plans for the future together. When Milena asked Grete what her ideal of freedom was, she described walking in the mountains.

"Oh, you are such a nature child!" Milena laughed. "I am just a city slicker. My idea of freedom is going to a little café together in Prague. And finding the perfect table where we can sit and talk and watch the world go by."

Much of their daydreaming centered around when and how and where they would write their book together. Milena imagined they would share a big desk, one sitting on either side. And together they would describe everything they were seeing. "It will be hard to describe these horrors, but I'll make you pots of tea and buy delicious cakes that you so love," she said.

"And you will always eat my cake!" Grete laughed, kissing Milena on the nose.

"Yes, because yours is always better."

Would they be living in Germany, in Potsdam? Grete was not sure since it depended on where the Soviets ended up. Milena wasn't sure she could live anywhere but in Prague. But would the Soviets allow them to return to their democracy? Maybe they could live together in Mexico or Paris when this war was over. Grete would find her sister and her brother-in-law there, she said. Maybe she hoped to be reunited with her daughters, who were in Palestine. Milena described the little apartment they would share with Honza and her cats, not far from a park where Milena would no doubt "organize" flower collections. They would have pots of flowers on their desk to keep their spirits up while they described the darkness of the camps. Honza would go to a good French school.

"Will there be nuns running the school?" Grete asked, laughing.

"There are good nuns, enlightened nuns," Milena protested. Their fingers laced together as they dreamed, and Grete tried to gently rub Milena's knuckles with her free hand.

Grete worried about Milena's swollen joints and increasing pain. Milena's skin had become the color of the overcast lidded gray sky. But when they whispered together their dreams of the future, she thought they might just make it out alive to the other side. It seemed possible, at least during those few shared moments.

Milena shifted closer to Grete so she could lay her head on Grete's shoulder.

"Do you like my postcard?"

They both looked at the colorful Impressionist postcard that Milena had managed to attach to the wall next to their bunk. It was a mystery to Grete where Milena got such things. But it was true she was constantly given gifts by the Polish women and some of her old friends from Prague. Someone had given her this picture of a brightly colored landscape. "Maybe we won't go to Paris where there are too many nuns. We will go there," she said, laughing. Together they looked at the image on the small card.

Grete began to see things emerge in the landscape that she hadn't noticed before. Here was a valley, a stream coming from the mountains, a lake.

"I don't see a lake," Milena said.

"Here, can't you see it." Grete pointed to a colorful spot on the card.

"It's not a lake and that's not a stream." Milena lifted her head to look Grete in the eye.

"But look, Milena, I see it so clearly." Grete tried to point out the color pattern.

"No, you don't!" Milena's voice was harsh.

"What do you mean?" Grete whispered, frightened by the tone in Milena's voice.

"You really don't see clearly! The things I see, you cannot see!" And with those words, Milena sat up, ripped the postcard down off the wall, and tore it into tiny shreds.

Grete was startled. What had happened? One moment they were so close, laughing together, and then Milena had this sudden outburst. What had she done wrong? Grete began to cry.

Milena, seeing Grete's tears, was panicked. "Don't cry! Please. Gretuška, stop these tears. Please, you must stop."

Milena's pleading only made Grete lose all control of herself. She rolled away from Milena and sobbed into the hard boards of their bunk.

"Come, come." Milena tried to pull her back toward her. "Please, forgive me."

Grete feared losing Milena all the time, and here it had happened so suddenly. But now Milena was pulling at her shoulder, begging her to turn back and face her. Grete turned to look at Milena. Her face was a blank. She looked older and so distant. She seemed to be staring into the void.

As Grete described it later, "I stopped crying instantly and started talking, trying to pass the incident off as a trifle. But Milena said sadly, 'It's awful to see someone you love crying. It makes me think of last farewells, of my tears in cold railroad stations, the heartless taillights of trains . . . the end of love . . . please don't ever cry again . . .'"[21]

"What did I do?" Grete asked. What had just happened? It had come out of nowhere, Grete thought.

"Was that our first quarrel?" she asked Milena. "You were wondering why we never quarreled." She paused and asked, "Milena, why were you so angry with me?"

With her thumb, Milena wiped away the tears rolling down Grete's face. She quietly explained that in the moment of disagreement between them, Milena had panicked because of an overwhelming feeling of isolation. A huge chasm opened up. She felt that they were worlds apart. That somehow they would never understand each other and just talk past each other and "that nothing either of us said could reach the other's heart."

Milena was terrified at the thought of separation, at the smallest hint of isolation, perhaps because it was so close to reality. What she was witnessing in the *revier* was unbelievable. The world was not seeing clearly what Milena, with her unflinching gaze, was observing day after day.

MILENA SAW THE horror around her, she saw the misery, and it drove her to despair that there was so little she could do. Every evening, she returned to their bunk with gruesome tales from the *revier*. "She was a journalist, and nothing escaped her. Despite the tension in which we lived," Grete wrote, "she never lost her ability to store up impressions. Perhaps it was her fear of violent death that sharpened her senses. Besides, we were determined to write our book, and for that it was necessary to cultivate our memories. There could be no question of closing our eyes or shutting ourselves off."[22]

In the hierarchy of the camp society, Czechs had been relatively privileged along with political Germans. But this would change in May 1942 when two agents from the Czechoslovak Resistance bombed the car of Reich Protector Reinhard Heydrich, known as the "Butcher of Prague." Earlier in the year, Heydrich had chaired the meeting at Wannsee, and he is seen as one of the principal architects of the Final Solution. He had been sent to Prague to quash national resistance movements and keep up the quotas of Czechoslovak productivity, the manufacture of motors and arms that were essential to the German war effort. He also pledged to make Prague "Jew-free."

The Czechoslovak government in exile, headed by Edvard Beneš, wanted to inspire the Czechoslovaks to resist. And they hoped that by demonstrating Czechoslovak bravery, the UK government after the war would understand that the Czechoslovaks deserved to have their nascent democracy restored. After training by the British SOE

(Special Operations Executive), seven Czechoslovak soldiers in exile in the UK were air-dropped into the countryside near Prague.

On May 27, 1942, two of the Czechoslovak soldiers ambushed Heydrich during his daily commute at a tram intersection where his chauffeur-driven convertible would have to slow down. At the vital moment, Jozef Gabčík's Sten submachine gun jammed, but Jan Kubiš threw an anti-tank grenade at the car.

Heydrich tried to give chase but collapsed. Karl Gebhardt, Himmler's top surgeon, was summoned to save his life. Heydrich did not die immediately of his wounds and even seemed to improve, but he succumbed to infection on June 4.

Hitler demanded revenge, and violent reprisals followed. In Prague, 500 Czechoslovak citizens were executed, and in Mauthausen, 294 prisoners were killed, including family members of the agents and Czechoslovak politicals. The manhunt for the killers and all involved was the priority of the Nazi Gestapo. They placed the trench coat, briefcase, and bicycle that had been used by Kubiš and Gabčík in the front window of the Bata shoe store, demanding citizens come forth with any information about men seen with these items. The radio announced that if they didn't find the killers, 100 Czechoslovak citizens would be killed each day. They considered killing 10,000 Czechoslovak citizens, but Himmler felt such widespread indiscriminate killing could hinder Czechoslovak productivity. It is estimated that around 5,000 Czechoslovak citizens were killed, and more than 13,000 arrested.

German intelligence falsely believed that the killers had taken refuge in the town of Lidice, so the SS lined up all the men of the village and executed them. Then they burned the village to the ground. The town's 195 women and 95 children were taken away. Eight children who looked "Aryan" were sent to German families for adoption; the rest were later murdered in gas vans at the Chelmno extermination camp. The surviving women from Lidice were transported to Ravensbrück. They were brutalized by the guards, who had been told these were the people responsible for the assassination of Heydrich. One woman gave birth in the *revier* soon after arriving. "It was a little boy who arrived in good health and his mother heard the baby and saw him enter the world with a happy face," recalled Czechoslovak camp survivor Vera Hozáková. "A few hours later the doctors announced to the mother that the baby was dead and they brutally beat the mother."[23]

Hanka Housková, who was caught in the struggle between her party loyalties and her friendship with Milena, wrote about the arrival of the women from Lidice. When she wrote her memoir, in March 1992, it was finally politically safe to speak about Milena. By then, the Lidice massacre had become an emblem of Czech national identity. Hanka wrote that at the camp in 1942, the Czech communists welcomed and supported the bewildered women from Lidice, who were initially confused as to why they were there. Hanka rebuked Milena for not having gone to the women more than once or twice. The communists used this as another charge against Milena, "'You see,' Ilsa said to me, 'how far Milena has distanced herself from the people.' And I kept quiet," Hanka wrote.[24]

One can imagine that Milena had many thoughts about the Heydrich assassination and the heavy cost of the reprisals on the civilian population. She was also not willing to put on a show for the communists to demonstrate her Czech patriotism, by visiting the Lidice women. Milena would have seen it as self-serving to use the tragedy of these poor bewildered women as a loyalty test.

SINCE THE DISCOVERY of sulfonamides in 1935, it was hoped that they would be an effective treatment against gas gangrene and infection. By 1942, clinical trials with animals showed promising results, but it was not clear if these results transferred to human infections, especially battlefield wounds. There were positive anecdotal stories from the front lines, but Nazi doctors wanted to test the new drugs methodically to determine the parameters of how and when to use sulfa drugs.

At the postwar Doctors' Trial at Nuremberg, Gebhardt would testify that Heydrich's assassination was the catalyst to the human experimentation at Ravensbrück. According to Gebhardt, Hitler was furious; his good friend had died from infection. But this appears to have been an attempt to shift the blame to outside political forces. The experiments were already planned. Himmler, always the enthusiastic and ghoulish amateur scientist, encouraged experimentation on camp prisoners. They were perfect test subjects, being biologically and scientifically human and yet, by Nazi standards, morally less than human.[25]

While the Nazi doctors were creating methodical human trials that broke with all ethical standards, the Allies had decided to use sulfa drugs on the battlefield even though their efficiency was still inconclusive. By the early 1940s, the Allies were testing a new drug, penicillin.[26] But wartime made research and development difficult.

By August, Dr. Gebhardt had installed a secretive ward in the *revier* at Ravensbrück where he would begin medical experiments on seventy-five young Polish students from the town of Lublin. In small groups, the young women underwent a terrifying and mysterious surgery. Their legs were cut open, and bacteria, dirt, glass, and splinters were introduced into their open wounds. Some were treated with sulfonamides, and some with other drugs. But the results were inconclusive. Gebhardt and the doctors decided to make bigger wounds, introduce more bacteria. Some women were injected with tetanus, and survivors remembered them slowly dying in agony. The pain was excruciating. Their legs turned gray-black and swelled to four times their normal size.

Every few days, the women were rolled in for inspection. Their heads were covered with a sheet so they could not see the doctors, while their bandages were ripped off and their wounds scraped. One of those inspecting doctors was Ernst Grawitz, Himmler's chief surgeon and the head of the German Red Cross. Many of the women passed out from the pain. They were all thirsty. The smell of their infected putrid flesh was awful. At night, when the ward was closed and they were locked in together, they tried to help each other. The stronger ones hopped on their wounded legs to soothe the feverish and the dying.

When the experiments began, Gebhardt was there, but as time went on and there were no real results, the task of inspecting the guinea pigs fell to the lowly female doctor Oberheuser. When it was clear that the end was near for a patient, she casually injected them to finish them off. Other patients and survivors remember how she sneered at the patients while flirting with the male doctors.

These experiments were meant to be kept secret, but secrets were hard to keep in Ravensbrück. *Revier* staff were banned from the experiment ward, but the other prisoner doctors and people passing through the *revier*, like Milena, got wind of what was happening. They heard the terrible screams coming from the ward. Some of the prisoner doctors spied through the keyholes; they listened at the doors; they saw the putrid bandages and the emptied vials labeled with strains of bacteria and tetanus. There were Polish prisoners working in the lab where the samples were sent. Everyone pieced the information together. And the news spread around the camp. Prisoners snuck up to the young Polish girls' window and tried to pass them bits of food. The young women now had a camp nickname—"*Kaninchen*," "rabbits." Later experiments on the *Kaninchen* involved breaking their bones and leaving broken bones unset to see how they might heal.

Milena witnessed all of this. And it wasn't just the *Kaninchen*. The doctors had become more and more casual about killing "useless mouths."

Gerda Quernheim and Dr. Rosenthal, who had worked together doing abortions on pregnant prisoners, now seemed to be liberally killing patients with injections. Milena kept an eye on them. Every evening, she counted the bodies. She told Grete the corpses had "marks of hypodermic needles, smashed ribs, bruised faces and suspicious gaps in their teeth."[27]

Quernheim was the only prisoner allowed in the *revier* at night, and it was clear that she and Rosenthal went there to be together. During these nightly trysts, they murdered patients, "not only for the perverse pleasure of it" but for profit. Milena furiously whispered her findings to Grete: "They chose them for their teeth."

"What? What do you mean?" Grete hated that Milena's days were in that place while she was in the greenhouse playing with the aquarium of lizards and toads.

"Gretuška, they remove the gold teeth and crowns from their victims. They are pocketing the gold."

They looked at each other. There was nothing else to say.

"Please be careful, Milena." It was her usual plea.

"It's also the Jews. They are killing them for little or no reason. They used to pretend to have a reason at least."

One group of Jewish women were injected simply because they came to the *revier* for dysentery. Hitler had announced that Germany was to be cleared of Jews, and Himmler ordered all the camps on German soil had to be *judenfrei*. The remaining 522 Jews at Ravensbrück who hadn't been killed by brutal labor or lethal injection were finally deported to Auschwitz in October.

The steady descent into horror continued, with Milena as witness. The *revier* became even more gruesome, with prisoners being lethally injected on the surgery table and their limbs amputated. From her *revier* window, Milena saw doctors driving away with limbs wrapped in sheets.

In testimony after the war, it was revealed that healthy limbs from "lunatic" women prisoners were to be used for "special experiments," in transplants onto wounded German soldiers.[28] One of these "lunatics" destined for this horrific surgery was a Czech woman from Lidice who had been driven mad when her house was burned to the ground with all her children inside. Milena had sat by her bed and listened to her "ravings" in Czech before she was murdered on the surgery table for the harvest of her limbs.

BY LATE SUMMER, the days were punctuated by air-raid sirens. In the distance, they could see the glow of lights searching the sky above Berlin. Milena and Grete squeezed each other's hands in the dark as squadrons of Allied bombers droned overhead. Rumors were passed around about German losses and groups of German soldiers surrendering to the Soviets. There was an atmosphere of tentative optimism. But Grete felt ambivalent about the bombing of German towns. She knew that there were many Germans who hated National Socialism as much as she did. They would be unprotected under the Allied bombs while the SS higher-ups would be safely ensconced in their shelters. Both Milena and Grete wanted the war to end, but they were under no illusions about the prospect of a Soviet victory for the future of Germany and Czechoslovakia.

Milena, in the *revier*, was witness to endless horror. She warned Grete never to go there if she were sick. What remained unspoken between them was that they were really terrified of Milena ending up there as a patient. She'd had serious medical issues even before her deportation, and she was already in her third year of imprisonment.

Grete was working in the garden when a Jehovah's Witness prisoner rushed in, breathless and bursting with the news: "Milena has collapsed. They've put her on a bed in the *revier*."

"I need to go to her!" Grete was frantic.

But her friends held her back. "You can't. It's too dangerous."

"But I need to make sure she's safe."

"Grete," Lotte said, calmly holding her shoulders, "if you go now you will get in trouble, and then how will you protect Milena?"

They turned to the Jehovah's Witness messenger. "You have to go stand by her side."

"What about my job?" the messenger pleaded.

"This is your real job," Lotte emphasized.

Grete reminded the messenger about how good Milena had been as a block elder, how she had protected the Bible Students. Finally, the messenger agreed to go to the *revier* and stay by Milena's side. "Don't let anything happen to her," Grete begged.

Grete had to wait a few excruciating hours before they were marched back from the gardens. Then she rushed to the *revier*, where she found Milena "burning with fever and terrified of being killed by injection."[29]

But Milena had many friends in the *revier*. They were all keeping watch over her and protecting her from lethal injections. At great risk, Grete and her greenhouse friends stole gladioli from the garden, hiding them flattened under their clothes against their emaciated bodies. When Grete saw the smile on Milena's face at the flowers, she knew the risk had been worth it. The flowers seemed to cheer her up, and she recovered from what would become the first of many kidney crises, or as Grete would later write, "It was her first attack of nephritis." It was her first in the camp, but as early as January 1937, Milena wrote to a friend about a kidney crisis.[30]

Milena recovered, but the attack marked her. She wasn't the same. She lacked her old spontaneous vitality. The mischievous look that had made her push the siren button was gone. She confessed to Grete that she had a strange disembodied feeling when it came to her emotions. It was as if they were no longer real, more like copies from memories of authentic feelings she had once felt. This confession hurt Grete a little. She wondered if Milena still felt their love. But Grete reminded herself that at least Milena was alive and she shouldn't ask for more than that. "You just need to get your strength back," Grete told her.

Soon after returning to the block and to their bed, Milena told Grete that she had seen herself in a mirror. "I look just like the sick monkey that begged for the organ-grinder who used to station himself outside my house. Whenever I passed, he would give me his little cold hand. Every time I saw him he looked more miserable. . . . Those same sad eyes looked at me in the mirror today." And then she shrugged and said, "Oh well, life is short, but death is long."[31]

Despite Milena's waning strength, and to Grete's frustration, Milena did not stop her constant risk-taking to help others. A group of male prisoners were brought to the infirmary for X-rays, no doubt because they were suspected of having tuberculosis. Walking by the men, who resembled feverish skeletons, Milena thought she recognized one of them. She walked past again and nodded; the man nodded back. It was Milena's old friend Záviš Kalandra, a Czech historian from Prague.

"Please, Milena," Grete said when Milena excitedly reported her discovery, "there's nothing you can do to help that man."

"If you had seen his state, Gretuška," Milena answered.

"No! As miserable as he is, I wouldn't think I could help him!"

Milena didn't listen. There was an SS pharmacist who worked in the men's camp and had a good reputation. After Milena found a way to speak with him, he agreed to take a note to Kalandra.

A few days later, Milena received an answer, the same Grete would have written if she could: "Milena, I beseech you for your sake and mine. Don't write again. You're risking our lives."

IN OCTOBER 1942, SS Senior Overseer Langefeld returned from Auschwitz to her previous post at Ravensbrück as *Oberaufseherin*. As at Ravensbrück, she had quickly found herself in conflict with Auschwitz's SS camp commandant, Rudolf Höss, over questions of who had authority over the women. Some of the female prisoner kapos, whom Höss controlled and who would not take orders from Langefeld, had sexual relations with the male SS guards. One of Langefeld's female guards had a relationship with a male prisoner kapo who traded sex for the jewelry stolen from the newly arrived and murdered Jews. SS officers were also involved in the lucrative trade in pillaged goods, including Höss himself, who reportedly was having sex with an Austrian prisoner from Ravensbrück. She worked at the jewelry depot and helped him smuggle the loot out of the camp.

At Auschwitz, Langefeld lost control of her guards. She heard rumors of debauched evenings in the canteen with SS officers. When Himmler visited on July 17, 1942, four months after her arrival, she asked him to transfer her back to Ravensbrück. He refused. Himmler informed Höss that the extermination of the Jews needed to go faster. The killing centers of Treblinka, Sobibor, and Belzec were murdering thousands, and the construction of Birkenau, two kilometers from Auschwitz, was now complete, with two working gas chambers. Himmler confessed to Höss that while inspecting the Birkenau gas chambers, he had felt "weak at the knees," but as good Nazi officers, they must soldier on.[32] Himmler and Höss agreed on the system whereby prisoners would be sorted upon arrival so that those who could be exploited for their labor would not be killed outright.

During Himmler's long visit to Auschwitz that day, Langefeld hoped for her chance to speak with him. She was kept waiting while

Johanna Langefeld with the daughter of an overseer friend and her son, Herbert,
February 20, 1941

Himmler observed a flogging of ten women prisoners. Near the end
of the day, when Himmler was anxious to end his visit, she had a
few moments of rushed explanation. She tried to tell him how the SS
had manipulated her female kapos and guards. He did not appear to
listen to her. A few moments later, speaking to Höss, he undermined
her authority by saying that the prisoner kapos, who were loyal to
Höss, needed to "vent their evil on prisoners," particularly the Jews.

At a small subcamp a few miles away from Auschwitz called Budy,
where female prisoners were draining a swamp, the conditions and
treatment were particularly appalling. The SS goaded the female
kapos to beat the Jewish women. In early October, the brutality of the
kapos finally went "too far" and created a scandal at Budy. The kapos claimed the prisoners rioted and this led to a massacre of ninety
women. It is telling and sickening that Höss, a hardened SS commandant who was overseeing the murder of a thousand lives a day
in the gas chambers, was horrified by the sight of the aftermath of
the massacre. "The Budy bloodbath is still before my eyes. I find it
incredible that human beings could ever turn into such beasts. The

way the kapos knocked the French Jewesses about, tearing them to pieces, killing them with axes and throttling them—it was simply gruesome," he wrote.[33] Apparently orderly mass murder was fine, but chaotic killing was just too much for Höss.

Here was proof that there was disarray among Langefeld's female guards. Höss wanted to be rid of her as much as she wanted to go. Langefeld had also appealed to Oswald Pohl to move her back to Ravensbrück. A few days after the massacre, she was allowed to return to her favorite camp.

During her six months at Auschwitz, Langefeld had seen the gas chambers and knew firsthand what happened to Jews there. This does not seem to have upset her. It was what happened to the other prisoners. "Auschwitz is the most horrible place the mind of man could conceive of," she later confided to Grete. "I can never get over that the Bible Students I took there came to their end. But at least Teege and Maurer were saved."[34] Teege and Maurer were the two political prisoners who had served as her personal secretaries when she was at Ravensbrück. They had gone to the new camp with her. She had asked and gotten their release for good behavior from Himmler on his July visit.

Langefeld was in her early forties. Raised in the Rhineland and deeply patriotic, she regretted not being a man so she could fight for her country during the First World War. She followed Hitler's rise to power with admiration. He was her ideal and her hero. She had married early, had a son, and then her husband died. During the period of economic collapse after World War I, her family was ruined, and she went to work in the prison system. She firmly believed that Hitler and Himmler were wonderful men. In her mind, the brutality and inhumanity she witnessed in the camps were separate from her idealization of Hitler. The lower-level SS officers were to blame. They were stupid thugs, nothing like her dear Führer. Among the prisoners, she had a reputation of being relatively "decent," with her soft spot for the Poles and Jehovah's Witnesses. She could even show kindness to the Roma and Sinti, and occasionally toward other *Asoziale*. But she remained a true Nazi as far as Jews were concerned. Grete witnessed how Langefeld's face contorted into hatred when she wrote a list of Jewish names for a transport.

Langefeld returned from Auschwitz a changed woman. Her nervous tics were amplified. Before she spoke, she had to clear her throat once or twice. She endlessly stroked her dress as if ironing out the wrinkles. She constantly brushed away nonexistent hair from her face. The horrors she had witnessed at Auschwitz, and the conditions at Ravensbrück upon her return, destabilized her. She had always maintained that her role was to reeducate and reform the women prisoners, besides the Jews, who were unsalvageable. But the camp she found upon her return was clearly designed to do something else entirely.

There was the new commandant, Fritz Suhren. Young and slim, fair-haired and handsome, he was known to be a rule-follower, brought in along with the new Gestapo chief, Ludwig Ramdohr, to root out corruption. The camp population had swelled with all the new arrivals from the east. And physically, it had changed dramatically with the newly built Siemens factory just outside the walls. There was now a small men's camp, for the male prisoners who had been brought from Buchenwald to build the *Siemenslager*.

Siemens was not alone in building a factory next door to a concentration camp in order to profit from the endless cheap labor. Three other major German manufacturers—IG Farben at Auschwitz, Steyr-Daimler-Puch AG at Mauthausen, and Heinkel at Sachsenhausen— were also benefitting from partnerships with the SS. The plant managers came from Berlin and were not used to working with camp prisoners. They were not nearly as vicious as the SS guards. Working in the factory was considered a plum job, as you were inside, dry, and relatively warm. Siemens also sought out women with administrative skills. Grete was one of the first prisoners chosen to work at the factory. She was pulled from the lovely greenhouses to serve as secretary for the plant director, Otto Grade. Once again, she was in a position of power with its concomitant privileges. And as Milena pointed out to her, she would be in a position to help others.

In the factory's head office, Grete was able to observe Grade up close. He calculated how much each prisoner produced and kept meticulous records of each and every pfennig. Siemens paid the SS around five Reichsmarks a day for the labor of a woman prisoner.[35] This was relatively low-cost for Siemens, which was enjoying record orders in the war economy boom. And the money represented a fortune for Himmler and the SS coffers since the cost of feeding and housing the women was minimal, and they seemed to have a constantly renewed supply.

Siemens also offered incentives. If a prisoner worked more than her quota, she was given a coupon for the camp shop. If she worked under her quota, Grade ordered the guard to beat her. If that didn't work, he would send a report to the camp and have her replaced. The rejected prisoner would then face the punishment block, flogging, and possible special transport. Each month, he sent detailed reports about output and prisoners back to headquarters. Grete understood that Grade was a slave driver with a clear motivation. As long as his bosses back in Berlin were pleased with his work, he would get an exemption from the fighting on the Eastern Front that was fatal for so many.

Meanwhile, the Siemens plant was expanding, and male prisoners were being driven mercilessly to build more and faster. "In the short period of my work for Grade I heard five executions 'while attempting to escape,' and that was just from one work gang," Grete later wrote.[36]

Upon her return, Langefeld wanted Grete to work as her secretary. Grete's knowledge of Russian and other skills were useful to her. And as an old political, she knew the runnings of the camp inside and out. Milena and Grete talked it over. It's important to note the level of privilege Grete had that she could decide which job she would take. She had a choice because she had such an important job at Siemens. Taking the job with Langefeld would make Grete the most powerful prisoner in the camp, but this authority came with great danger. As usual, Langefeld was clashing with SS command, and aligning with her would make Grete vulnerable to the vicissitudes of power. Milena and Grete decided that because the job would place Grete in a position to help other prisoners, she must take it despite the risk.

There was also the fact that when she worked at Siemens, Grete slept in the Siemens block. Working for Langefeld meant she could return to Block 1 and Milena.

Sitting in the office day after day with Langefeld, Grete saw her insecurities and gnawing self-doubt as she presided over the chaotic camp and the ever-growing brutality. Once, Grete overheard her battle on the phone with an SS officer. Langefeld was trying to obtain winter clothing for the prisoners. She slammed down the receiver and bitterly exclaimed to Grete, "That man ought to be made to stand naked on the camp street for a few hours so that he could learn what it is to feel cold."[37]

As they became closer, Langefeld confided more in Grete, about her distaste for the SS officers in charge. And Grete gradually took more risks. One day, Langefeld, clearly upset, recounted to Grete her disturbing dream from the night before. She had dreamed that a squadron of bombers had landed in Ravensbrück and turned into tanks. Foreign solders climbed out of the tanks and took over the camp. "What do you think it means?" she asked Grete, blinking compulsively and ironing out the fabric of her skirt with her hands.

"You're afraid Germany will lose the war."

As she spoke those words, Grete startled herself. Saying something like this to a senior guard, and loyal member of the National Socialist Party, should have landed Grete in trouble. She could have been flogged, thrown in the *Strafblock*, but instead, Grete witnessed the look of fear on Langefeld's face. It was undeniable. Germany was losing the war. And Langefeld was losing confidence in the Nazi Party. Every Friday, Langefeld had to attend the ritual of floggings along with Suhren and the camp doctor. She returned from these weekly beatings tense and on edge. Throwing down her cape and gloves, she would sit down at her desk, unable to control the growing storm of tics and nervous compulsive motions. To Grete, it was obvious that Langefeld was close to breaking down.

As her ambivalence grew, Langefeld became more unsure of how to proceed. She would hesitate before making a command and put off important decisions. Grete was able to use these lapses to intercede on prisoners' behalf. All the disciplinary reports had to go through Langefeld. She would have to see the prisoners and make a recommendation to the commandant about the appropriate punishment. When the reports of disciplinary problems arrived in the office, the prisoners waited in the hall until Langefeld saw them. One day, an *Asoziale* was brought in for stealing a turnip. Langefeld questioned her.

"Did you steal the turnip?"

The prisoner was shivering with fear. Her clothes hung loosely on the skeleton of her body, and her face was covered in sores.

"Yes. But I was just so hungry," she wailed.

"But if everybody stole turnips there would be none left for anyone else? What would we do then?" Langefeld spoke to her as if she were a child.

The case clearly called for the woman to be sent to solitary confinement, and even a flogging. Theft of food was a serious crime. But Grete decided to try to intercede. After the woman was led out of the room, Grete explained, "I know this woman from when I was a room elder at the *Asoziale* block. She will never survive the *Strafblock*."

Langefeld said nothing. Her mouth twitched and she blinked nervously. Then, in a sudden movement, she took up the report and tore it to pieces, letting the torn paper fall into the wastebasket.

When Soviet prisoners were questioned by Langefeld, Grete served as interpreter. She was able then to answer the way she knew would please Langefeld. Grete discovered that Langefeld had a terrible memory, and Grete took advantage of this. She would put a report with damning information, something that would surely lead to a prisoner being flogged, at the bottom of the pile, and if Langefeld or the SS supervisor didn't ask or follow up on the report, she kept it buried there.

In the winter of 1942, a large group of women from the Soviet Red Army arrived at Ravensbrück. They instantly made an impression on the political prisoners who were communists and admirers of the Russian Revolution. Members of the medical corps, these nurses and doctors had been captured at the Battle of Sebastopol. They arrived in uniform and battle-worn. With astonishing army discipline, they followed their leader's orders, even though the Germans were unable to determine who their leader was. No one broke ranks.

Camp Commandant Suhren and Ramdohr had them stripped naked in the washroom and walked among the ranks. Langefeld returned to her office in a fury, loudly condemning this display of bad behavior; it was provocative and shameless. Even she had been moved by the dignity of the Red Army women.

The new arrivals were placed in quarantine, but the Ukrainian, Soviet, and Czechoslovak political prisoners were eager to communicate with their comrades. Ramdohr's camp police intercepted quite a few of their attempts to smuggle notes. The notes were brought to Langefeld, and Grete was made to translate them. It was clear from the notes that the prisoners were eager to make themselves useful to these women from the official Soviet Red Army and so they were providing them with intelligence about the camp: how many prisoners, how many guards, the security situation. They gave names and the past history of the executed. If Grete translated these notes correctly, the prisoners would be in trouble and perhaps be executed themselves. Instead, she translated them into sentimental messages of greeting and vapid praise for Mother Russia. Langefeld tossed the notes into the bin.

Grete had gotten used to her position of power. Though she constantly worried about Milena taking risks, she might have developed a false sense of invincibility. She did not realize that she and Langefeld were being watched.

Langefeld had protested Ramdohr's brutal methods. He was not answerable to the commandant, but only to his Gestapo bosses in Berlin. He rarely wore a uniform, preferring a dark flannel suit. And he never followed the protocol for punishments. He would put prisoners in the *Strafblock* with no report to justify doing so. He would beat them himself in his office—one of the most callous female guards was shocked at the blood on his office walls. With his ruthlessness, he had been able to acquire a network of spies among the prisoners. Langefeld had made her opinion of him known. And Ramdohr felt contempt for her and her nervous self-importance.

When no reports resulted from the intercepted messages, he had a few of them translated for himself. The contents were quite different from Grete's versions. Without her realizing it, the net was tightening around Langefeld. And if Langefeld fell, Grete would fall with her.

The commandant and the Gestapo chief, who did not like each other particularly, wanted to get rid of Langefeld, but Suhren knew that Langefeld had quite a bit of information on his SS officers. She knew about their embezzlement and corruption. There was a thriving black market outside the camp with the theft from the *Effektenkammer* and the parcels sent to prisoners. Suhren wanted to be careful about how and when they trapped Langefeld.

In the winter of 1942, two Polish women who were working in the kitchen managed to escape. They hid behind the refuse bins loaded on the back of a truck. When their absence was noticed, they were already far away. They had traveled all the way to Berlin by train. One was caught a year later and brought back to the camp. As more and more prisoners worked on gangs outside the walls, many on the local farms, there were more escapes.

Grete reported that during this period, about a dozen prisoners were able to make it out without being recaptured. She experienced a "feeling of delight when I had to take out their cards out of the general index and put them in a special box-file marked 'Escapes.'"[38]

Langefeld would inevitably be held accountable for these failures in security. Ramdohr blamed her for the kitchen's lax ways, "ruled by filthy Poles." Whenever Langefeld had a new functionary position to fill, she consulted her favorite block elders, the camp elders: Rosa Jochmann, Maria Fischer, and Helena Korewina. Langefeld was known to have a soft spot for the Polish politicals, and especially the *Kaninchen.*

Sympathy was growing camp-wide for the *Kaninchen*, and the SS knew it. Those women who had survived the gruesome butchery in the *revier* were now back in their block. They could not go out to work and so they had time to talk to each other. Sometimes they ventured out of their block for sunshine and the other prisoners saw them, these once-healthy young women bent over crutches, barely able to stand or walk.

The executions of Polish women continued just outside the walls of the prison. Two of the *Kaninchen* had been taken and shot.

The prisoners had to fight back.

"The sight of so many disabled women in one block had an effect on us and we suddenly had a growing sense of our own power," recalled Wanda Wojtasik.[39] They organized and managed to smuggle out secret messages in their official censored letters to their families. They hoped the news about these war crimes would reach the wider world.

In November 1942, the International Committee of the Red Cross held a crisis meeting. The question on the table was whether they should tell the world about what they knew. News had gotten to them with increasing frequency about the Final Solution. Through the Polish underground and the exceptional daring of the *Kaninchen* in Ravensbrück, they had learned about the "medical" experiments done on the young women. They had known about other atrocities for some time, but they had chosen to remain silent, preferring to use "quiet diplomacy." They wrote ingratiating letters to the head of the German Red Cross, Ernst Grawitz, the very doctor who had signed off on Gebhardt's human experiments.

The ICRC's lack of action and silence remains a black mark on the organization. One of the prominent committee members, Carl Burckhardt, was a great admirer of Hitler. Before the war and after inspecting one of the early concentration camps, he wrote to Hitler, signing the letter, "Your deeply devoted, deeply respectful, deeply grateful, Carl Burckhardt."

The Polish government wrote to the ICRC, pleading with them to respond and tell the world. The ICRC replied that the German Red Cross was not allowing them access to the camps and they "insist that such camps are not subject to the Geneva Convention of 1929." Hiding behind this excuse, they abandoned their mission to "protest the horrors of war." Later they would further endanger the lives of the surviving *Kaninchen* by hiding behind their "neutrality" and not delivering parcels to the seventy-seven known surviving *Kaninchen*. The policy at the time was that if the Red Cross had a name and prisoner number, they could send parcels to specific prisoners. Other prisoners in Ravensbrück, not the *Kaninchen*, were receiving parcels from the ICRC. The *Kaninchen* had gotten their names and numbers to the ICRC through their underground methods, as a kind of insurance policy. If the Nazis knew the ICRC knew about the *Kaninchen*, the logic went, they would be less likely to execute them. But the ICRC chose not to send parcels, fearing that it might offend their good friend Dr. Grawitz.[40]

Through multiple reports from escapees, the World Jewish Congress, the Polish underground, churches, resistance movements, and others, the fact that a horrific genocide and mass murder was occurring in Hitler's concentration camps could no longer be denied. In late November 1942, US newspapers hit the streets reporting on Hitler's mass murder of European Jews. On December 17, Allied leadership, which had long been skeptical about the Jewish genocide, decided to make a joint statement that there was no longer any doubt about Hitler's murder of Europe's Jews. It was the first official statement condemning "in the strongest possible terms this bestial policy of cold-blooded extermination." But like the ICRC, even this statement was mitigated by political leaders who wanted to soften the language. Some State Department officials suspected the news was untrue and wanted the Jewish leaders to "call off, or at least tone down" their accounts of mass murder. They worried if the public believed the news they would be forced to do "something more specific to aid these people."[41]

In Ravensbrück, Ramdohr was amassing a list of strikes against Langefeld, while Grete was pushing Langefeld to be more and more lenient. Ramdohr recruited spies from the kitchen who provided him with damning information about Grete and Langefeld's favorite camp elders like Rosa Jochmann.

Milena was also pushing Grete to do something about Rosenthal and Quernheim. Every night they were drinking, having sex, and picking out one or two prisoners to murder and extract their gold teeth. Milena urged Grete, "Say something to Langefeld, my darling. Tell her what they are doing."

For Milena, Grete "screwed up her courage" and recounted Milena's story to Langefeld. She erupted in hysterical anger, screaming at the top of her lungs, "These doctors are criminals. They're as bad as the Camp Commander."

Grete was surprised by Langefeld's vehemence. "Is that what you really think?" she asked her.

"Yes, that's what I really think."

"If you feel that way, how in God's name can you go on working here? Why don't you get out?"

Langefeld's response surprised Grete: "But isn't it important for the prisoners that I should stay here and try at least to prevent the worst?"

The internal moral trade-offs haunted everyone to varying degrees. Years later, in 1957, Langefeld would knock on Grete's door in Frankfurt. Langefeld had been arrested by the US Army after the war and was extradited to Krakow to stand trial as a member of the Auschwitz SS personnel, but aided by Polish prison staff, she escaped. She hid in a convent, and sometime around 1957, she moved to Munich illegally to live with her sister. She sought out Grete, desperate to be forgiven. Grete described an old woman, barely recognizable with missing teeth, babbling as she tried to justify her behavior.

PART FOUR

1943

The Dark Cell

Women in Ravensbrück doing hard labor

By early 1943, Langefeld's and Grete's fates were intertwined, and neither woman seemed to understand the growing threat against them. Suhren and Ramdohr were looking for ways to remove Langefeld, and Grete risked being caught in the power struggle. Ultimately, Langefeld's downfall would come from her soft spot for the *Kaninchen*.

When some of the *Kaninchen*, who had already been operated on twice, were called back to the *revier* for a third operation, they refused. The SS did nothing in response. The *Kaninchen* grew bolder. After much discussion, in mid-March 1943, they decided on a protest march to Langefeld's office. It was a long way for them to walk. Leaning over crutches, or carried by healthy companions, they slowly made their way toward the camp office building. It took them an eternity to cover the three hundred meters. They took one step and then gathered their strength for the next. They expected the guards to stop them, but there were no guards to be seen.

The SS clearly wanted to ignore the existence of the *Kaninchen*, but the other prisoners did not. Those who were coming back from their work details turned and stared in astonishment. Others looked out from windows of their blocks. The *Kaninchen* walked slowly in silence; the only sound was the clicking of their canes and crutches on the sandy campgrounds. Finally, they made it to the main square in front of the offices. Eugenia Mikulska was carried to the front: "They put me on the ground and went back to the ranks standing about fifty meters behind. I couldn't stand, so I kneeled on my sound leg and stretched the operated one out in front of me, as I couldn't bend it."[1]

They waited for a long time for a reaction. A guard appeared, and they said that they wanted to speak with the *Oberaufseherin*. They read out a simple statement: "We, the Polish political prisoners, categorically protest against the experimental operations performed on our healthy bodies."

There are conflicting reports about what happened next. Some recall that an SS officer came out and said that Langefeld knew nothing about the operations and they must be a figment of the prisoners' imaginations. Others recalled that Langefeld sent a message that she had referred the matter to the commandant. And still others recalled that Langefeld briefly came out of her offices and onto the main square, where she looked embarrassed, paralyzed, and awkward, as if she were in pain. Then she quickly turned and went back inside.

The protesters returned to the blocks. But their action awakened an atmosphere of tension and revolt in the camp. A few days later, when another group of Poles was called to report to the *Effektenkammer*, always a prelude to their execution, there was a near mutiny. Suhren considered this further proof that Langefeld had lost control.

The *Kaninchen* and their revolt did influence Langefeld. She believed they had been lied to, that they had "volunteered" for the experimental surgeries with the promise they would be released, and instead, they were being executed. Their plight would lead to the final straw for Langefeld and her SS career.

In April, Ramdohr put three of the political elders, Rosa Jochmann, Maria Fischer, and Maria Schwarz, in the *Strafblock*. This should have been a warning to Grete she was on thin ice. A few days later, Grete saw a memo on Langefeld's desk calling for ten Polish prisoners with numbers between seven thousand and ten thousand to report to the *Effektenkammer*. Both Grete and Langefeld knew what this meant; they were slated for execution.

A short while later, as Grete sat at her typewriter looking through the window, she saw the ten women being brought to the square in front of the offices. Two of them were on crutches. Without thinking, she called out, "Frau Langefeld, they are going to shoot the *Kaninchen*! They are coming now."

Langefeld jumped up to look out the window. She went swiftly back to her desk and picked up the phone, asking the operator to connect her to the commandant. Grete listened anxiously.

"Herr *Lagerkommandant*, do you have permission from Berlin to shoot the *Kaninchen*?"

Grete could not hear Suhren's response, but Langefeld put down the phone and ordered her to go out and send the two prisoners on crutches back to their block. It was perhaps Langefeld's first real act of rebellion. It was also her last.

Two weeks later, on April 20, 1943, Grete was in the office when Langefeld received a brief phone call from Suhren. She listened in silence, put down the receiver; then, with trembling hands, she picked up her cap and gloves. She came over to Grete's desk and did something she had never done before: She put her hand out for a handshake. "I'm afraid for you," she said as she shook Grete's hand in farewell. "Ramdohr is a beast."

Grete sat alone in the office, frozen in place, trying to calm her rising panic.

She looked out the window and saw Milena rushing across the main square, coming from the direction of the *revier*. What was she doing? Why was she walking out there during working hours? Something terrible must have happened, something she had to tell Grete. Grete rose and ran down the corridor to greet her.

Breathless, she threw her arms around Milena. "What has happened, my darling?"

Milena looked back at her with her dark searching eyes. "Nothing has happened. But I suddenly felt so worried about you. I had to come see you. I had to make sure you are alright."

"It's Langefeld," Grete said. "Something's happened to her."

"If she's in trouble . . ." Milena was thinking through the consequences of this catastrophe. They had worried about just this sort of scenario. If Grete worked so closely with the heads of power, she would run a great risk. Grete kissed her to stop her from talking. She felt desperate to protect Milena.

"Please, Milena," she said, pulling away and holding Milena by the shoulders, "You must get back to the *revier* before you are discovered. Please, I am fine. I'll see you tonight."

Just as Milena was leaning in close to Grete to kiss one last time, they both saw Ramdohr through the window coming around the corner toward the office entrance. "Get back into your office," Milena screamed.

Grete ran and made it just in time to sit down in front of her type-writer. Only a moment later, Ramdohr burst through the door.

"Buber, come with me," he ordered.

Grete stood and walked with him down the corridor in silence. As Grete stepped outside the building, she saw Milena standing mo-tionless like a pillar just a few feet from the door. Grete turned away quickly, not wanting to draw Ramdohr's attention in Milena's direc-tion, but the look on Milena's face in that brief instant seared into her heart. A look of abject fear and love.

Grete followed him to the *Strafblock*. "Why have I been brought here?" she asked.

He laughed. "You've got a nerve to ask. It's only because you sys-tematically suppressed reports and destroyed messages intercepted from prisoners; that's all. Don't deceive yourself: we've had an eye on you for some time, and we're on to all your tricks. You've interfered with official documents and conducted communist agitation."

Grete started to defend herself, but Ramdohr raised his hand.

"You'd better not say anything now. I'll leave you in the bunker for a while and then you can think about whether it is worth it or not to lie."[2]

Grete knew that "the bunker" meant she would be put in the ab-solute darkness of the solitary confinement cells. These cells within the *Strafblock* were ruled over by the guard Dorothea Binz.

Ramdohr handed Grete over to Binz. Beautiful and cruel, with her tight blond braid coiled in a crown on her head, she was known for her vicious pleasure in urging her dog to bite the prisoners' legs as they marched. Grete and Milena had watched Binz riding across the main square on her bike with the cape of her uniform flying behind her. "She loves that cape," Milena had commented dryly.

And for some reason, Milena's insight had made Grete laugh.

Grete was stripped and searched by one of the Jehovah's Witnesses who worked in the block. She was given a thin cotton shift with no sleeves and a towel. She was led barefoot down a basement corridor, past occupied cells, until an empty one was found. Then the door was slammed shut and she was left in complete blackness. Feeling her way around the tiny cell, she stumbled against a stool that was fixed to the ground. She sat and tried to get her eyes to adjust to the darkness. There was a faint sliver of light coming from under the door. But it wasn't enough to pierce deeper into the tiny cell. Low on the door was a hatch that could be slid open for food to be passed into the cell. There was a small peephole, but when she tried to look through it, she saw nothing. The peephole was so they could observe her. A small wooden flap could be lowered and raised to serve as a table. There was also a bed flap, but it was locked folded up against the wall. There was a toilet in one corner and cold heating pipes in another. There was a tiny window high up, but it had been closed and all light blocked. She paced the cell: four and a half steps by two and a half steps.

Grete sat back down on the stool. She wondered what Ramdohr had in store for her. She had seen women who had gone mad after stints in the bunker.

Up until now, she had been outside of herself, observing the situation. Now fear seized her. It came when she thought about Milena. Who would look after her? What if she got sick again? Milena needed her. At night sometimes, she would sob on Grete's shoulder, "If only I could be dead without dying! But to die in this place like a dog!" Grete consoled her. When they were together, Grete could get Milena to think about better times. Now, so cut off from Milena, would she lose her forever? Would she ever see her again?

The light in her cell was turned on from the outside. The brightness made her squint and shield her eyes. She saw there was an eye looking at her through the peephole. It was Ramdohr inspecting his latest victim. Then he switched the light off and she was engulfed in darkness.

As she blindly paced her cell, she began to focus her attention on the sounds. The loud brash voices of the guards. Binz breaking into sharp laughter. The sobs and cries of prisoners. Dogs barking. The distant muffled sound of the siren. Then came a familiar smell, the nightly soup. She heard the shuffle along the corridor, the opening of the hatches on the doors, and the scrape of tin trays sliding into the cells. The sound came closer, clanging as they approached her door with the soup. But then they passed by her door. There would be no soup for her.

Evening was coming on, and she grew colder in her cell. She sat on her stool and pulled her legs up to hug them against her chest. She rubbed her cold hands together, beat them against her body, jumped up and down to take the stiffness out of her joints. The cold floor hurt her feet. She tried to warm her bare arms between her thighs. She was exhausted, but no one had unlocked her bed, and the floor was too cold to lie down on. She tried sitting on the floor with her back against the cell wall, but soon she was chilled to the bone. She had noticed some newspaper behind the cold pipes. She spread the paper on the ground and lay curled on a small square. She was still too cold to sleep. The night was endless. But it did end when she heard the distant sound of the siren and imagined the morning roll call.

How was Milena coping? She wondered. The thought of Milena out there in the camp possessed her. After five years of confinement in prisons and camps, after the horrors of Siberia, Grete was tougher than most. She didn't scream, or weep, or hammer the floor with her fists. She repressed self-pity; she had to survive for Milena.

The day was no different than the night before. Her cell seemed even colder. The light was turned on for five minutes by two Jehovah's Witness prisoners who gave her a broom to sweep out her cell. For the rest of the time, she was in darkness.

Ramdohr came and turned on the light, opened the cell. "Well," he said, "how are we feeling today? Are you ready to make a statement now?"

Grete turned her back to him.

"Very well," he said, "I can wait." He left, slamming the door and turning off the light.

Her stomach cramped with hunger when she smelled the soup again. And again, they passed by her door. The second night, she slept a little, dreaming of bread, but woke when she was reaching for the hot loaves. Then she dreamed she was given a plate of macaroni, but as she bent to eat it like a dog on all fours, she woke up and hit her head on the cement floor.

By the third day, the hunger pangs had subsided. But the feeling of cold had taken over, overwhelming her. Every morning, one of the Jehovah's Witness prisoners opened the cell, turned on the light, and gave her a brush and pan to sweep out her cell. The Jehovah's Witness prisoner never said a word, her face a mask to protect herself from contact.

"Give me some more paper, please," Grete pleaded with her.

She nodded and rushed out, then quickly thrust some more paper into Grete's cell. Grete covered a small corner, and there she sat with her head in her hands. That way anyone looking through the spy hole would not see her face. She sat like that for days in a stupor. She began to hallucinate people, visitors, warm, soft quilts, plates of food. She no longer noticed or kept track of the days or the difference between day and night. Even the gnawing sense of cold drifted away with her mind. She was watching strange ghostly phosphorescent figures moving around her in the darkness, protecting her. As her mind drifted free into the world of hallucinations, she felt a sense of peace.

She was startled by Binz screaming at her, "Hey there! Don't you want your bread?"

She crawled to the door and took the warm brown liquid they called coffee and her portion of bread. With the first sip, she felt her mind restore itself. She was back in her body in the dark cell. It had been seven days with no food. She would now be given normal camp rations every fourth day, and on the days in between, she was given a piece of bread. It was a cruel metered torture—just when the pangs of hunger subsided, she would be given food again. It was just enough food to keep her feeling hungry all the time. Binz also let down the bed and gave her a sheet and a blanket. That was the end of what the Gestapo called "strict dark arrest with hard sleeping."

A day later, Binz took Grete out of her cell, and for a brief breathless moment, she thought she was being released. Instead, she was led up the stairs to the higher row of cells. These were better, as they weren't so damp and moldy and there was a touch more light seeping under the doorway. During the day, she sat staring at the thin strip of light, and once even lay down flat, pressing her lips to that faint glimmer of sun.

One night, Ramdohr took her from her cell to question her. He didn't bring up the suppressed reports. Her crime had shifted. He was accusing her of being part of a plot with Langefeld to set up a spy organization against Suhren. He told her that she would be hung "in full view of the whole camp." She gathered from this interrogation that Langefeld was under arrest.

Back in her cell, she pressed the Jehovah's Witness prisoner who came in each morning for the brief period of sweeping out for news. Did she know what had happened to Langefeld? She refused to say anything. But at last, one day, she whispered that Frau Langefeld was no longer working at Ravensbrück.

In the dark bunker, sounds became Grete's whole world. There were two tiers of cells arranged around a central court. She learned to distinguish where the sounds came from. The worst sounds came on Fridays, the day of floggings. The cries and screams could be heard throughout the building. She could not shut out the sound. She heard it no matter what she did. She heard it with her skin, with her whole body. The pain went straight to her heart.[3]

Grete was sometimes able to communicate with other prisoners, though this had to be done carefully since it was against the rules. By accident, she found out that her friend from the kitchen garden Eva Busch was also in the bunkers, and she called out to her without thinking. Grete had just been served her warm morning liquid when Binz heard her call out and stormed in, enraged. She grabbed Grete's cup and poured it out on the ground. "Three days starvation for you. No bed. No blanket."

Grete took up her position in the corner, and in her weakened state, her sense of reality seemed to drift away almost immediately. She was back in her world of hallucinations.

MILENA WAS BESIDE herself with worry for Grete. But getting her help gave her a purpose. She knew which of the Jehovah's Witness prisoners worked in the *Strafblock*. She was resolved to get them to pass a message and some food to Grete. Several times, Milena found them on the camp street and begged them to help her. But they were adamant in their refusal. What she was asking them to do was too dangerous; she risked getting them all killed. Eventually, when they saw her coming, they would turn away.

If they wouldn't meet her on the street, Milena would find another way. One night, she snuck out, the way she used to do to visit Grete, that first year when Grete was the block elder for the Jehovah's Witness prisoners. That was a happy year, she thought. She knew the way in the dark. She had done this so many times. It was harder for her to move now that her rheumatism had gotten so bad. But the urgency of her mission carried her through.

She had found out what bed they were in. They were on the top, on the third tier, and it was hard for her, with her swollen joints and bad knee, to climb up there quietly in the night. But she did it. They startled awake to find Milena on top of them in their bunk! She implored them to help her dear Grete.

They were angry. She was going to get them into trouble. She was crazy. They really could not help her. If they did, they risked the *Strafblock* themselves. And what if their block elder found Milena here? Their current block elder was not like Grete. They would all be in trouble.

"Yes," Milena agreed, whispering, "Grete is not like the block elder you have now." Milena reminded them of all the things Grete had done for the Jehovah's Witness prisoners as their block elder. Had they forgotten how to be grateful?

But they insisted they could not break the rules. It was just too great a risk.

"Yes, I understand you are afraid." Milena shifted her argument. She was nothing if not persuasive. She began to talk to them in their own language, the language of Jehovah, the God of vengeance. She preached to them about Christian charity and described the torments of hell in the next world if they kept their hearts hard and turned away from helping a friend in need. Wasn't it their duty as good

Christians, now more than ever? This reduced them to whimpering. "God is calling you to this task! Will you refuse him?"

With a yelp of fear, one of them agreed; they would do it. Grete pulled out a squashed package and placed it into their hands.

"Tell her I love her," she whispered urgently before crawling away.

GRETE WAS HALF-CONSCIOUS on the floor of her cell. It was the third day, just before the end of her supplementary punishment for trying to speak with another prisoner. Before the usual distribution of bread, the hatch on her door slid open and a voice whispered breathlessly, "Grete, come quick, I've brought you something from Milena."

Grete crawled on all fours to the door. The woman pulled out a parcel from under her dress. "Take it quick. Milena sends you all her love. But hide it, for the love of God."

Grete grabbed the package and wept. Milena was helping her instead of the other way around. In the package was a handful of sugar and two buns she must have gotten from a parcel from her father.

IN THE DARKNESS of her cell, Grete dreamed in vivid colors, and now her dreams were about escape, about real freedom. She was running, her heart pounding, through the streets of Berlin. She had a train to catch. A train that would take her to Prague, where she was meeting Milena. She went into a shop, and there were books, but also all kinds of reproductions of paintings she and Milena had talked about. There was a painting by Brueghel, and beautiful Impressionistic landscapes. She picked one after another to bring to Milena. Then there was a soft, warm fur coat. She knew the coat had magic properties and that it would heal Milena, so she bought it too. And then, at the train station, she bought armfuls of colorful magazines that they could leaf through lying in bed together. The train was leaving; she had to rush to jump up into the car. And then the light went on in her cell.

Ramdohr took her for questioning again. This time he menaced her with Auschwitz. He was sick and tired of all her denials. He could arrange for her transport there, "return undesirable." Back in her cell, she thought this threat was more likely than the public hanging he had threatened the first time. She remembered what the Jehovah's Witness prisoner who had been to Auschwitz had told her about the smell of burning flesh. And it seemed to her that she could smell it in the air. Was she completely losing her mind?

She asked the woman in the cell next to her if she could smell burning flesh. The woman responded, "Yes, of course. Didn't you know the crematorium they've built behind the bunkers has started up?"

Grete had been in dark arrest for two months and had not been aware of the newest addition to Ravensbrück. The death rate now had become too substantial to send the bodies into Fürstenberg village to the local crematorium.

Again, one morning before the serving of breakfast, the hatch of her door slid open and the Jehovah's Witness prisoner produced another package from Milena. Grete laughed with joy. But the woman shushed her, miserable with fear. "Grete! Please let me tell Milena you don't want her to send you any more packages! It's too dangerous. Please, let me tell her. Please, Grete! Milena's going to get herself thrown in here!" The woman was almost hysterical.

"Very well, OK. Tell her I forbid her to send me anything more."

GRETE FORCED HERSELF to fight, to keep herself from falling into a stupor, into self-pity. She developed a strict routine for each day. Walking, crawling, gymnastics, and reciting poetry and stories to herself.

One story about a boy and woman in a small hut by the Black Sea took over her mind. Every day, she allowed herself to daydream into the story. She would open the door of the hut and see the ocean. She was both people in the story. They were both refugees hiding in a perfect place by the sea. They had a protector, a hunter who sometimes brought them food. Grete drifted for days with the protagonists, two people perfectly happy in their little hut together. They loved each other; they held each other tenderly. Sometimes Grete's neighbor would tap on the wall and bring her back to reality. But she longed only to dive back into her story.

After ten weeks in the *Strafblock*, Grete was released and sent back to the camp without further questioning or any explanation. She would later write that the exhilaration she felt at that moment of liberation was greater than what she felt when she was finally liberated from the camp less than two years later. But the very next day, she fell ill. Her body couldn't stand regular meals. Milena arranged to get her assigned to "inside work," and most of the day she rested on the bed she shared with Milena.

Milena recounted Langefeld's fate. After she had halted the execution of the two *Kaninchen*, Himmler himself had given the order to have her removed. She was separated from her son and taken to Breslau to stand before the SS tribunal. She was charged with being "a tool of the Polish political prisoners and having shown sympathy for Polish nationals." Her main Polish block elders were thrown into the *Strafblock*. Langefeld was let off for lack of evidence, but she was dismissed from service.

Only a week later, just as Grete was beginning to get some of her strength back, she made a fateful mistake. Helena Korewina in the Polish block wanted to see her. Helena had a leaflet about the Nazi Deputy Führer, Rudolf Hess, flying to England. Polish workers in the forest gang had found it where it was probably dropped by the Royal Air Force.

The story of Hess's flight is one of the weird twists in the history of World War II. To this day, what really was behind his flight has not been completely resolved. What is known is that on the night of May 10, 1941, he flew a German Messerschmitt to Scotland. The plane crash-landed in a field when he ran out of fuel and parachuted to safety. Hess claimed he was there to negotiate a peace agreement with England. This was astonishing coming from a man of his rank. Hess was a longtime friend of Hitler's. As Deputy Führer, he was third in command after Göring. He had joined the Nazi Party in 1920, participated in the Beer Hall Putsch, and served in prison with Hitler, where he took dictation for much of *Mein Kampf*. His

self-described peace mission was just weeks before Hitler would attack Russia. Hess believed that the British nobility would go against
Churchill and sue for peace with Germany in order to allow Germany
to defeat the greater evil of Bolshevik Russia. Closely tied in marriage and blood to German nobility, many of the titled class in the
United Kingdom were just as antisemitic as the Nazis and fundamentally believed that a certain class of people were genetically superior
rulers. But Hess had miscalculated. The British were not going to
sue for peace on Hitler's terms, and once Hess said that Hitler knew
nothing about his mission, he was promptly thrown in jail.

Hess was moved around to various locations and even spent a
moment in the Tower of London. He was transferred back to Nuremberg after the war to stand trial. He was not hanged but given a life
sentence. He spent forty-six years in Spandau, where he remained
long after other Nazi war criminals were freed. For twenty years, he
was the only prisoner there. He finally killed himself at the age of
ninety-three.

Did Hitler know about Hess's mission, or was he working behind
his back? Some theories describe the affair as a trap by the Soviets,
who lured Hess on the mission, or a trap by British Intelligence, who
used Hess's flight as propaganda. Some key investigative documents
about Hess's exploit have disappeared or stayed top secret, further
fueling speculation and suspicion.

Hess's flight was used as propaganda. The leaflet that Grete described was found by the prisoners, who considered it "like a magic
talisman."[4] Here was a crazy man, high up in the Nazi hierarchy,
asking the British for peace. It was a sign of how unhinged the
German war effort had become. But possession of such a paper was
dangerous.

The very next day, Grete was awakened roughly, pulled from her
bed, and searched. The mattress was pulled up, everything turned
inside out. Clearly, they were looking for something in particular.
Grete worried it was the leaflet. As she was marched back to the
Strafblock, she felt her anxiety grow. And then, outside the interrogation room, she saw Helena Korewina with her daughter and another

Polish woman from their block. It was clear one of Ramdohr's spies had learned about the leaflet and mentioned Grete's visit.

She was returned to the *Strafblock*, where Binz greeted her mockingly, "What! You here again! That didn't last long, did it?"

Once again, it was a week without food, dark arrest and hard sleeping. Then the regular routine of food every fourth day. The same hunger and cold. The same noises. The same sounds of flogging and cries of pain. The same suffering and misery all over again. The same darkness. But Grete's mind slipped away quickly this time. She wasn't sure she had ever been let out. Maybe that week was just another hallucination. She lived in "feverish dreams peopled by the characters of song and poetry."[5]

At some point during the following five weeks, while Grete was in the *Strafblock*, she was taken out and brought to Ramdohr's office.

There she almost collapsed from the shock of it: the sight of Milena in the office standing next to Ramdohr and smiling. Had Ramdohr arrested her too?

Milena read Grete's thoughts. "No," she said, "I haven't been arrested." The sound of her voice was like food. "I've only come to see how you are getting along. Everything is alright."

The visit was over quickly. Grete was led back down to her cell. Her mind spun frantically. How was it possible that Ramdohr let them see each other? Still, Milena was out there, fighting for her. She had to keep going for her sake.

GRETE SLID EVER more deeply into mania. She lived almost entirely in her fantasy story of the hut by the sea, of her two imaginary people loving each other. Sometimes the prisoners in the cell next to her would call out to Grete and pull her away from the dream. It was almost a nuisance to talk with them. As soon as the conversation was over, she dove back into the universe of her imagination. She lost her sense of time, the count of days, the reason she was there.

When one Sunday the cell door opened and she was released, it felt so abrupt and sudden she could not understand what was happening to her. She did not feel the exhilaration she had felt before. She did not want to leave her fantasy world. She hated the bright flat light and the ugly gray reality of the camp. She hated the dirt and the blocks and the people staring at her from their sunken eyes. What were they looking at? She wanted to scream at them. Where was her hut and the ocean view? She wanted to close her eyes and try to get back to the place of darkness and dreams.

Grete would have done it, gone completely mad, but Milena was there. And she understood the danger. Anyone talking with Grete for more than a few moments could see that she had lost her mind. Mentally ill prisoners were put to death, chosen for the next *Sondertransport*, or simply shot. Milena managed to get Grete put into a corner of the *revier* overseen by a trustworthy Czech block elder.

Whenever Milena could, she would slip away from her desk and visit Grete. She listened patiently over and over again to the story of the boy and the old woman in the hut by the sea. Slowly the two people in the story became Grete and Milena.

Milena listened and stroked Grete's forehead and kissed her, saying, "Yes, it is beautiful, your world, but Gretuška, now that you are back, let me tell you what has happened here while you were away." With her voice and her touch, slowly, tenderly, Milena coaxed Grete from madness. When she had recovered enough, the memory of Milena in the office returned. Grete asked, "Did it really happen that I saw you in an office with Ramdohr?"

Milena explained that after Grete was taken away a second time, Milena began to really fear that she would die in there. For three weeks, she waited for Grete's release. But when it did not happen, Milena got up her courage and asked for an appointment with Ramdohr. It was audacious, but he agreed to see her, maybe hoping she was going to denounce someone. Ramdohr operated completely out of the control of the SS. He was a force unto himself and very dangerous. Every prisoner knew to avoid him. Milena knew she was risking everything when she walked into his office.

She got straight to the point: "I would like to speak to you about my friend Grete Buber. She is in the *Strafblock*."

Grete could image her standing up tall and regally in front of the beastly Ramdohr. He was so used to people trembling in front of him. Normally he would slap a prisoner for such forwardness, but not Milena. He nodded, curious for her to continue.

"If you promise me," she said slowly and carefully, "that Grete Buber will leave the *Strafblock* alive, and that is in your power, I can do you a great service."

Ramdohr was flustered by this woman. "What are you saying to me?"

"Horrible things are taking place in this camp. If nothing is done to stop them, you can say goodbye to your career."

Ramdohr's face turned red, and he stood up, pounding a fist on the desk. "Who do you think you are talking to?"

But Milena did not flinch.

She looked him straight in the eyes. "I beg your pardon," she said calmly. "You don't seem to understand. I have come here to help you. But if you are not interested in what I have to tell you, I beg your pardon. Just send me back to the *revier*."

He could have exploded, knocked her head open against the wall, sent her to the *Strafblock*. This was what he normally would have done, but he didn't. She had piqued his interest.

"What are these horrible things you think I don't already know that are happening?"

But she kept him in suspense. "Serious criminal offenses," she said. "Both prisoners and members of the SS are involved. But before I give you the details, I want to know if you are prepared to meet my conditions?"

"Do you think you can blackmail me?" He was astounded, almost amused.

"Of course not, Herr *Kriminalassistent*. How could I, a mere prisoner, think of anything of the kind? But I thought that you, as a German, would know the meaning of friendship. Grete and I are friends. Tell me, I am sure you would never abandon a friend in such a situation?"

Milena knew that friendship—*Freundschaft*—was a central theme in German literature. Still, it was a gamble, appealing to his higher moral values. Ramdohr turned to look at her, and she saw that her intuition had hit the mark. Somewhere deep down, this beast had once felt friendship. "Can you tell me if Grete Buber is alive?"

"Of course, she is."

"Can I see her? This very day?"

"Hold on, wait a moment, one step at a time." He was trying to regain control of the conversation, but it was too late. Milena started to explain to him what kind of friend Grete had been. What kind of person she was. How she had stood up against the communists. Ramdohr made the mistake of listening to Milena. He was pulled into the story. She still had her exceptional powers of persuasion.

At last they came to an agreement. He would let her see her friend, and she told him about the crimes being committed in the *revier*, the injections, the stolen gold teeth, the nightly drinking and sex, between prisoner and SS doctor. She told him about the murders, but he didn't care about the murders—he himself had killed plenty of prisoners—but the other things were a threat to his career. He had been brought there to root out corruption, and Dr. Rosenthal was stealing gold that belonged in the SS coffers. Furthermore, he was having sexual relations with the prisoner Quernheim. Uncovering this blatant theft and breaking of the rules about sexual relations would show that Ramdohr was doing his job.[6] Milena had given him useful information. He might have already known about Rosenthal and Quernheim, but Milena presented the information in such a way that he saw the advantages of using it.

AFTER MILENA WAS granted her brief visit with Grete in Ramdohr's office, she went back to her block and collapsed. She had used all her force and willpower to convince him. She had managed to navigate safely through the treacherous encounter. While she was doing it, she was acting in a play, a bit of high-stakes theater, but now all that energy was gone. What if he changed his mind? What if he decided to cover for Rosenthal? She would be shot the same day. Or perhaps Quernheim would come in the night and kill her with a lethal injection. She didn't sleep, paralyzed with fear, until a few days later she heard the news that Dr. Rosenthal and Gerda Quernheim had been arrested. Rosenthal was sentenced to seven years, and Quernheim was sent to Auschwitz.

Ramdohr would later testify in the postwar trials that he was responsible for exposing the "appalling conditions" in the *revier* after Milena Jesenská had come to him with the evidence.

With Langefeld gone and her block elders in the *Strafblock* out of the positions of privilege, most of the people experienced in running the camp were gone. Ramdohr was at the height of his power. He continued to grow his impressive spy network. There was a new level of chaos. Groups were able to "organize"—the camp lingo for theft—everything. And there were shortages of everything, straw for mattresses, bowls, food. The camp was seriously overcrowded. Built for three thousand, it now housed eighteen thousand women, with new arrivals every day. The roll call lasted three hours, starting at four instead of six A.M. The entire camp, even the privileged blocks, was infested with lice.

With the influx of thousands of new prisoners, the crowding had reached even Block 1. In much of the camp, four people shared one bed. In Block 1, there were three people to the space of two beds. Grete and Milena chose Tomy Kleinerová, a friend of Milena's, to share their sleeping space. Tomy was a character in Ravensbrück. She worked as a street sweeper, always carrying her bucket and broom. She had a contagious laugh with an endless supply of jokes.

Contributing to the sense of disarray, the camp had run out of the striped uniforms issued to new arrivals. Now the prisoners were dressed in civilian clothes. Often these came in truckloads from Auschwitz. In front of the *Effektenkammer*, there were heaps of clothes and piles of shoes with the shoelaces tied together. Women picked through the piles looking for clothes that fit. Then white crosses were painted on their backs to mark them as prisoners.

THE WAR WAS going badly for the Germans in 1943. They had lost the Battle of Stalingrad in February. With an estimated two million deaths, the battle was the deadliest of the entire war and one of the deadliest battles in all of history. With hindsight, it is now considered the turning point of the war. By May, the Germans had lost the North African campaign. And in July, their massive tank offensive near Kursk in the Soviet Union was blunted within a week, the Soviets turning it into an offensive attack. German cities were being bombed to rubble.

Germany was losing men, and they needed more weapons. There was added pressure to use the concentration camp slave labor to keep German industries producing arms. The network of Himmler's subcamp *Kommando* units grew, and the women at Ravensbrück were in danger of being picked at any moment and shipped off to a *Kommando*, or forced labor camp.

Sudden change in the routine was what prisoners hated most. As Grete wrote, "A prisoner is strangely conservative. Once he is settled down, even in our lousy, dirty huts, he is unwilling to move and have his life disturbed. What comes may be, and probably will be, worse. And, in any case, it is upsetting."[7]

By the end of the summer, Ravensbrück prisoners worked in more than twenty *Kommandos*, and the main square where roll call took place began to look like a slave market. Factory managers would come to shop for the labor they needed. Suhren would treat them first to a lavish feast with plenty of wine, champagne, and schnapps. Then the men, captains of German industry, would drunkenly stumble along the lines of women—who might have been standing there, waiting for hours—groping at and choosing the women at their whim. It was terrifying. Grete and Milena feared they would be separated at any moment. As soon as Grete had recovered enough, they had to get her a safe job where she wouldn't be picked up in one of these "labor mobilizations."

Through their Polish friends, Grete was able to get a job on the forestry gang. The Poles called the leader of this work gang Mother Liberak. A kind woman, she was on good terms with the young Polish guard named Eugenia. Mother Liberak would bring one or two *Kaninchen* with her gang each day as long as they could walk there and back. Once in the forest, she would allow them to lie down and rest. They had to pass the SS quarters and go down the road toward Fürstenberg until they came to the woods. The pace was slow and easy so that the *Kaninchen* could keep up. Grete loved it, walking in the woods with the soft mossy ground underfoot and the fresh air in her lungs. They kept their tools in a hut so they didn't have to carry them back and forth each day. Eugenia was the rare guard who trusted her gang. She would retire to the hut with her dog while the women worked. A civilian forester met the women each day. He was also on friendly terms with Eugenia and Mother Liberak. He brought the women bread, smuggled out their letters, and treated them kindly. He would tell them which trees to cut. They never went too fast or pushed too hard. At midday, the forester would call a halt to the work, and they built a campfire. The forester brought them a few potatoes to roast in the fire. Once again, Grete and Milena had managed to use their privilege and connections to find a good situation for Grete. She quickly recovered her strength. But as Grete got better, Milena's health was deteriorating.

BETWEEN 1943 AND 1944, the secretaries in the *revier* counted around sixty *Sondertransporte*, about two to three a month. Milena understood that as soon as she was unable to work, she would be sent on a transport or given a lethal injection. She and Grete lived in fear of that possibility.

To maximize the profit from slave labor, hygiene, medical care, and camp conditions needed to improve. At Ravensbrück, it was decided to put the Red Army medics and prisoner doctors to work in the *revier*, something that had not been allowed before. For Milena, this change presented a glimmer of hope. Her condition was clearly getting worse, but now there was a slight chance she would get the treatment she needed. And in August, a new SS doctor arrived who was said to be better than the previous ones.

Dr. Percival Treite had specialized in gynecology and was considered a good surgeon. He was hoping to get a professorship in medicine in Berlin when he got word that he was being sent to Ravensbrück instead. He came from a religious family; his English mother (hence the name Percival) and his father were devout Christians. His father had been a preacher in the Salvation Army, and young Percival marched in the band. He joined the Nazi Party a little later than most, perhaps because of his religious upbringing, which had included pacifism and a belief in the sanctity of life.

He quickly reorganized the *revier*, establishing an infectious disease block, a block for dysentery, and another for skin diseases. He organized a system of cards, allowing the older prisoners to be given rose-colored cards for inside work, where they could knit socks for German soldiers. And he created a bandage station to help alleviate the long waiting lines. He also recruited staff from incoming prisoners. The camp was becoming international, with prisoners arriving from all corners of Europe. The *revier* became a polyglot place with Czech, Yugoslav, Polish, Russian, and French doctors and nurses. Treite was a snob, and he was especially pleased when he found a prisoner from the nobility with medical training.

Perhaps his most important recruit was Dr. Zdenka Nedvědová, a pediatrician who had arrived in Ravensbrück from Auschwitz. Many who arrived from Auschwitz at this time had survived the typhus plague that had devastated the women's camp. The new arrivals were immediately recognizable with their bald heads and enormous sunken eyes. Treite would go to the square where new arrivals were lined up and call out, asking if anyone had medical training. He was pleased when he found Nedvědová. Having survived typhus, she was immune and could work with infectious patients. She was an excellent doctor, a devoted Czech communist, and despite their political differences, she would take good care of Milena.

Treite recognized Milena's name and discovered that he had studied under her father, Professor Jan Jesenský, in Prague. He fell under her charm and immediately began to treat her as his patient, showing her great care and attention. Even Milena was impressed with Treite.

Grete wrote that Treite was different from his predecessors: "He inspired confidence, especially after he had set up a special barracks for mothers and their infants."[8] Having a *Kinderzimmer*, or nursery, was a big shift in policy at Ravensbrück. Suddenly it appeared that women would be allowed to give birth and the babies would be allowed to live.

The nursery might have been set up because there was such a large influx of pregnant women from Warsaw and other parts of Poland. Most of the women had been raped. Many did not yet know they were pregnant. The new nursery was quickly full. But the babies needed to be fed and, as Grete went on to explain, their undernourished mothers did not produce the milk necessary, nor were they given the time to nurse. The women had to immediately go back to the same hard work schedule as every other prisoner.

The camp commandant refused to give the babies milk, so almost all of them starved to death within the first three months of their lives. Marie-José Chombart de Lauwe wrote about the horrors of the nursery in her account of her time in the war, *Toute une vie de résistance*. Working in the French Resistance in Brittany, Marie-José and her entire network were caught by the Gestapo, and she was sent to Ravensbrück. The daughter of a pediatrician father and midwife mother, she had been a medical student. At first sent to work in the Siemens factory, she was then recruited by Treite to be a nurse in the new *Kinderzimmer*. It was one room with two levels of wooden bunks and up to forty newborn babies lying across the bunks. They had no real hygiene, no bottles, no diapers, no nipples. Prisoners in the camp tried to make diapers from scraps of cloth, bottles and nipples using rubber medical gloves, and they tried to scrounge milk or powdered milk from the Red Cross parcels. But the powdered milk was usually stolen by the SS inspectors, and there was never enough to feed the babies.

Marie-José felt powerless to save the babies and had to witness their slow suffering and starvation along with the near hysterical despair of their mothers. Out of roughly five hundred births during that period, only thirty-one babies survived, and those were the ones born just before liberation. It is unclear how many children were born during deportation, but the French organization Fondation pour la Mémoire de la Déportation found the records of twenty-three French babies who were born in Ravensbrück. Of those, three survived. Years later, Marie-José would maintain that the time she spent in the *Kinderzimmer* was "the worst memory" of her entire deportation.[9]

Grete, wanting to believe that Treite was a possibly decent person, wrote that he could not have done anything about the babies as the order came from higher up. She doesn't mention his later brutal sterilization of Romani and Sinti children. In an experimental and cruel method developed by Carl Clauberg at Auschwitz, Treite sprayed caustic substances into their fallopian tubes. Clauberg had experimented for three years on women in Auschwitz, killing hundreds. When Auschwitz closed ahead of the invading Soviets, he came to Ravensbrück, eager to carry on into the last months of the war.

The prisoner doctors were horrified at the sight of young healthy children going into Treite's office, only to emerge maimed, bleeding, and in extreme pain. Many of the young ones died. When the prisoner doctors pleaded with him to stop, he responded, "Orders from Berlin." According to figures from the British war crimes investigators, between Christmas 1944 and February 1945, five hundred Romani and Sinti women were forcibly sterilized; at least two hundred of them were young girls. Milena was no longer in the *revier* by late 1944, so Grete might not have known about those events.

In 1943, when Percival Treite arrived as the new camp doctor, Grete needed a miracle to save Milena. She hoped it would be Treite. It was true that during this period, women could go to the *revier* for treatment without risking their lives. Grete wrote that some of the *revier* doctors shamelessly cared only for the sick from their own country or political group, but in general, she was impressed. "Most did their best with great devotion and in extraordinary circumstances."

Grete even struck up a friendship with a staunch Czech communist named Inka when she had an attack of boils. She worried that Inka would treat her badly as she had been rejected by the communists, but instead, she found a friendly, caring person. "The conditions she worked in were appalling. She had no proper room and the bandages were piled up high all around her as the women queued up between the mass of bunks." Grete would return to visit with Inka to catch up on gossip, and they later became close friends.

Treite's *revier* was an improvement, but the bar was low. He was still a doctor for the Nazi Party. He enjoyed surrounding himself with intelligent women. And they saw the dark side of what he did. He liked to show off, making them watch him perform surgeries, sometimes unnecessary Cesarean sections or high forceps deliveries just because he felt like operating.

One prisoner doctor, a skilled surgeon, was kept busy sewing up dog bites and lacerations from beatings. Women who had gotten floggings came to the *revier* with burst kidneys or other serious hemorrhaging. Treite would not have been involved in caring for these women. He would have assisted in the flogging, watching them and taking the victim's pulse during the beating procedure to determine if the punishment could continue.

A prisoner doctor recalled the madhouse block organized by Dr. Treite. The mentally ill women waited there for the transport to their deaths. She described the scene of two mattresses full of excrement on the floor. Six women covered in sores and bruises, practically naked and raving.

Carrying out unethical medical experiments on prisoners was a recurring theme among Nazi doctors. Treite was no different. He asked Nedvědová to gather cockroaches, boil them up, and feed the liquid to women suffering from swollen legs. When Treite wasn't looking, Nedvědová poured out the liquid and gave them water instead.

In another pointless experiment, she was supposed to inject pregnant women with the urine of other pregnant women. When Treite caught her trying to fake it, he lost his temper and threatened her with flogging and the *Strafblock*. But Nedvědová stood her ground, saying that she was trained at Charles University in Prague and she could not mistreat her patients. He relented, no doubt because he needed Nedvědová and he was scared that Ramdohr would find out he was carrying out unauthorized experiments.

Prisoners soon knew that they could get good medical treatment from the prisoner doctor Nedvědová, and increasingly they turned to her for help. One such prisoner was the French ethnographer Germaine Tillion, who would later become a close friend of Grete's. Germaine arrived sick with one of the first transports of French Resistance fighters. Her block elder brought Germaine to the *revier*, where she lay slumped and immobile against the wall. Dr. Treite nudged her with his foot, pronounced that she didn't have scarlet fever, and sent her back to the block. The block elder contacted the prisoner doctors, and that night she brought Germaine to Dr. Zdenka Nedvědová, who diagnosed her with diphtheria and treated her with serum. Germaine was admitted to the infectious disease block, the diphtheria ward. Later Germaine would reflect on how lucky she was to have arrived at that particular time, when the *revier* was being run by these talented courageous women.

AT NIGHT, ONCE the SS had left the *revier*, the prisoner staff had the rare privilege of being able to talk freely among themselves. The atmosphere might have reminded Milena of the days when she would meet with writers and intellectuals in Prague cafés. Now they gathered around a bed in the *revier*. Sometimes Milena would recite a story by Kafka, or they would sing, or someone would recite a poem. The Polish politicals and the Czech communists often talked, and debated, about the war. It was going badly for the Germans. Political controversies were not infrequent among the Czech prisoners, between the communists and those who wanted to reinstate the prewar Masaryk-style democracy. There was discussion about the Soviets versus the Americans. They wondered which army would reach them first and what would be the best outcome for them. The Poles preferred the Americans, and went so far as to say that Stalin was worse than Hitler. This infuriated the Czech communists. How could they say such a thing when they were sitting in Hitler's concentration camp? Furthermore, where was their Catholic God? If he was all-powerful, how could he allow this horror?

The Poles had equally strong feelings about how Hitler and Stalin had divided up their country. The Russians had treated them brutally throughout history. The Americans at least would bring them freedom. Stalin would just bring more violence and prison camps.

The discussion was getting heated; Milena stood up. "Enough. Stop it," she said. "If the *Oberschwester* or the others hear there will be trouble."

"Milena, how can you be worried about that," someone answered her. "This is important. What will happen to us after the war?"

"No, here and now is important," she answered matter-of-factly.

Hanka, the young Czech nurse, spoke up: "Milena, you can't stay neutral. You must say what side you are on. You can't stand in the middle."

"Oh," Milena said quietly. "Side? Side? Why do you have to be on one or the other side of the barricade? No, Hanichka, you don't understand a thing."

"It's you I don't understand, Milena. Who do you belong to? Which side are you on? Tell me. Tell us. Who do you belong to?"[10]

Milena might have responded, *To myself.* She had always claimed for herself the direction of her life. And even in the camp, she had been able to maintain her inner freedom. Perhaps in an intimate moment with Grete, she might have said she belonged to their love, to her daughter, to her friends and family. She did not belong to a political party. Milena's politics were more subtle and less polemic than Grete's clear anti-communism. Grete's hatred for the Soviet system was animated by the fury of someone who had been betrayed. She had so fervently believed in the revolution that when she lost her faith, it had crushed her whole world. Milena had believed too, but only for a short while. When she began to hear about the show trials, and when Jaromír returned with the disillusioning reports from the Soviet Union, she had no trouble accepting this information. Milena did not need to believe in the goodness of humanity as a lofty ideal; she loved human beings as they were, limited and broken. She had little tolerance for those who took refuge in blindly following a political system or a religion; she saw these extremes as equally inhumane.

A friend of Milena's, Nina Jirsíková, the Czech dancer and choreographer, described Milena:

> She was large, even robust. Despite her stiff leg, she held herself straight . . . her eyes were particularly expressive. They shone through with her strong character. One sensed a spirit that would not submit and that dominated over a body already weakened . . . In that place where there were so many people who were morally as well as physically broken, her force was surprising . . . She had the power to bring others along with her spontaneity, to get others interested, to forget for a moment the conditions we were living in. It was for us a great blessing. Milena was one of the rare people capable of morally aiding others.[11]

The hard-line communists in the camp could not forgive Milena's friendship with Grete, nor her renunciation of the party before the war. But many Czech prisoners, even some communists, admired her. Some fellow Czechs were a little jealous of her closeness with Grete. It was not unremarked upon that Grete was a German.

Milena would talk with the young communist prisoners about the Moscow show trials, or other contradictions in the Soviet actions, and they would be charmed by her intelligence, but unable to accept her "Trotskyite" views. They believed that individual needs must be sacrificed for the greater good. Inevitably, one would offer the catchphrase excuse: "When forests are felled, splinters fly."

Milena would respond sadly, "They were not splinters; they were people."

August 10, 1943, was Milena's forty-seventh birthday. Her friends knew she was not in good health. She was old by concentration camp

Camp Couples, drawing by Nina Jirsíková

standards. Her rheumatism made it difficult for her to move. And her kidneys were inflamed, causing her debilitating pain. Worrying that this might be her last birthday, her Czech circle of friends decided to throw her a birthday party.

The Czech prisoners maintained a lively and active cultural life, which centered around Block 8. From 1942 to 1944, the block was almost exclusively Czech and run by a sympathetic block elder. Within the group of Czech women, there was an elite of professional artists and cultured prisoners. Milena, though she did not live in Block 8, was part of this circle. She had known many of these women before the war, when they were part of her avant-garde social milieu. Like Milena, they were considerably more emancipated than many other women in the camp. Educated and professionally active, some of them had had important careers before the war.

Nina Jirsíková was an artist and a dancer. Prisoners would "commission" her to decorate their tiny corner of the block with a drawing, or to illustrate the cover of a small booklet of poems. One of her popular commissions was a drawing of a Madonna and child Jesus in striped concentration camp clothing with a red triangle and halo. She made many drawings of camp life. One drawing shows three tiers of bunk beds crowded with bodies. A woman is stepping on the face of another as she tries to climb down. In another drawing, Nina illustrated the lack of privacy as the women try to bathe. Her drawings have a sense of humor and even tenderness. She made a "fashion" magazine of caricature drawings. Malnourished and bareheaded, barefoot women were posed confidently and defiantly. The drawings were accompanied with ironic commentary: "This year, on Summer Sundays, washed underpants are worn over the arm (to dry), and as a particularly tasteful accessory, a spoon effectively stuck in the buttonhole and a food bowl at the waist. Motto: *Omnia mea mecum porto* (so that no one steals it from me)."[12] Nina's drawings also show couples walking arm and arm and depictions of "passionate friends."

When Nina arrived in the camp in 1941, she was sure she would never dance again. It took about a year for her to recover from the shock. Then, as she recalled in her later memoir, on Christmas Eve 1942, she improvised her first dance performance. Standing in front of her blockmates,

> disgusted with myself, in my camp clothes and my feet in my clogs as if they were stuck to the ground by their weight. And that weight in me and around me was the first impulse to start moving-dancing. . . . I began to pantomime our common suffering. It was a very unmoving expression, its principle was the feet as if they were embedded in the ground. As if I were suddenly carrying the weight of our common woes on my back. . . . then I threw off and kicked off my clogs, and I danced in those hideous grey camp stockings. . . . The women . . . stood up, began to clap rhythmically. The dance de facto ended with us being one body, one soul, defiantly confronting our suffering.[13]

Nina's performances became a weekly event in Block 8. Almost every Sunday between 1944 and 1945, she choreographed and performed dance solo and in groups.

Anička Kvapilová was the main organizer and initiator of the Czech cultural scene. She was the prisoner who remembered how Milena had welcomed them with so much humanity when they first arrived. Hidden in her parcels, Anička received poetry and literature. She circulated these clandestine books, and she wrote and made her own collections of poems. Her poetry was nostalgic and tender about missing home but also about the passionate friendships in the camp. The poems were published after the war in Brno in 1947 under the title *Krajíček chleba* (*A small slice of bread*). Anička dedicated the book to Milena Jesenská, and to the actress and writer Milena Fischerová, who had been one of her closest friends in the camp.

In 1947, when Anička was able to publish her poems, they were appreciated not only for their literary value, but also because of her work among the women in the concentration camp. But only a year later, the political climate would change. Anička Kvapilová would be expelled from Communist Party affiliations, and she would flee into exile in Norway in June 1948.

Another writer among the Czech cultural group, Františka Věra Sojková, was older, already fifty-three, and in danger of being selected for *Sondertransport* for her gray hair. But she survived and later published a collection of poems, *Poor Women in Mud*, during the brief period after the war when such histories were allowed. Her poems are bitter and despairing. In 1964, she wanted to publish a memoir of her camp experience, but she was discouraged by her fellow survivors from Ravensbrück: "According to the directives from above at the time, it was not considered appropriate to continue to return to the memory of the concentration camps, instead of dealing with building the present."[14]

Květa Hniličková was also part of the Block 8 group. She had organized a puppet show for the children in the camp. The simple stage was made out of slats; the curtain sewn from scraps stolen from the sewing workshop floor. Workshop 1 was the first large factory to use prison labor at Ravensbrück. It was built right against the prison wall, and thousands of women worked there on twelve-hour shifts making SS uniforms. After working the night shift, Květa, together with Věra Fialová, made puppet heads out of paraffin and cotton wool and decorated them with stockings, pieces of fabric, string, and watercolors.

For Milena's party, the table in the block elder's room was piled with gifts: a handkerchief with tiny hearts embroidered with Milena's name, a carving of a little elephant and other figurines from a toothbrush handle, a booklet of poems from Anička, flowers that had been smuggled into the camp.

They had planned the party as a surprise. When Milena walked in and saw everyone smiling at her, she burst into tears. By then, she was very ill, and she had not been able to go around the camp and visit with her friends as she had done in the past. Now, whenever she was not working, she was resting.

Milena had missed Nina's performance of Karel Hynek Mácha's epic love poem *May* just a few weeks earlier, on May 1. While the communists around the camp were celebrating May Day with Soviet songs, the Czechs in Milena's circle were treated to Nina's staging of Mácha's *May* as a choral recitation. The text of the entire poem had arrived in the camp in one of Anička's parcels. Nina had rehearsed it with twenty-four women for almost a year. Milena was distressed when she couldn't make it—it had been one of those days. The pain in her back and legs was almost unbearable. It was all she could do to make it through work and get to her bed. Grete was with her, trying to console her.

"Oh, my blue angel," she said to Grete between tears, "it is such a beautiful poem."

"I wouldn't understand a word of it." Grete was happy to be alone with Milena. She didn't want to be at any celebrations, not with this feeling of dread, the lump in her throat that never went away. The only time she felt some relief was when she was close to Milena.

"I'll teach the poem to you later. It's the story of tragic love, of two young people, it's a poetic masterpiece of Czech literature. Next May,

I'll teach you. We will go to the statue of Mácha, in Petřín Park. And like all lovers we will put our flowers there. Petřín is so romantic in May when its cherry trees are in bloom."

At her birthday party, surrounded by her friends, Milena spoke through her tears, "What a surprise! And I thought you had forgotten me and weren't friends with me anymore. Forgive me for not coming, Nina. Forgive me, all of my dear friends, that I could not see you more often but from now on I'll be better."[15]

Grete stood off to the side and watched Milena surrounded by laughter and the happy chatter of her Czech friends. They were so expressive, Grete thought once again, perhaps a little jealously. Nothing like the austere German family birthdays of her childhood. This was Milena in her natural setting.

The party was a magic moment carved out of a cool summer night. The friends laughed and told stories, and then they sang. The actress Milena Fischerová was known for her beautiful recitations of poetry. And because Milena lamented missing Nina's May 1 performance, she recited the poem. Tomy Kleinerová recalled after the war: "I can still see her, reciting Mácha's *May*. We closed our eyes and absorbed the infinite beauty of the Czech language." This would be one of her last recitations. Milena Fischerová was stricken with tuberculosis, and in March 1945, she was sent to the gas chamber.

Grete could not understand the words, but she felt the song grow more sorrowful. Heads bent down, bodies swaying. There were a few tears.

It was time to go back to the block; the siren would ring out soon. Milena looked at Grete across all her friends, and they locked eyes. Milena's eyes shone feverish and alive; her cheeks were smeared with tears, but she was happy. They gazed at each other in recognition. This was a moment they had to hold on to. Grete wanted to remember the look of satisfaction and love on Milena's face. Milena made a sign and gesture with her head. Grete knew she was asking for her help. As they walked together across the camp to the block, to their bed, Milena held on to Grete tightly. The evening had taken so much energy out of her. "That was the best birthday I have ever had,"

Milena whispered, leaning more heavily against Grete. "Imagine, it happened here in this place!"

"It was beautiful," Grete agreed. "To see all your friends. They were so pleased with their gifts."

"Gretuška, don't misunderstand me, it was wonderful because you are with me."

WHAT NEITHER GRETE nor Milena knew was that outside of Ravensbrück's walls, Joachim von Zedtwitz was working to get Milena released. Joachim had formed the small resistance group that Milena worked with helping Jews escape from Czechoslovakia at the start of the war. After Milena was arrested, Joachim had spent fifteen months in prison—he had been arrested for potentially compromising letters found in his apartment—but the Gestapo had never found anything in the letters to tie him directly to the resistance network. Since his release in 1941, he had not been able to stop thinking about Milena. He desperately wanted to help get her released. Joachim, as a noble and a shrewd political player, had cultivated a network of friends and acquaintances. One was a Berlin lawyer who was well-connected with the Gestapo.

The lawyer felt that there was a good chance they could get Milena released from the camp. Joachim put together a file showing that she suffered from mental illness, and on those grounds, she should be released to the custody of her father. He was in close contact with Professor Jesenský. They secured a copy of Milena's medical records from when she had been in the asylum in Veleslavín back in 1917. The file was ready and had been sent to the lawyer in Berlin. The lawyer, feeling confident, assured Joachim that they had all the paperwork they needed. It was only a matter of time, and Milena could be back in Prague with her father and her daughter, Honza.

ONLY A FEW letters written by Milena from this time have survived through the vicissitudes of history. In 1950, a young woman, probably

Honza, visited a café in Prague and forgot a manila envelope containing a little more than a dozen letters written by Milena. When the young woman did not return to claim the envelope, the café owner turned it over to the local police. This was during the height of the Cold War. The letters were mostly written in German, but they noticed that one was written in English, which raised their suspicions. It was addressed to Jaromír Krejcar, Milena's ex-husband and Honza's father. They alerted the security police, who confirmed that Krejcar was a deserter from the Soviet Union. The envelope was sent to the head security office, where it was added to the dossier on Krejcar and where it stayed for another fifty years until the Iron Curtain was no more and a young Polish doctoral student doing research on Krejcar discovered the poorly microfilmed images of the letters.

The letters from Ravensbrück are short because there was a strict line limit. There were many forms of censorship involved in the writing of the letters: the obvious censorship carried out by the German authorities but also the self-censorship of Milena, who wanted to write something that would pass the censor and also protect her father and daughter from their worst fears. Even as she was hiding the harsh reality of her own situation, she was castigating her father and daughter to write her more truthful letters with real details, not the vague platitudes they were sending her. She probably wrote over forty letters to them during her time in Ravensbrück, but only seven remain. It is clear her principal concern was Honza.

Milena was desperate to be involved in her child's life. Honza was moving homes, and Milena wanted to know why.

The letters from Honza had to be legible, or the German censors threw them away. A letter from Honza in May was discarded by the censors for this reason. Milena peevishly wrote to her father that other mothers received beautiful letters written in good handwriting from their children. The only reproach she had received from the camp authorities was to let her know her daughter's letters had been discarded due to her sloppy handwriting. Milena's frustration and longing are palpable. In letter after letter, she pleads with Honza to write more often. Imagine, she pleads, since she was allowed only one letter a month, what it was like when everyone else was getting a letter, and Milena got none, how sad it made her feel.

Furthermore, Milena wanted answers to her specific questions. Where exactly was Honza living? Why was she no longer with her grandfather? Who was taking care of her? What was she studying at school? It must have been terrible for Honza to read those reproaches from her mother.

In an earlier letter from when Milena was in prison, before being deported to Ravensbrück, she wrote to Honza, "Write real letters, Honza, about important things. Everything that has to do with you interests me, every little detail."[16]

Kafka once wrote to Milena, "Writing letters is actually an intercourse with ghosts . . . written kisses never arrive at their destination; the ghosts drink them up along the way."[17] Honza was haunted by those ghosts.

Even the unwritten letter could haunt her. Later Grete would write to Honza that her mother had wanted to write her a long letter to tell her how proud she was and how happy she was that Honza had not been discouraged or given up her music studies. By the time Honza read this letter from Grete, she had abandoned her study of music.

Years later, Honza would write an essay titled "The number of lines is limited," illustrating the mental torture and psychological ambivalence involved in trying to compose a suitable letter for her mother. In the essay, Honza contrasted a series of anodyne lines in italics from her cookie cutter "good letter," the kind her mother hated, with the *real* context and why she could not write the truth to her mother. For example:

I have grown so much. When you see me you will be surprised by how much I have grown! In fact, I am not that big, and I myself have no idea if I am big or not. But my aunt keeps hiding the spice cake and complaining that I eat too much and that it's bad for my health. And I have started to grow breasts. Other girls are starting to wear bras.

Grandfather doesn't notice and I can't tell him. If mamma was home she would have already bought me a bra, but I can't go alone into a store to buy a bra . . . and I don't have the ration tickets for it![18]

Honza knows her words are vapid and the letter is stupid, but she can't find a way around it. She writes the letter only because it is demanded of her. But her mother, who is a true hero, would never write such a stupid letter even if it was demanded of her. Honza recognizes she is not a hero like her mother, nor will she ever be. But she can be just as stubborn as her mother, so at least she will not write such a stupid letter. She ends by not writing to her mother.

Milena wanted precise details of Honza's life, real information. But then she wrote to Honza, "I am good. I am thin and very mobile. My hair is long, almost grey and my skin is tanned by the sun. Here the air is beautiful, we are in the middle of a forest with its murmurs and perfume. I think when I am free, I will not be able to handle the happiness."[19]

It is possible to see why Honza would "forget" or lose the stash of letters later in a Prague café; the pain in them was made more unbearable by all that was unsaid and unspeakable. Milena's letters are rose-colored and vague.

The last letter, dated September 1943, was typed. Milena was granted permission, perhaps by Dr. Treite, to use the *revier* office typewriter because the rheumatism in her fingers made it too difficult for her to hold a pen. She wrote, "I am doing very well," but the letter, and what we know from accounts, makes it clear that she was not. The letter reads almost like a deliberate goodbye to her father. "If anything should happen to me, know that you were always with me . . ." She thanked him for all the packages and letters and his care of her. She said her physical ailments didn't represent an immediate danger, but they were difficult to endure. She needed warmth and heat for relief, but there was only cold: "This region is cold, even in summer." She asked if he could get her some specific medicine, perhaps suggested to her by Zdenka, and anything else he might suggest that could help her with the rheumatism, because she wrote tellingly, "I cannot let myself be unable to work . . . One has the right to live as long as one works"—to get this line through the censors, she added, "This is understandable, it is a war."[20] She needed something for the pain, but it needed to be injectable because her stomach and heart no longer tolerated the pills she had been taking. She asked that he send it to Margarete Buber, number 4208.

Later in the letter, she admitted to being hungry: "It's one thing to be hungry and quite another to be hungry for *four* years."[21] Again she thanked him for the packages of food, admitting that hunger risked transforming her into a kind of savage, but she was able to control herself. She asked about certain foods she missed dearly, Czech dishes. The end of the letter was a description of what she would love to eat. She wondered if maybe he could send certain foods to her. Like many starving people, Milena found food an irresistible subject.

The winter of 1943–44 was especially harsh and difficult. Overcrowding had reached new levels. The death rate was rising. Many women who had survived for three years were reaching their limit. The long roll calls alone took their toll. Women suffered frostbite standing in the cold. The doctors in the *revier* could not keep up with the amputations, and women died of gangrene.

The new orders to cull the population of "useless mouths" was first made apparent in the *revier*, where once again the use of the lethal injections occurred regularly and the SS doctor, this time Treite, was seen in the pharmacy filling a syringe with lethal serum. Treite also announced that no bandages would be given to the elderly women and no medicine for tuberculosis. If you did not work hard enough, you risked being shot on the spot. Tuberculosis was now rampant. Women in the sewing shop and at the Siemens factory were being carted away on stretchers and then dispatched in the *revier* with a lethal injection.

Adding to the desperation, a new list was being prepared for a large selection for another transport. This led to a frantic month of haggling and scrambling, trying to get people off the list. The terrible truth was that to remove a name, another name had to be provided in its place. Treite explained to one German political that at the very least they needed eight hundred names, and if they removed German prisoners, she should find replacements from the "asocial elements." Suhren and other SS authorities promised the panicked prisoners they would not be sent to Auschwitz. Treite even said there were no gas chambers in Auschwitz. Prisoners were told the selected would be transported to Lublin, a place where they would be cared for by the Polish Red Cross. In fact, they would be sent to Majdanek, an extermination camp on the edge of Lublin.

Milena and Grete were terrified during this period of panicked selection. Milena's condition meant that she was exactly the kind of prisoner being picked for the deadly transport.

ONE OF THE perks of being in Mother Liberak's forestry gang was that she allowed each person to take a day off occasionally. When it was Grete's turn, she chose to spend the day with Milena.

They walked around the camp lost in conversation about Honza. Milena hadn't seen Honza in four years. She had been a child then, and now Milena knew her daughter must be a young woman. Grete had not seen her daughters since Judith was twelve and Barbara was fourteen—now they were young women, nineteen and twenty-one years old.

A common grief of mothers in prison was that their daughters kept growing without them. "They grow up into girls and young women," Milena said, sighing, "and naturally they almost forget their mothers. And their letters get so formal. You hear that they're learning to play the piano and getting on very nicely, and doing very well at school, and things like that. But I wish Honza would sometimes tell me what sort of a dress she has and whether she's started wearing silk stockings."[22] Essential intimacies were lost. Milena and Grete walked with their arms linked together.

Only on a few very rare occasions in Grete's books does she mention that she has two daughters. This is contrasted against the many times she describes conversations with other mothers about their grief of separation from their children. Grete often wrote about Milena's longing for Honza. But about Grete's own longing for her daughters, she says nothing. The omission is complicated. Perhaps she did talk about her daughters with Milena, but refrained from writing about them out of a sense of privacy or of wanting to protect them. Perhaps she felt she could not draw them into her story after she had lost custody of them when she followed Neumann into the Communist Party. Perhaps she had to compartmentalize for survival. Perhaps she felt an unconscious shame. For whatever reasons, in her accounts, Grete chose very carefully what could be seen and what had to stay hidden.

In Grete's recollection of the conversation with Milena that day, she says they got so lost in their exchange that they forgot to pay attention to where they were. They allowed themselves to be caught by surprise. Coming to the end of a camp street where they were just about to turn around and head back, they ran face-to-face into the SS guard in charge of the labor gangs. Suddenly she felt Milena's arms pull away. Grete gasped—she couldn't let Milena be caught in any act of "lesbianism."

"What are you doing walking in the camp during work hours?" the guard bellowed at Grete.

"I'm sick and on 'inside work.'" It was a feeble lie, the only thing she could come up with at the spur of the moment. Because Milena had the yellow armband of the *revier* worker, she was allowed to be out on the streets. To Grete's relief, he ignored Milena and focused on her. "Did you not have enough time in the punishment block? Maybe you need another dose? Report to me tomorrow, otherwise you will be in trouble."

The next day, Grete was thrown off the easy forestry gang and assigned to sewing in the dreaded Workshop 1. This was a work assignment she had managed to avoid until now. Hundreds of machines made so much noise that Grete could barely hear herself speak, and the place shook with the vibrations. The windows were all closed and blacked out to hide from the Allied bombing raids. The air was stuffy and full of the dust of fabric and thread; it was difficult to breathe.

The women in the sewing workshops had strict quotas, 180 shirts a night, and so they rushed and worked with focused speed. Each prisoner sewed one thing and passed the in-process uniform to the next one. One did the sleeves, one did the back, the next did the collar, and so on down the line until a finished product emerged and was inspected. They worked twelve-hour shifts with one half-hour break in the middle.

Grete heard the word "quota" and immediately thought with dread about her time in the Gulag. Having never touched a sewing machine before, she was hopeless. Nothing worked. Her seams ran away with her, her needles broke, she lost the thread. If she hadn't been an old Ravensbrück prisoner, she would have been badly beaten by the overseer. But because she had friends everywhere, she was looked after. A Czech forewoman surreptitiously sewed a pile of bands and put them on her table. Another friend who was from the repair workshop and whose job it was to go from machine to machine making repairs watched over Grete, and quickly repaired Grete's broken needles before the overseer saw them.

The overseer, SS *Unterscharführer* Gustav Binder, terrorized the women in Grete's workshop. Usually once a night, he would go on a rampage. He would pick out one woman working at her sewing machine and pull her by her hair, then smash her face into her machine until she was bloodied and had fallen from her seat. He would step over her in a heap. Everyone continued to sew as if nothing were happening, terrified to miss the quota. They dared not look directly at Binder. They didn't want him to notice them. Grete recalled with admiration one Frenchwoman who was often Binder's prey. She would curse Binder with a stream of French insults no matter how much he beat her.

Grete made friends with a Ukrainian girl named Nina sitting at the machine next to her. She taught Grete folk songs that they would then sing during the sewing; it helped them stay awake, and the machines were so loud no one else could hear them.

They had one break at midnight for a half hour to drink the black liquid coffee substitute and eat a piece of bread, if they had managed to save a piece from the earlier meal. Then they would lay their heads on their machines and try to sleep for a few minutes.

The many air-raid warnings were a source of great pleasure. The lights would be cut, and Grete and Nina would make their way to a dark storeroom where the SS uniforms were piled up. They lay on the uniforms like a bed. Exhausted, they slept soundly through the bombings and the rattling of the factory windows.

Perhaps during one of those air-raid warnings, while Grete slept on the pile of SS uniforms, an Allied plane flying far overhead was making its way to Berlin. This was the plane that dropped a bomb on the offices of a lawyer in Berlin, killing him and destroying the dossier that had been prepared to secure Milena's release. With that total ruin, the possibility of Milena's release was also destroyed. But neither Grete, nor Joachim, nor Honza, nor Milena's father, nor Milena herself would know this for a long time, if ever. After the planes passed, there was silence; then the lights were turned back on and the all-clear called them back to their hated machines. The work of making more uniforms ground on through the night.

Most were too exhausted or terrified to attempt sabotage, but the sewing workshop offered many opportunities to hinder the German war effort. The more experienced sewers would sew the buttons on in such a way that they would not line up, or the cutters would cut the fabric so that there was terrible waste, or the furs that were recovered from the murdered Jews were ruined so they couldn't be used for the uniforms for soldiers freezing on the Russian front. But there were some German prisoners who had family members conscripted into the army and sent by force to the cold steppes of Russia. Those women were less likely to take part in sabotage.

Once again, Grete's lucky timing had served her well. Not long after she had been thrown off her beloved forest gang, Ramdohr and his spies found out about the easygoing life of the women on the gang. All the prisoners were arrested along with the SS supervisor Eugenia and put in the *Strafblock*. Eugenia was put in a bunker in dark arrest, where she would stay until the very end of the war.

After the liberation, on the road full of war refugees, when Grete was trying to make her way home, she would run into Eugenia. The former Ravensbrück guard was being sought for collaborating with the Germans. Grete, promising to help her, wrote a letter explaining that Eugenia had been a good guard and had been brutally punished by the SS for her kindness.

PART FIVE

1944

❧

Release

Grete at her typewriter, 1950

I N THE EARLY DAYS OF RAVENSBRÜCK, HERR WENDLAND, THE UNDER-
taker from Fürstenberg, the town across the lake, would come to
take the dead. He would bring a coffin and wrap the dead person in a
paper shroud that had frills on the end where it was tied, "something
like a frill round a hambone," Grete wrote. And the body would be
carried to the village for cremation.

Over time, Wendland made enough money from the thriving business to buy a truck. But then the SS authorities decided to save money
and build their own crematorium in the camp. They would later build
a second one when the new gas chamber produced too many dead for
only one crematorium.

The dead were so thin they could easily fit two into one coffin, flat
boxes of rough-hewn wood. At first, it took four prisoners to carry the
coffins to the crematorium, but then they had too many bodies to move
and so they were given a cart. With the cart, they could fit around three
coffins, or half a dozen corpses, with each cartload. At the crematorium, the bodies were removed from the coffins and put in the ovens.
The brief journey in the coffin piled in the cart was all the funeral pro-
cession a prisoner could hope for. Afterward, their ashes were dumped
into the lake.

Milena's health was steadily getting worse, and Grete was mostly
working long, harrowing shifts in the sewing workshop. From time to
time, someone brutally beaten in the workshop by Binder would arrive in the *revier*. When Milena saw the injured, she would feel panic
for Grete, as if she were once again in the *Strafblock*. The two women
were apart and consumed with worry for the other.

Occasionally they found a way to see each other. Milena lamented
that she was not going to make it. "I won't survive this camp," she
confessed to Grete. "I know it now. I will never see Prague again. If
only Herr Wendland had come for me! He always looked so friendly
in his duffle coat."

Grete's tongue felt thick in her mouth. It was harder and harder for
her to find the words to contradict Milena. It felt too much like lying
when she said, "The war will end soon and you'll be better then. You
just need to hold on a little longer."

She knew the war would end, but would the end come soon enough?

Milena dragged herself to work. She feared the lethal injections or being selected for transport if she did not go to work each day. But the pain in her back and stomach was terrible, debilitating. She often collapsed, and her friends would have to help her back to her feet.

In the sewing workshop, Grete, again through the network of old Ravensbrück prisoners, was promoted from the sewing machine to the job of distributing thread and buttons. This was much easier and gave her a little more freedom. She was able to move around and talk to people.

In early 1944, Treite expressed concern about Milena's degrading health. Zdenka had already diagnosed an ulcerated infected kidney. She knew from Milena that the condition was aggravated by gonorrhea. Zdenka was doing her best to treat Milena with whatever medicine she could get her hands on, often medicine sent by Milena's father.

Treite decided that the situation was dire and that Milena needed an operation. He offered to do the surgery himself and remove the infected kidney. That Treite would put so much effort into saving one prisoner while systematically carrying out the orders to murder thousands of others might appear on the surface to be improbable. But the Nazi system was full of contradictions and gruesome ironies, like a maternity ward that condemned newborns to starvation.

Treite respected Milena and had shown her great deference because of her father. Milena agreed to let him operate, despite her fears that he would simply give her a lethal injection. He could easily dispatch her, as she now knew he was doing to so many others. But Milena had not lost that inner will that made her write in 1921, "How sweet, how sweet, how sweet it is to live!"[1]

During the operation, she woke up from the anesthetic, and ever the journalist, she asked to see her infected kidney. Treite showed it to her and then she was put back under to finish the procedure.

On the morning of the surgery, Grete was desperate to be with Milena. She pulled some strings and during a noon break rushed to the *revier* for a few moments. There she found Milena lying silent and deathly pale. To Grete's shock, Milena was reciting a prayer in Czech. Grete fell to her knees by her bed and clutched her hand. Milena noticed her and squeezed. "Is that you, Gretuška?"

"I'm here, my love."

"Yes, and so am I," Milena whispered. "I'm still here. Sing one of your silly Russian folk songs to me." By the time Grete had finished, Milena was asleep again and Grete had to rush back to work before she got caught and was thrown into the bunker.

Dr. Zdenka Nedvědová and the prisoner nurse Hanka Housková found a healthy Polish girl who worked in the kitchen, was well fed, and had the same blood type as Milena. She agreed to donate blood, and they administered the transfusion.

Milena's health and her spirits improved gradually and steadily. She had returned to her old habits. She distributed the contents of a package that had come to her from her father, handing out to each woman in the ward some little prize until there was very little left for her. Grete teased Milena with a hint of exasperation, "Must you be Mother Milena to all the others?"

"It makes me happy," Milena admonished Grete.

There was a festive atmosphere among the dying women. Grete found it comforting that Milena was back to her old ways, but there was the familiar frustration. When would Milena learn to take care of herself, not sacrifice everything for others?

When a young French girl who clearly had only a few days left to live nibbled a bit of a candy from Milena's parcel, she started to sing "La Marseillaise," and they all joined in with their wispy, weak, but defiant voices.

For the next four months, before the morning roll call, when it was still dark outside, Grete ran to Milena's bedside. She had fifteen minutes that she could spend with her before the siren went off. She brought her breakfast, and at noon, she would sneak over to Block 8 with the Czech block elder, who would have organized some warm food for Milena. Grete was breathless and anxious and hopeful. The fifteen minutes she spent each day with Milena were all she lived for.

And Milena was getting better. Her friends believed she was going to recover. They brought a tiny deck of playing cards that they had made, and they played card games with her or sang songs together. Often she did not have the strength to join in, but she enjoyed the chatter. One day, she was able to stand and walk to her office. She sat at her desk and looked out the window, where she could see the bars of the entrance gate. Later she whispered to Grete that she had enjoyed looking at freedom just past those gates.

Milena was focused on living for Honza. With a Czech friend who had a daughter the same age as Honza, Milena planned how they would be reunited with their children in Prague as soon as the war was over.

Grete sat next to her bed during stolen moments and pretended to be optimistic and swallowed down her anguish. It was against the rules for her to be in the *revier*, but she felt some invisible force protected them from being caught.

Then, in April, Milena's steady improvement stalled. Zdenka suspected that Milena's other kidney had ulcerated. Just as Grete had caught Milena praying that one time after the surgery, Grete now prayed. They had both sworn to each other that they were atheists; they would never take refuge in political or religious fanaticism the way the communist and Jehovah's Witness prisoners did. But now Grete prayed. She would do anything to keep her Milena alive. They had survived so long, and the war was going badly for the Germans. If only Milena could hold on for just a little bit longer, they could make it to the end together.

Indeed, they would soon learn that the Americans were on French soil; then it would be just a matter of time before the German Army was defeated.

Grete reminded Milena of the book they had to write together, the projects they had dreamed up, the places they had promised to show each other. "You have to show me Prague," Grete said as a way of encouraging her.

Milena's father sent her three postcards depicting scenes from Prague. She would look at the postcards and guide Grete through the streets of her city. "Come this way down these narrow streets with the bumpy cobblestones, over there it will open up into the big market-place . . ." She moved through the city in her memory and described to Grete each doorway, each fountain or church. She crossed the bridges she remembered crossing as a young girl in love. She had them climb the church tower so they could view it all, but she told Grete to go slower—she couldn't keep up or climb that fast with her stiff leg. She described them walking through the Kinský Garden and stealing flowers, "to fill our little apartment."

She walked with Grete along the Vltava River, as she had done so often with her father. "What are we wearing?" she asked Grete, and then she described their outfits. "We look so good together, don't we? A handsome couple."

This was how they would visit her beloved city, with Milena holding up the postcards and describing to Grete where they were.

In frightening lucid moments, Milena realized she was dying. "Look at the color of my feet," she said. "Those are the feet of a dying woman. And the hands!" She held out her hands to Grete. "The lines are disappearing. That's what happens just before you die."

Milena asked Grete to visit Honza: "If I can't do it, you must go to her." She asked Grete to tell Honza all about the camp, everything they had been through. She trusted Grete to let Honza know all the fears and desires she had for her daughter.

"I know that you at least will not forget me. Through you I shall live on." Milena instructed Grete, "You will tell people who I was, you are my indulgent judge."[2]

According to Nedvědová, the final catastrophe was Treite's fault. Seeing that Milena's recovery had stalled, he decided, without consulting Zdenka, to do another transfusion from the same Polish girl. It was too soon. Milena's body had developed antibodies to the foreign blood, and she went into shock. She lost consciousness. Still, Nedvědová was able to keep her heart going. And it seemed she might recover.

Grete brought her a bouquet of blue pansies, and they discussed the color blue. Milena loved the color, she told Grete, "since it is your eyes." She assured Grete that she was going to be fine, that she was going to get better. They talked about Honza and the letter she needed to write to her.

On May 15, Milena received a letter from Joachim von Zedtwitz. Her eyes were failing, and she was drifting in and out of consciousness, but upon hearing his name, she sat up and asked Grete to repeat the name over and over again. She smiled and sighed, "Oh, thank God he's alive. It's a miracle. I was sure he had been shot."

Perhaps the card held a coded message for Milena about her release. The release that Joachim still thought was going to happen because the last he had heard, the lawyer in Berlin was feeling very confident that they had all the paperwork they needed. Perhaps if Milena had been more alert and healthier, she would have noticed the coded message and felt encouraged by it. As it was, she felt joy at the simple news that Joachim was alive.

Later that same day, Grete was told that Milena was dying. She rushed to the *revier* to find Milena in a febrile state with a euphoric look on her face. "She was radiant, her dark eyes were shining." Grete went to her; "she held out her arms in that beautiful gesture of hers." She was surrounded by her friends and she was blissful. At one point, she said, "I have only happy thoughts . . ." Later that evening, she lost consciousness.

Milena died two days later on May 17, 1944.

HER DEATH, THOUGH expected, caused waves of grief through the different prisoner groups. Treite allowed her to have a coffin to herself. Her friends gathered flowers and put them in the coffin around her body. Grete asked for and got permission to accompany her on the short journey to the crematorium. She walked behind the cart that was pushed by two male prisoners with green triangles. There was a warm spring rain. The ground was muddy, and the two men complained about pushing the cart through the thick mud. They talked to each other, everyday banter about nothing. In the distance, Grete heard the sound of birds on the lake. When they got to the crematorium, they would remove the bodies from the coffins since they reused the coffins. They opened the box with Milena. One man said to the other, "Get a good hold of her, she can't feel anything."

Grete collapsed.

DESCRIBING THE NEXT days, Grete wrote, "With her it was impossible to believe in death. It is inconceivable that she is no longer here."[3] For four years, Grete's every waking moment had been about Milena. She had looked for her each day, and her eyes were trained to spot her in any crowd. She had spoken to her whenever she could, touched her, caressed her, felt her presence. They had built their little world together inside that hostile place. Now that world was gone.

Only a few weeks later, they would hear about the Americans landing in Normandy. Women all around the camp celebrated. But Grete sobbed alone in her bunk. Without Milena, it didn't matter. Life had been drained of meaning. The cruelest thing of all was that life would continue. Grete would stumble through the days, amazed that people went on with their petty squabbles, their small triumphs, in mud and misery. Nothing had changed for them, and yet everything had changed.

GRETE WOULD SURVIVE another terrible year in Ravensbrück. It would be the worst year of the camp, with the highest death rates occurring in the final four months of the war.

The overcrowding, murder, and horror increased. With each new atrocity, Grete thought, *At least, Milena did not see this.* In the adjacent small subcamp, called Uckermark Youth Camp because it had originally been built to house adolescent girls, the SS created a death camp with a gas chamber. The SS had tried to keep it secret, but the word got out, as it always did, about what happened when you were sent to Uckermark.

In May, when Milena died, there were 28,078 prisoners in the camp. By August, there were 39,258 prisoners. All throughout August, thousands arrived from Auschwitz. And by September, there were 41,802 prisoners, 14,000 of them Polish women arriving from Warsaw.

There was no room for them, and so a large tent was erected on the swampy ground edging the lake. Many died before being registered and remained uncounted. Along with these uncounted deaths were the many births and infant deaths that inevitably followed a few short months later in the *Kinderzimmer*. *At least*, Grete thought, *she didn't have to see the babies.*

By December, there were 43,733 prisoners. Prisoners from the death march from Auschwitz were all transferred to Uckermark, which was now the extermination camp of Ravensbrück.

January 1945 was one of the coldest months on record. *At least*, Grete thought, *she is not in this cold.* That January, all the elderly women who had been given rose-colored cards allowing them inside work knitting socks for German soldiers were sent to Uckermark to be killed.

In the first fourteen days of February 1945, four thousand women were gassed at Uckermark. There were large executions by firing squad of Red Army soldiers, some French SOE, and three English prisoners. These, along with gassings and poisonings in the *revier*, were still not enough for Suhren; the execution rate was too slow.

Grete found some peace in repeating to herself, *At least Milena does not have to see this.* Grete also found some solace with a few good friends. She fell ill from blood poisoning. She wanted to die. But the communist nurse Inka saved her life with her careful attention. She befriended two French prisoners who arrived in early 1944. Germaine Tillion, whom she called Kouri, and Anise Postel-Vinay, whom she called Danielle, were NN prisoners, or *Nacht und Nebel*—"Night and Fog"—a special designation that Hitler gave to certain prisoners who were meant to disappear completely so that their families would never know what had happened to them.

Kouri was a noted art historian and member of the French Resistance. Her mother, Émilie Tillion, arrived a few months after on a later transport, which upset Kouri. She had hoped her mother would be spared. Émilie was as strong as Germaine, but because of her gray hair, she was always in danger of being selected for gassing.

Kouri was an ethnologist who had done fieldwork in Algeria. She returned to Paris in 1940, and immediately joined the resistance as part of the network of the Musée de l'Homme. When she was being deported to Germany, she had in her luggage her massive doctoral thesis, which she was finishing. Not understanding where she was going, she had imagined she could work on it while in prison.

Once she arrived in Ravensbrück, and once she got over diphtheria and the shock, she began to work as an ethnologist, taking careful notes of everything she saw. She recorded the number at each roll call, calculated the death rate. Her notes and records were invaluable after the war, when so many documents from Ravensbrück had been destroyed. She was able to counter the claims that there were no gas chambers in Germany and certainly none at Ravensbrück. She would live to be one hundred, and soil from her grave would be interred at the Panthéon in 2015. She and Grete remained lifelong friends.

In March, there was another roundup for a transport; this time, the rumor was they would be sent to Mauthausen. Perhaps they were transporting prisoners to Mauthausen because the gas chambers at Ravensbrück were functioning at capacity. They were sending 170, 172, or up to 180 women to the chambers per day. The transport to Mauthausen was to take all the remaining Roma and Sinti, a large number of the sick and old, as well as the NN prisoners. Kouri and Danielle were saved from this roundup because Milena's Czech friend, Anička, got their names taken off the list. Once the transport left, they had to stay hidden. There was going to be a general roll call the next day, and everyone who had escaped the transport was looking for a hiding place. Danielle hid in the attic of Émilie Tillion's block. Grete hid Kouri under her sheet in the bed where she lay in the *revier*, still recovering from blood poisoning.

There was a siren for the general roll call. Everyone had to line up outside while there was an inspection of the entire camp, looking for the deserters. General roll calls were known to be especially dangerous times; the SS would choose people for gassing at whim, and anyone old or sick was especially vulnerable. But Grete was in the special privileged section of the *revier* that was safe from this sort of selection. Outside in the main camp square, over thirty thousand women stood in rows for hours. They had the women undress so they could look at their legs. Anyone with gray hair, swollen legs, or a wrinkled body was made to stand to the side. "Before our eyes the women were taken away in trucks," Zdenka wrote later. "Women who were led away cried and fought . . . within an hour I observed flames spurting high from the chimneys and a thick suffocating smoke spread over the camp."[4]

Kouri squeezed in tightly against Grete's side, and Grete was lying half on top of her when the door of their sick ward opened. Treite entered with two other SS doctors.

"How many sick in this room?" he asked Grete. His head was about at the level with her bunk.

"Two, Herr SS Doctor," she answered in a weak voice.

"What's wrong with you?" he asked her. She explained, and he looked briefly at the sick women in the bunk beneath her. He turned with the two other doctors and left the room. A little while later, they heard the siren again, marking the end of general roll call. They exhaled with relief. They had made it through. Just as they were thinking about how to smuggle Kouri back out of the room, Danielle appeared at the window, distraught. "They took your mother!"

Kouri was overwrought with horror. "Oh my god! Oh my god! My mother! My mother!" she wailed.

Terribly shaken, she could barely climb back out the window. She frantically tried to get word and a package of food to her mother. But a week later, the package and notes were returned to her. She was told that it had been impossible to save her mother; she had gone straight to the gas chamber. Kouri's grief was devastating, and in their grief, she and Grete found a common bond.

On March 30, 1945, a number of Swiss Red Cross buses arrived to liberate a group of French prisoners. On the very same day, two selections of women, 350 in total, were gassed at Uckermark. On April 1 and 2, there were at least two gassings each day. Kouri noted in her carefully kept records that over 500 were killed in one day. While the killing was going on, the empty Red Cross rescue buses waited outside the camp gates. Finally, on April 3, Suhren allowed 299 carefully selected Frenchwomen to leave the camp. Anyone showing signs of illness, starvation, or beatings was kept behind.

Now it seemed more than just rumors: The Soviet Red Army was approaching. Grete knew that there was a chance the Soviets, with the encouragement of some of the communist comrades, would shoot her when they reached the camp. She was glad Milena was not there to suffer this anxiety. Grete began to spend her time writing her notes about what she had seen and experienced. She gave these to Kouri in case she didn't make it. There were rumors that another release of French prisoners was being prepared, and Grete wanted her account to go with them.

The camp was no longer functioning in any orderly way. There was no more electricity to run the Siemens factory. The SS were looting the *Effektenkammer* and leaving the camp, laden with stolen goods. The gas chamber was destroyed and new saplings quickly planted where it had once stood. But killings continued in the mobile gas vans. The murders were slowing down because the new urgency was to destroy all the records. The crematorium was being used to burn documents while the bodies piled up. Other more faithful and delusional Nazis believed that on April 20, Hitler's birthday, Germany would unleash a new secret weapon that would turn the entire war around.

On April 21, Cilly, Rosa's companion and Grete's block elder, read out a list of names. Grete was on the list, along with sixty German and Czech prisoners, all of them old-timers who had been in the camp almost since the beginning. They were being released. Their friends cheered and hugged them. They were given a release paper that stated they were to report to the local Gestapo office of their town or village within three days. They did not know whether to laugh or cry.

Binz marched them in rows of five outside the gates of Ravensbrück. Just outside the perimeter, she called out her last order to them: "*Halt!*"

"Frau Binz," someone in the group called back to her, "I live in Cologne. Can you please tell me the address of the local Gestapo there? I don't want to be late in reporting."

Everyone burst into laughter, and Binz's face turned red. "You can do what you like. Go where you like. But just remember you are fugitives." She turned on her heels and returned to the camp.

Two days later, on April 23, Kouri and Danielle, along with the rest of the French prisoners, were liberated by columns of white buses, the humanitarian operation negotiated by the Swedish diplomat Folke Bernadotte with Himmler.

And on April 30, the Soviet Red Army liberated the camp.

GRETE DID NOT feel elated to find herself free at last. Instead, she felt dread and confusion. Milena and Grete had planned to greet freedom together. They would walk into the first towns together, through the first fields, hear the birds singing. Then they had planned to settle down and write their book together. Freedom without Milena was empty.

Grete did not know where to go. She could not return to Potsdam. The Soviets were there. She began a journey by train, then on foot; then later, for a time, she had a bicycle. Everywhere she went, the roads were full of refugees, some still in the striped pajama-like clothes they had worn for years, others like her in clothes marked with a white cross painted on their backs. She sought shelter with farmers and in towns. Some of the people were kind; some were bitter and afraid. Everyone was hungry. There was chaos, and there were policemen trying to maintain order. She met ardent communists who awaited the Soviet Red Army with great anticipation, and former communists who had lost their faith, like Grete, but who were searching for a new cause to believe in. How to make the world a better place if not through a revolution? She would tell them about Stalin and the Gulags, the show trials, the similarities between Hitler and Stalin. She knew this particular feeling of loneliness and banishment when a communist lost their faith. She knew what it was to lose your one love.

In the village of Boizenburg, the US Army set up a refugee center. They could get money, food coupons, and a voucher for soup each day. There was a huge sanitarium where they could sleep in a clean bed. Grete rested there for a few days. She was standing in line at one of the shops, enjoying this newfound moment of normality, when she heard the sound of his boots on the ground, and then she saw only the back of his head and neck. She felt the blood drain out of her face and a cold sweat wash over her.

She left her place in the line and began to follow this man, keeping a certain distance from him. She could do nothing when they were alone on a small street. She had to wait until there were some American soldiers. The man was going down a side street, and she might lose him forever. She ran and jumped over the barbed wire fence to the yard where she knew she could find Americans. "There is a Gestapo man from the KZ Ravensbrück. Arrest him!"

The soldier put his rifle on the ground and began running with Grete toward the man. Four other American soldiers joined the chase. Ramdohr realized he had been spotted, and he began to run. It took some time for them to catch him and bring him back to where Grete was standing out of breath. Then she saw his face. And he recognized her. "Frau Buber, you are doing me wrong. I also once was a Social Democrat . . ."

"Shut up!" the American soldier interrupted him. Grete gave her account of Ramdohr. In 1947, he would be executed along with Binz and some of the other former SS guards at Ravensbrück.

GRETE BEGAN TO take stock of all she had lost. There was her belief in the beautiful dream of the workers' revolution. For that dream, she had lost custody of her children. Then the life she built as a faithful party member crumbled. She lost her second husband to Stalin's purges. And then she lost her Milena, the most beautiful, passionate person she would ever know. With the war over, she had to rebuild her life. She asked an American Jewish soldier to mail a letter to her daughters in Palestine. She would find out a year later that he did mail the letter. As a German, she was not allowed to use the regular mail. At a Red Cross center, she asked to send a letter, but was told that Germans had no right to use the international aid organization. She was told, "If you have waited for so many years without sending your children a message, you can be patient a little while longer."[5]

Knowing that Potsdam had been destroyed, she thought perhaps her mother was in Bavaria at her grandparents' home in the tiny village of Thierstein. Grete traveled there mostly on bicycle and foot, like so many other refugees trying to get to some place they could claim as home. Along the way, a woman from the *Asoziale* block recognized her as her old block elder and took her in. She helped Grete get a ration card. Grete met other "KZers," refugees from the camps, and people who had no idea what the prisoners had been through.

As she neared her destination, she became panicked that she would not find her family there. She had already heard from a soldier that the street in Potsdam where her family had lived was bombed to ruins. Maybe her mother was dead. She had no idea where her sister was. When she was only a few miles away, she asked an old farmer if he knew her village, Thierstein, and if it had been destroyed. He confirmed her worst fear: The village had been burned to the ground.

With a broken heart, she continued anyway. She had to see for herself that all was lost. She saw the castle tower in ruins, but the village was still hidden behind trees. Just before arriving, she asked an old woman if she knew her grandmother. And the woman replied, "The house of Joannes Thüring is one of the few houses of the village that was not destroyed. And living there is your mother, your sister, your brother-in-law Dr. Fleiss, and many children." With tears streaming down her face, Grete arrived at the house and fell into the arms of her sister, who was standing in the yard. From inside the house, Grete heard the voice of her mother crying out, "Has she come? Has she really come?"

HONZA WOULD LATER write about the day she finally met Grete. The war had ended. Her grandfather had received a telegram over a year earlier, in May 1944, from the doctor in the German camp where Milena was being held. But Honza had not believed the news written on that flimsy piece of paper delivered to her grandfather's trembling hand. They must be mistaken. Her mother could not be dead. Surely now that it was all over, one day soon, Milena would walk through the door with her singular limp.

She had last seen her mother four years earlier, when Honza was twelve. Just before the Germans transferred Milena to Ravensbrück, Honza had waited with her grandfather on a wooden bench in a long corridor in the dark stone Petschek Palace. A neatly dressed office worker holding a stack of files walked past them, her heels sharply clapping the parquet. Her grandfather frowned and stared at the floor. Honza did not dare speak. She peered down the corridor and waited. When a woman appeared flanked by two Gestapo agents, Honza thought, *Who is that?*

The woman was thin with shoulder-length rust-colored hair. Her mother had kept her hair cut short, and she had been soft and round. This person walking toward her had high, sharp cheekbones that made her eyes seem as if they had sunk into her face. And those eyes were fixed on Honza, gazing at her as one would someone who was beloved. Then Honza recognized the limping gait.

The commissar, showing deference to her grandfather, invited the three to use his office to talk. Honza remembered how she chattered nervously, trying to fill in the gaps, her mind whirling. She wanted her mom to be pleased with her; she wanted to make her laugh. She told her mother that she deliberately sabotaged the German lessons at school. Honza and her friends pretended not to understand a word. She hoped this would please her mother, but instead, Milena gave her a tired smile and said, "You're a silly donkey, Honzičko. German is one of the most beautiful languages. You can't blame the language for the people who speak it."[6]

Honza saw her grandfather frown at this comment. She knew that he hated the Germans and everything German in his beloved Czechoslovakia.

The visit passed in a flash. There was a moment at the end when Honza took her mother's white hands with their swollen red joints and kissed them in the old-fashioned way. She wasn't sure why she did this, and both her grandfather and Milena watched her, surprised by the formality of the gesture. But then Honza saw two fat tears roll down her mother's cheeks.

Recalling that moment, Honza could not believe it would be the last time she ever saw her mother. Milena had to be alive. There was still the odd story of some survivor finally making their way home, often on foot. And with Milena's bad knee, it would take her even longer. Sometimes survivors had come all the way from Russia.

Honza looked around their small apartment. She had filled it with stolen flowers from Letná and Stromovka parks, just as her mother used to do. The apartment was ready for Milena's return.

Then there was a knock at the door.

A compact, middle-aged woman of medium build stood at the door. She introduced herself as Margarete Buber-Neumann, Milena's closest friend in Ravensbrück. "Please, call me 'Grete,'" she said. "I feel I already know you."

Once she was inside and seated at the small table, Grete's piercing blue eyes and her eyebrows seemed to slope down with tenderness as she looked at Honza. "I am thankful for having been sent to Ravensbrück, because it was there I met Milena."[7]

Honza did not know what to say. After a pause, Grete announced that she had brought a keepsake for Honza. Unfolding a handkerchief that she pulled out of her pocket, she placed a tooth on the wooden table. It was a yellowed jagged pebble. She said that Milena had given it to her during a bout of gum infection brought on by the malnutrition and lack of hygiene in the camp. Milena had pulled out her teeth one by one from her sore infected gums. Honza stared at the tooth. In front of her was a piece of her mother's smile, a part of the mouth that once spoke to her. Here it was: proof that her mother was dead.

"That's all that remains of Milena," Grete said. "I brought it to you, because I thought it might please you."[8]

Honza couldn't breathe. This unbearably cruel gift was the truth. Her mother could always stare the truth right in the face. Honza hated it, but her mother would have appreciated this gift, the succinct truth of her death. This keepsake.

Honza wrote that she didn't know what to do with the tooth. How to live with a piece of her mother. She could not figure out where to put it, how to keep it safe. She could neither live with it in her house nor throw away the only relic of her mother's body. It was a torment. In the end, forgetfulness came to her rescue. She put the tooth somewhere, then promptly forgot where it was. She lost her mother's tooth.

Honza believed in the freedom to forget, to lose the past. Forgetting should be recognized as a human right. She was grateful for her willful forgetting because the little she remembered was only just bearable. Too much memory was a curse. And her mother was haunted with precisely this kind of memory, recalling every detail. It was a burden she had shared with her friend Grete. As Grete explained to Honza, they had made a promise to each other, to use that memory to write a book.

The years after the war were difficult for Grete. She had to reconstruct her life from ruins. In June 1946, she began corresponding with daughter Judith in Israel, and she wrote, "My life is now very lonely."[9] A year later her daughter visited her in Sweden. On an island south of Oslo in Norway, Grete wrote *Under Two Dictators: Prisoner of Stalin and Hitler*. It was a difficult experience to recount the seven long years of violence and captivity. How many times she looked up from her desk on that remote, beautiful island at the sun sparkling on the water and wished she had Milena there to help her find the words. Sometimes, alone with the memories, she broke down and sobbed. She remembered Milena saying, "Yes, go ahead and cry, there is everything to cry about."

The book was published in 1948. Her old friend from the camp Anise Postel-Vinay (Danielle) translated the first half for French publication.

The decisive moment in Grete's postwar life came in 1949, when Grete was a witness at the Kravchenko trial in Paris. Victor Kravchenko was a middle-ranking functionary in the Soviet Union who had escaped to the United States and written a scathing account of life behind the Iron Curtain entitled *I Chose Freedom*. It became an international bestseller, and in the impassioned early years of the Cold War, it became a central polemic. Soviet sympathizers, the French left, and the French leftist press hated Kravchenko and carried out a campaign of character assassination. They reported that he was an alcoholic, and a lying stooge of the CIA. Kravchenko sued for libel in the French courts. The ten-week trial was a political sensation, filling the newspapers in both the national and foreign press.

Grete barely knew Kravchenko and didn't like him all that much. But she did know about the Gulags and the Soviet penal system. Grete proved to be the most important witness in the trial. Her even-handed, straightforward descriptions of the Gulag, and her suffering under Stalin, including the way she was traded to Hitler, was decisive. The German paper *Der Spiegel* noted, "In its simplicity, the testimony by Buber-Neumann was the most devastating judgement on the Bolshevik regime made during the trial."[10]

The trial helped focus worldwide attention on Grete's book, which was then published in English. She had found her voice and role. She spoke out against the Soviet regime throughout her life. And she was hounded by the Soviets who tried to discredit her. She had not been handed over to Hitler but thrown out of Russia for being a Trotskyite and Nazi sympathizer, they said. The Karaganda Gulag wasn't a prison, since there were no wire fences, and she was just a bourgeois CIA agent. During the Kravchenko trial, her friend Inka Jindřichová, the Czech communist who had saved her life from blood poisoning in Ravensbrück, would testify that Grete was an SS collaborator. But Inka was living in Czechoslovakia behind the Iron Curtain and had been sent by the Soviets to Paris, pressured to give false testimony.

Margarete Buber-Neumann being sworn in during the Kravchenko trial
in 1949 in Paris

Inka would later say that she deeply regretted her words. Even Lotte
Henschel, one of Grete and Milena's closest friends in Ravensbrück,
was recruited by the Stasi to spy on Grete.

Grete remained a commanding presence, and she was unwavering
in her insistence to live in the truth. She continued to write tirelessly
about power and the corruption of the Soviet Union. Because of that,
she was never allowed to return to the site of the camp, which was
now in East Germany, or to participate in any memorial activities
there. She lived in Frankfurt and worked as an activist and editor.
In 1948, she married a journalist, Helmuth Faust, but the marriage
was brief. She later lived with a woman who was believed to be her
partner. Grete wrote to Judith that she felt compelled by the promise
she had made to Milena to bear witness to "the tragedy of my generation." She died in 1989, just weeks before the Berlin Wall came
down.

Her daughter Judith was able to go to Ravensbrück for the fiftieth
anniversary of the liberation, and, inspired by her mother's life, she

began a sociological study of the Jewish women of Ravensbrück. In 2001, in part because of Judith's work, the Ravensbrück Memorial prepared an exhibition about Grete on the hundredth anniversary of her birth.

THREE YEARS AFTER the war ended, Ravensbrück was flattened by Soviet tanks and moved into the shadows of World War II history. Because it was for women, it was considered a minor camp. What remained of the memory of the camp was a memorial to the martyred communists who fought against the fascist, capitalist West. There was no mention of the deaths of Jews, Roma, Sinti, *Asoziale*, or any other category.

Milena's reputation in the Eastern Bloc and behind the Iron Curtain suffered along with Grete's. Immediately after the war, during the small window of time when Czechoslovakia was once again an independent country, a few of the survivors wrote admiring tributes to her, about her importance as a journalist and her courage in the resistance and in Ravensbrück. Anička Kvapilová and Jiří Weil wrote about her bravery. But by 1948, with the communist takeover of Czechoslovakia, she was sidelined in any history of the camp. The timing coincided with Grete publishing the book they would have written together, comparing Stalin and Hitler as two of the century's violent dictators, and placing both Milena and Grete on the Western side of the Cold War divide. Behind the Iron Curtain, in her beloved Prague, Milena was purposely erased from history. Franz Kafka was considered a deplorable bourgeois writer expressing tendencies that would undermine the good revolutionary, and Milena was an enemy of the state, a nonperson.

The memory of Ravensbrück was recorded in a collective document by the central committee of the Czechoslovak Union of Anti-Fascist Fighters, first published in 1960 and later 1963. Milena, rarely mentioned, was noted only as a problem for good communist prisoners. She, along with Grete, "tried with displeasing demagogic phrases to influence the young politically inexperienced comrades."[11]

In the second edition of the anthology in 1963, most of the passages where Milena had been mentioned had been deleted. But also in 1963, there was an international conference in Liblice Castle outside of Prague to discuss the work of Franz Kafka. This conference marked a shift—the moment when Kafka was recognized as an important writer after having been heavily criticized by the Eastern Bloc countries. The conference was the beginning of the liberalization in Czechoslovakia that would reach its climax in the Prague Spring of 1968. At the conference, Milena was publicly discovered by literary historians as the first translator of Kafka's work, but also as a politically engaged journalist. This limited "rehabilitation" of Milena irked some of the communist survivors. According to Božena Holečková, Milena did not deserve the attention that was paid to her at home and abroad just because of her relationship with the famous writer: "It was then claimed that her letters that she had with Franz Kafka were found, which somehow pretended that she was a friend of Franz Kafka, and they even wanted to publish them, I think it didn't happen after that because order had been established in the republic, but the right-wingers wrote about her as a great anti-fascist. That's all I know about Milena Jesenská. I say that she tried very hard to get to know me, but she did not succeed. Since they had already warned us and said, she was an enemy."[12] When leading Czech communists in the camp warned their younger comrades upon arrival about their ideological opponents Milena Jesenská and Margarete Buber-Neumann, they also pointed out their "depravity," using their alleged lesbian relationship to discredit them.

In the 1960s, Czechoslovakia was experiencing the slow, gradual thawing of hard-line communist rhetoric. Some Czech thinkers, leaders, and artists thought they could find a middle ground between the harsh censorship of the USSR and the open but degenerate, capitalist West. The liberalization of Czechoslovak culture reached a climax in the Prague Spring, with a series of mass protests starting in January 1968, calling for democratic elections, free speech, and open borders. The hopes for reform ended violently in August 1968, when the Soviets invaded with tanks and half a million troops to occupy the country. Resistance continued for eight violent, bloody months, but against such an overwhelming force, Czech citizens had no hope. What followed was a period known as "Normalization" when "order had been established." The official view once again swung back to seeing Milena as an ideological opponent of communist women and therefore worthy of condemnation.

The Czech communists would experience the same sorts of swings and purges that Grete witnessed in early Soviet Russia. During the period of Normalization, the authors of the first collective histories would be dismissed from the leadership of the Ravensbrück camp committee. They were pushed out as "carriers of right-wing opportunism" who "lost their class perspective" and betrayed their ideals. Dr. Zdenka Nedvědová, who had worked with Milena in the *revier* and tried to save her life, was one of the members to lose her leadership role. She had been a loyal party member, and the feeling of disillusionment and betrayal was very painful.

In an unpublished memoir written in 1972, Zdenka reflected on the attitude of the communist women prisoners toward Milena: "Milena did not believe in the socialist policy of the USSR . . . However, these political differences did not have a general effect on our human relations. We were all fighters against fascism, we were its prisoners." In her forced retirement, Zdenka was able to reconsider Milena's anti-Soviet warnings: "It's only the revelations and tragic events of recent years that have convinced me that Milena was more right than I was at the time."[13]

IN 1947, A very small circle of people knew that Kafka's letters to Milena existed: Milena's longtime childhood friend Staša Jílovská, Max Brod, Willy Haas, and Milena's first husband, Ernst Polak. Max Brod had promised Kafka he would destroy all his letters, but he had not done so, recognizing their literary importance. Ernst and Willy, living in London, wrote to Staša about getting the letters out of Czechoslovakia. Willy claimed that Milena had given them to him, but he had left them behind in Prague when he fled the Nazis.

(Honza would later question this claim.) Staša was the only one still in Prague. She thought the letters had no literary or monetary value. To her, he was no longer important—"the old acquaintances who were in his circle have died and the literary circles today in Prague, sadly, barely show any interest in Kafka."[14]

Ernst and Willy both had an interest in the letters since both of them were talked about in them:—Ernst because he was married to Milena at the time she was writing to Kafka and Willy because he was having an affair with Milena's friend Jarmila—an affair that led to the suicide of her first husband. Staša was in Prague and working in the government. She had a way, through diplomatic pouch, to get the letters out of the country and to London, where Ernst and Willy were able to read them.

In 1952, Willy Haas published an edited version of the letters, cutting passages (without indicating there were omissions) that he feared might hurt the feelings of people still alive, or hurt his own reputation. The publication was a literary sensation. Kafka was already a giant in the literary canon after the war for the way he expressed the sense of anxiety and guilt of a generation. In his letters to Milena, Kafka wrote intimate details that he had revealed to no one else. The publication of Kafka's *Letters to Milena* brought her to the West, but Willy left out Milena's full name. She was merely the muse, the passive receiver of the letters. In the West, she would be known as "Kafka's Milena."

In 1968, Milena's daughter, Jana "Honza" Černá, wrote an account of her mother, which she titled *To Milena* (republished later in the West as *Kafka's Milena*). One thousand copies were rushed to print during the tiny window of the Prague Spring. Only a few copies made it to West Germany before the book was banned.

Honza's book was flawed, as any work would be that was written by a forty-year-old woman trying to remember her mother whom she last saw when she was twelve. But it provided a rich portrait of Milena as a mother and insight into her life during those years leading up to the war. Honza appreciated her mother's eccentricities and powerful character, the influence that Milena had on others. But when Honza was writing her book, her mother's articles were strictly banned. She

wouldn't have had easy access to them, and perhaps didn't understand the influence Milena had on her milieu in the 1930s. Honza's
son Jan Černý wrote, "We knew from the age of nine or ten that our
grandmother was someone who was faithfully remembered by her
circle of friends. They would visit us regularly to see Milena's grandchildren, but mostly to help her daughter who was always in some
distress or another."[15]

Honza never spoke about her mother to her children. And they
learned never to ask. When the book appeared, its contents came
as a shock of discovery for Milena's grandchildren, according to Jan
Černý. He understood his mother's silence about her own childhood
was due to the suffering she endured from Milena's imprisonment and
death. Honza's grandfather died soon after Milena. He never really
recovered from her death. Honza inherited some money from him,
which, like her mother, she squandered. At nineteen, she was on her
own. And life under Soviet rule was as difficult for her as one can
imagine it would have been for Milena.

Honza was at the center of the underground anti-Stalinist movement in Prague. She never conformed to the Soviet Communist Party,
nor held a permanent job. She supported herself by odd jobs such
as tram worker and house cleaner, and later by making ceramics
and selling them door to door. She survived in the margins, scrambling. She was a writer, poet, and feminist. With Egon Bondy, she
co-organized what was probably the first ever Czech samizdat publication. In the USSR, samizdat were clandestine periodicals, often
written by hand, of forbidden or censored texts. The small publications were passed from reader to reader in grassroots groups.

Jan Černý writes that Honza's children "always felt loved by her.
She talked to us like we were adults and expected us to act that way.
But she was incapable of taking care of the little daily details of life."
Yet her writing remains powerful, brazen, piercingly honest, and
subversive. Her long erotic epistolary work addressed to Egon began
with the first line: "I will not take it in the ass today." Protofeminist
and anarchist, it remains a much-admired work in Czech. She hated
intolerance and weakness, and shunned easy sentimentality. Like

her mother, she could not lie or obscure the truth. She could not accept the doublespeak of Communist Party rhetoric. Perhaps writing about Milena had eased the burden of her mother's shadow over Honza. Jan Černý writes that in the last six years of his mother's life, she found a peaceful balance with her fourth husband. She enjoyed making beautiful ceramics and playing with her grandchildren.

With the collapse of the Soviet Union, old friends who had known Milena, but who had remained silent during the years when she was considered a decadent bourgeois traitor, could finally speak of her. Books, articles, and collections of her journalistic writing were published. Joachim von Zedtwitz, living in Switzerland, prepared a testimony about Milena. Marie Jirásková recovered Milena's Gestapo file and collected her archives. Marie was able to document in detail the resistance work Milena had carried out to rescue Jews. Joachim's testimony and Marie's documents were sent to Yad Vashem. In the spring of 1995, Milena was honored as Righteous Among the Nations for her actions saving Jews in Prague in 1939.

DECADES BEFORE MILENA become known to the world, on May 17, 1944, Dr. Treite sent a telegram to Professor Jesenský. In a highly unusual act, Treite invited Jesenský to Ravensbrück to collect Milena's ashes. But Honza recounted that her grandfather was absolutely devastated by the news of his daughter's death. He was an old man, unable to function in his grief, much less travel to Germany among the bombardments and through ruined cities in rubble. Honza wrote that she worried he would kill himself. Grete later confirmed in her letter to Dr. Jesenský that she knew Treite's telegram gave him permission to come to Ravensbrück, and she didn't know the reasons why he hadn't come, but that it was much better that he hadn't. Milena would not have wanted him to come to that place.

After her mother's death, Honza had to tell the news to Milena's friends; to her father, Jaromír; and to others. She was comforted by one of her mother's lovers and her old tutor, Lumír Čivrný, who was arrested together with Milena by the Gestapo. She had saved his life. When Honza arrived in her black dress and black stockings, she didn't have to say anything. Lumír instantly realized what had happened. He walked with Honza for hours around Prague, talking about Milena as if she were still alive, wandering through the streets she had so loved.

Twelve days after Milena's death, Grete was finally able to write a letter to Dr. Jesenský:

May I tell you about Milena, Milena to whom I owe the most beautiful and also the saddest years of my life? No one has known such a life force, no one has experienced such intense feelings, but no one has known such great sufferings. Milena understood the tragedy of our generation, because she knew how to think. She intended to put these thoughts on paper, because for years she had suspected that she would never see freedom again, that she would never get there. How many times did she say: "I still have to write a book, the book, I have to create something eternal."

With her life Milena created eternity.[16]

AUTHOR'S NOTE

Many years ago, when I was young and living on a small sailboat, I cherished a paperback copy of Kafka's *Letters to Milena*. There were only two of us on the boat, and I often felt alone at sea. I read and reread my windblown, salt-sprayed copy, trying to figure out *who was Milena?* I was trying to discover who I was. On our little boat, tortured with fear and anxiety, I felt both an alliance and frustration with Kafka. Milena seemed to have the courage that Kafka and I lacked. But she remains offstage in the letters, a powerful absence.

When I was researching my last book, I discovered that Milena's final years were in Ravensbrück. It was like stumbling upon a long-lost friend. The historian Agnès Treibel first talked to me about Milena. She lit the spark, telling me that there was an untold story in Milena's friendship with Margarete.

Scholars have recognized that for too long history was written about kings, conquerors, and colonizers. The narrative left out the story of the majority—everyday people, the enslaved, the colonized, and of course, the marginalized. To rectify this imbalance, in telling this story, I engage in an act of recovery and imagination.

One must acknowledge that claiming to be a lesbian was taboo, and in the Nazi Era more than taboo, it could lead to death. After the war, that status didn't change much. The label could ruin a reputation, end a career, sever ties with one's family, and banish a person to the margins of society. I had to take that context and read between the lines to find the sub-rosa story. If we accept the archive as it was written and recorded, we are playing into the hands of the powerful who worked to repress and erase the stories of certain types of people. By imagining their lives, we recover the stories that were forbidden to be told. In a concentration camp for women all the people are oppressed and silenced, first as prisoners, and then as women. With the added layer of same-sex couples, you can be sure that the record or sources in the traditional sense will not be clear.

Many survivors claimed that Milena and Grete were a couple. But in doing so, they were often trying to damage their reputation. It is difficult to parse the political agendas. There was a tacit understanding that "passionate friends" was the acceptable way to avoid the label of "lesbian." And I avoid using the term "lesbian" for Grete and Milena because it is too essentialist—that is, it reduces them to a simple sexuality when I think they—and all of us—are much more complex. If they had the words, and were allowed to speak their truth, I think they may have said they were queer.

As I state in the book, we can never know the exact nature of the sexual relationship between Grete and Milena. That remains private, their secret. But what I can see, reading between the lines, is that they loved each other, that their friendship went beyond "normal" friendship, and, as Grete would later say, it became "the content of my life." It was physical, tender, and profound. I am using their beautiful love story to shine a light on sexuality in the camps and how it was seen, hidden, and the important role it played in survival. To have found love in a concentration camp is extraordinary.

ACKNOWLEDGMENTS

I would like to thank Elisabeth Dyssegaard, my excellent editor, for encouraging me to pursue the story. And I wish thank the talented staff at St. Martin's: Jamilah Lewis-Horton, Danielle Fiorella, Lauren Riebs, Michelle Cashman, Paul Hochman, Ginny Perrin, Meryl Sussman Levavi, Jessica Zimmerman, Kiara Ronaghan, and Hannah Dragone.

My agent, Andy Ross, is always a blessing and a friend. I feel lucky to work with him.

For the research of this story, I was honored to be able to speak with some excellent scholars, who gave me wise guidance and direction. At every exchange, they deepened my understanding. I am grateful for the careful insights, edits, and commentary from Anna Hajková. Her input was absolutely invaluable. I also wish to thank Insa Eschebach, Andrea Genest, Suzette Robichon, and Laurie Marhoefer for taking their valuable time to talk with me and give me much-needed advice. And I wish to thank Uta Rautenberg for sharing her brilliant doctoral thesis. All these historians were unfailingly generous and helpful, and any errors that remain are entirely my own.

I received help with understanding Czech and Czech history, and in the research of Milena, from Hanka Pauerova, Jindra Schiff, and my dear George Bauer. Emmanuel Lanternier gave me some valuable insights on Germaine Tillion.

I want to thank my staff at the Dora Maar Cultural Center, who held down the fort when I was writing: Thank you, Laurence Varenik and MacKenzie Mercurio.

I am blessed with wonderful friends who continuously support me and my writing efforts. They have listened to me as I tried to work out the knots of storytelling. When writing about difficult subjects, it was vital to have friends who brought me joy. Thank you: Nicky Dingwall-Main, Dawn Michele Baude, Lauren Sandler, Nicholas Boggs, Dorothy Spears, Sylvia Peck, Caleb Penniman, Crista Cloutier, Maxine Swann, Andrew Dey, Mary Callahan, Allegra Biggs, Mary Flannagan, Joe Havel, Karine Cariou, Celeste Schenck, Ebba Langenskiold, Kiko Lopez, Laurie Fendrick, Peter Plagens, Cloe Guerin, Ella Hickson, Siena Powers, Mike Turoff, and, last but far from least, Marc Spyker.

This book could not have been written without two blissful winter residencies. The first was provided to me by Janet Nichols and Erik MacPeek, who generously lent me their jewel box cabin in Mystic, Connecticut. The second winter I was given the great privilege of a fellowship at MacDowell in New Hampshire.

I am lucky to have a truly supportive family. My sister Tilly Strauss once again traveled with me on the research trip to Berlin and Prague, and tirelessly helped me track down each and every address where Milena lived. Her curiosity and wonder make her the perfect traveling companion. My other siblings are equally important in their unflagging support: Kate (Annie) Long, Suzy Strauss, Lise Charlier, and my brother, Willy Strauss. My father, Julian Strauss, and my stepmother, Betsy Strauss, are inspiring with their love of history and their own writing projects.

My three children, Sophie, Noah, and Eliza, have put up with me working through family vacations and talking on and on about these dark subjects. They are not only my favorite people to hang out with, but they also take care of me, often summoning me from my writing desk for warm delicious meals, giving me encouragement in times of doubt, and always reminding me to have a good laugh. I could not have written this book without them.

And finally, my mother, Kate Cowles Nichols, who passed away just as I was finishing the manuscript. Throughout my life, she was my most loyal and fierce cheerleader. She framed my early poems. Her flair for storytelling was the seed for my calling as a writer. I miss her; she was my first reader, and always as excited as I was when the finished book arrived.

NOTES

Part One: 1940

1. Margarete Buber-Neumann, *Milena* (London: Collins Harvill, 1989), 2.
2. Sarah Helm, *Ravensbrück: Life and Death in Hitler's Concentration Camp for Women* (New York: Nan A. Talese/Doubleday, 2015), 65.
3. Judith Buber Agassi, *Jewish Women Prisoners in Ravensbrück* (Lubbock: Texas Tech University Press), 49.
4. Nikolaus Wachsmann, *KL: A History of the Nazi Concentration Camps* (London: Little, Brown, 2015), 228.
5. Helm, *Ravensbrück*, 19.
6. Wachsmann, *KL*, 227.
7. Helm, *Ravensbrück*, 51.
8. Margarete Buber-Neumann, *Under Two Dictators: Prisoner of Stalin and Hitler* (London: Pimlico, Random House, 2009), 164.
9. Vissarion "Beso" Lominadze was a Georgian revolutionary and close friend of Stalin's. He had worked with Heinz as part of the Comintern in China during the disastrous uprising there. He later become critical of rapid collectivization and was part of a group that openly questioned Stalin's policies.
10. Laurie Marhoefer, *Sex and the Weimar Republic: German Homosexual Emancipation and the Rise of the Nazis* (Toronto: University of Toronto Press, 2015), 97.
11. Buber-Neumann, *Under Two Dictators*, 193.
12. Buber-Neumann, *Under Two Dictators*, 171.
13. Buber-Neumann, *Under Two Dictators*, 172.
14. Buber-Neumann, *Under Two Dictators*, 179.
15. Buber-Neumann, *Under Two Dictators*, 177.
16. Buber-Neumann, *Under Two Dictators*, 180.
17. Buber-Neumann, *Under Two Dictators*, 188.
18. Buber-Neumann, *Under Two Dictators*, 189.
19. Buber-Neumann, *Milena*, 11.
20. Pierre Rigoulot, "Margarete Buber Neumann," *Actualité* 40 (January 2010), 110.
21. Buber-Neumann, *Under Two Dictators*, 4–5.
22. At the start of the war, Willi was rounded up along with all German nationals in France and sent to the Chambaran camp. Babette was sent to the Gurs camp. In June 1940, with the approach of the German forces, the prisoners in Gurs were released. In the general confusion, Babette could not find Willi and decided to continue with their plan, which was to immigrate to Mexico and find each other there. Around the same time, Willi was able to get out of Chambaran with the

help of some of his organizers. He went underground into the French Resistance. On October 17, 1940, his corpse was found hanging in the woods near the Isère River. It was ruled a suicide, but Babette and all his friends, and later biographers, believed he was murdered by Soviet agents, just as Trotsky had been killed two months earlier in Mexico.

23. Robert Beachy, *Gay Berlin: Birthplace of a Modern Identity* (New York: Vintage, 2015), xii.

24. Claudia Schoppmann, *Days of Masquerade: Life Stories of Lesbians During the Third Reich* (New York: Columbia University Press, 1996), 133.

25. Marhoefer, *Sex and the Weimar Republic*, 173.

26. Isabel Meusen, *Unacknowledged Victims: Love between Women in the Narrative of the Holocaust. An Analysis of Memoirs, Novels, Film, and Public Memorials* (PhD diss., University of South Carolina, 2015), 4.

27. Milena Jesenská, "Judge Lynch in Europe, 30 March 1938," *Přítomnost*, in *The Journalism of Milena Jesenská*, ed. Kathleen Hayes (New York: Berghahn Books, 2003), 156.

28. Milena Jesenská, "Hundreds of Thousands Looking for a No-Man's-Land, 27 July 1938," *Přítomnost*, in *The Journalism of Milena Jesenská*, 172.

29. Milena Jesenská, "Beyond Our Strength, 12 October 1938," *Přítomnost*, in *The Journalism of Milena Jesenská*, 180.

30. Ian Ona Johnson examines in detail these agreements and how they led inevitably to World War II in *Faustian Bargain: The Soviet-German Partnership and the Origins of the Second World War* (New York: Oxford University Press, 2021).

31. Johnson, *Faustian Bargain*, 236.

32. Buber-Neumann, *Under Two Dictators*, 126.

33. Buber-Neumann, *Under Two Dictators*, 143.

34. Extract from Milena's article "A Dream," (written under the pseudonym A. X. Nessy), in *Tribuna*, June 14, 1921. From Milena Jesenská, *Vivre*, ed. Dorothea Rein (Paris: Éditions Cambourakis, 2016), 69. (Translated from French by author.)

35. Buber-Neumann, *Milena*, 168.

36. Germaine Tillion, *Ravensbrück* (Paris: Éditions du Seuil, 1988), 187.

37. Tillion, *Ravensbrück*, 186.

38. Milena Jesenská, "The Art of Standing Still," *Přítomnost*, April 5, 1939, in *The Journalism of Milena Jesenská*, 212.

39. Buber-Neumann, *Milena*, 151.

40. Buber-Neumann, *Milena*, 11.

41. Buber-Neumann, *Milena*, 11.

Part Two: 1941

1. Buber-Neumann, *Milena*, 9.

2. Helm, *Ravensbrück*, 105.

3. Buber-Neumann, *Milena*, 159.

4. Pavla Plachá, *Torn Lives: Czechoslovak Women in the Ravensbrück Nazi Concentration Camp in 1939–1945* (Prague: Ústav pro studium totalitních režimů, Puchra, 2021), 64.

5. Johnson, *Faustian Bargain*, 238.

6. Helm, *Ravensbrück*, 111.

7. Insa Eschebach, "Milena Jesenská and Ravensbrück: A contribution to the history of remembrance of the women's concentration camp," in *Milena Jesenská: Biography—Contemporary History—Memory*, eds. Pavla Plachá and Vera Zemanova (Prague: Aula, 2016), 132. Cited from an interview with Sigrid Jacobeit, recorded August 22–23, 2000.
8. Buber-Neumann, *Milena*, 39.
9. Buber-Neumann, *Under Two Dictators*, 182.
10. Buber-Neumann, *Milena*, 153.
11. Buber-Neumann, *Milena*, 158.
12. Alena Wagnerová, *Milena*, translated by Jean Launay (Monaco: Anatolia/ Éditions du Rocher, 2006), 177.
13. Buber-Neumann, *Milena*, 91.
14. Wagnerová, *Milena*, 26.
15. Jana Černá, *Kafka's Milena* (London: Souvenir Press Ltd., 1985), 29.
16. Milena Jesenská, "The Café," *Tribuna*, August 10, 1920, in *The Journalism of Milena Jesenská*, 66.
17. Mary Hockaday, *Kafka, Love and Courage: The Life of Milena Jesenská* (Woodstock, NY: Overlook Press, 1997), 27.
18. Wagnerová, *Milena*, 60.
19. Wagnerová, *Milena*, 64.
20. Hockaday, *Kafka, Love and Courage*, 32.
21. Milena Jesenská, "Superficial Small Talk about a Serious Subject," *Tribuna*, June 17, 1922, in *The Journalism of Milena Jesenská*, 100.
22. Hockaday, *Kafka, Love and Courage*, 36.
23. Buber-Neumann, *Milena*, 51.
24. Franz Kafka, *Letters to Milena*, translated by Philip Boehm (New York: Schocken Books, 1990), 8.
25. Kafka, *Letters to Milena*, trans. Boehm, 44.
26. Kafka, *Letters to Milena*, trans. Boehm, 44.
27. Kafka, *Letters to Milena*, trans. Boehm, 51.
28. Kafka, *Letters to Milena*, trans. Boehm, 63.
29. Kafka, *Letters to Milena*, trans. Boehm, 70.
30. Excerpt from Milena's letter to Max Brod, *Letters to Milena*, trans. Boehm, 251.
31. Excerpt from Milena's letter to Max Brod, *Letters to Milena*, trans. Boehm, 254.
32. Milena Jesenská, "Modern Dances," *Tribuna*, February 14, 1924, in *The Journalism of Milena Jesenská*, 22.
33. Kafka, *Letters to Milena*, trans. Boehm, 192.
34. Milena Jesenská, "Mysterious Redemption," *Tribuna*, February 25, 1921, in *The Journalism of Milena Jesenská*, 91–94.
35. Černá, *Kafka's Milena*, 180.
36. Hockaday, *Kafka, Love and Courage*, 133.
37. Wagnerová, *Milena*, 121.
38. Černá, *Kafka's Milena*, 117.
39. Milena Jesenská, "Prague, the Morning of 15 March 1939," *Přítomnost*, May 22, 1939, in *The Journalism of Milena Jesenská*, 205.
40. Buber-Neumann, *Milena*, 134.
41. Jesenská, "Prague, the Morning of 15 March 1939," 209.

42. Scene recounted from Jana Černá, *Kafka's Milena*, 144.

43. Milena Jesenská, "Soldaten wohnen auf den Kanonen . . . ," *Přítomnost*, June 21, 1939, in *The Journalism of Milena Jesenská*, 218.

44. Milena Jesenská, "Children," *Tribuna*, January 9, 1921, in *The Journalism of Milena Jesenská*, 81.

45. George M. Weisz, "Starvation Genocide in Occupied Eastern Europe 1939–1945: Food Confiscation by and for the Nazis," *Journal of Law and Medicine* 28, no. 4 (December 2021), 1105–1113.

46. Buber-Neumann, *Milena*, 156.

47. Buber-Neumann, *Milena*, 166.

48. Wagnerová, *Milena*, 172.

49. Buber-Neumann, *Under Two Dictators*, 160.

50. Wachsmann, *KL*, 248.

51. Helm, *Ravensbrück*, 132.

52. Buber-Neumann, *Under Two Dictators*, 210.

53. Helm, *Ravensbrück*, 134.

Part Three: 1942
1. Wachsmann, *KL*, 295.

2. Helm, *Ravensbrück*, 144.

3. Helm, *Ravensbrück*, 148.

4. Wachsmann, *KL*, 248.

5. Buber-Neumann, *Under Two Dictators*, 210.

6. Buber-Neumann, *Under Two Dictators*, 220.

7. Buber-Neumann, *Under Two Dictators*, 221.

8. Buber-Neumann, *Milena*, 175.

9. Discussion about Rosa Jochmann and homophobic accusations against her from Uta Rautenberg, *Homophobia in Nazi Camps* (PhD diss., University of Warwick, October 2021), 96–104.

10. Buber-Neumann, *Milena*, 34.

11. Buber-Neumann, *Milena*, 40.

12. Wanda Półtawska, *And I Am Afraid of My Dreams*, translated by Mary Craig (UK: Hodder & Stoughton, 1987), 60.

13. Amicale de Ravensbrück et Association des déportées et internées de la Résistance, *Les Françaises à Ravensbrück* (Paris: Éditions Gallimard, 1965), 156.

14. Insa Eschebach, "Homophobia, deviance and female homosexuality," in *Homophobie und Devianz* (Berlin: Metropole, 2012), 69.

15. Erika Buchmann, *Frauen im Konzentrationslager* (Stuttgart: Verlag das Neue Wort, 1946), 22. Quoted in Eschebach, "Homophobia, deviance and female homosexuality," 67.

16. Anna Hajková, "Sexual Barter in Times of Genocide: Negotiating the Sexual Economy of the Theresienstadt Ghetto," *Signs* 38, no. 3 (Spring 2013). I am indebted to Hajková for her work on sexuality in the camps and her concept of sexual barter.

17. Buber-Neumann, *Milena*, 42.

18. Buber-Neumann, *Milena*, 59.

19. Buber-Neumann, *Under Two Dictators*, 224.

20. Buber-Neumann, *Under Two Dictators*, 225.
21. Buber-Neumann, *Milena*, 175.
22. Buber-Neumann, *Milena*, 169.
23. Helm, *Ravensbrück*, 211.
24. Eschebach, "Milena Jesenská and Ravensbrück," 142.
25. Volker Roelcke, "Sulfanomide Experiments on Prisoners in Nazi Concentration Camps: Coherent Scientific Rationality Combined with Complete Disregard of Humanity," in *Human Subjects Research after the Holocaust*, eds. Sheldon Rubenfeld and Susan Benedict (Springer, 2014), 51–66. This paper covers the history of the human experiments with sulfa drugs in the camps.
26. Penicillin was not yet in large-scale production at the outset of the war. In 1941, the United States did not have sufficient stock of penicillin to treat a single patient. By September 1943, however, the stock was sufficient to satisfy the demands of the Allied Armed Forces. The Germans would only successfully make penicillin in October 1944, but due to Allied bombing, they would never be able to produce it at scale. Robert Gaynes, "The Discovery of Penicillin—New Insights After More Than 75 Years of Clinical Use," *Emerging Infectious Diseases* 23, no. 5 (May 2017), 849–853, http://dx.doi.org/10.3201/eid2305.161556.
27. Buber-Neumann, *Milena*, 181.
28. Helm, *Ravensbrück*, 233–35. Helm cites several sources for this information, including *Beyond Human Endurance: The Ravensbrück Women Tell Their Stories*, edited by Wanda Symonowicz; *The Death Doctors*, edited by A. Mitscherlich and F. Mielke (translated by James Cleugh); and the Records of the Polish Research Institute, Lund University. These are detailed reports of Polish survivors who arrived in Sweden in 1945.
29. Buber-Neumann, *Milena*, 177.
30. Wagnerová, *Milena*, 140.
31. Buber-Neumann, *Milena*, 177.
32. Helm, *Ravensbrück*, 190.
33. Helm, *Ravensbrück*, 238.
34. Buber-Neumann, *Under Two Dictators*, 230.
35. The conversion rate was then roughly 2.50 Reichsmarks to 1 US dollar. One dollar in 1940 is worth $18.60 today. In other words, 5 Reichsmarks a day in today's terms cost Siemens $37.20 daily.
36. Helm, *Ravensbrück*, 241.
37. Buber-Neumann, *Under Two Dictators*, 229.
38. Buber-Neumann, *Under Two Dictators*, 233.
39. Helm, *Ravensbrück*, 246.
40. Helm, *Ravensbrück*, 389.
41. Memo by R. Borden Reams, December 10, 1942, from United States Holocaust Memorial Museum, "Declaration of December 17, 1942," https://perspectives.ushmm.org/item/declaration-of-december-17-1942, accessed on September 1, 2024.

Part Four: 1943

1. Helm, *Ravensbrück*, 254.
2. This scene taken from Buber-Neumann, *Under Two Dictators*, 235.

3. Buber-Neumann, *Milena*, 188.

4. Buber-Neumann, *Under Two Dictators*, 244.

5. Buber-Neumann, *Under Two Dictators*, 244.

6. This scene taken from a description in Buber-Neumann, *Milena*, 194.

7. Buber-Neumann, *Under Two Dictators*, 87.

8. Buber-Neumann, *Milena*, 201.

9. Marie-José Chombart de Lauwe, *Toute une vie de résistance* (Paris: FNDIRP, 1998).

10. Scene recounted from Helm, *Ravensbrück*, 303.

11. Wagnerová, *Milena*, 172.

12. Plachá, *Torn Lives*, 211.

13. Pavla Plachá, "Muses in Ravensbrück: Cultural and Artistic Activities of Czech Women Prisoners," *Memory and History* 11, no. 2 (2017), 10.

14. Plachá, "Muses in Ravensbrück," 12.

15. Buber-Neumann, *Milena*, 199.

16. Černá, *Kafka's Milena*, 205.

17. Kafka, *Letters to Milena*, trans. Boehm, 230.

18. Milena Jesenská, *Lettres de Milena Jesenská 1938–1944: De Prague à Ravensbrück* (Villeneuve d'Ascq, France: Presses Universitaires du Septentrion, 2016), 157.

19. Jesenská, *Lettres de Milena Jesenská 1938–1944*, 145.

20. Jesenská, *Lettres de Milena Jesenská 1938–1944*, 151.

21. Jesenská, *Lettres de Milena Jesenská 1938–1944*, 152.

22. Buber-Neumann, *Under Two Dictators*, 248.

Part Five: 1944
1. Milena Jesenská, "Mysterious Redemption," *Tribuna*, February 25, 1921, in *The Journalism of Milena Jesenská*, 94.

2. Buber-Neumann, *Milena*, 206.

3. Margarete Buber-Neumann's letter to Professor Jan Jesenský, May 29, 1944, in *Lettres de Milena Jesenská 1938–1944*, 153.

4. Helm, *Ravensbrück*, 550.

5. Buber-Neumann, *Under Two Dictators*, 334.

6. Černá, *Kafka's Milena*, 140.

7. Buber-Neumann, *Milena*, 3.

8. Černá, *Kafka's Milena*, 36.

9. Buber-Neumann, *Under Two Dictators*, xviii.

10. Quote from "In vielen schönen Worten," *Der Spiegel*, April 9, 1949, 12.

11. Plachá, *Torn Lives*, 62.

12. Plachá, *Torn Lives*, 79.

13. Wagnerová, *Milena*, 174.

14. Wagnerová, *Milena*, 183.

15. Jan R. Černý, postface to *Vie de Milena*, by Jana Černá (Clamecy: Éditions La Contre Allée, 2014), 243.

16. Jesenská, *Lettres de Milena Jesenská 1938–1944*, 154.

BIBLIOGRAPHY

Amicale de Ravensbrück et Association des déportées et Internées de la Résistance. *Les Françaises à Ravensbrück*. Paris: Éditions Gallimard, 1965.

Baldacchino, Adeline. "Margarete Buber-Neumann—survivre au siècle des barbelés." *Ballast*, March 19, 2018. https://www.revue-ballast.fr/margarete-buber-neumann-survivre-au-siecle-des-barbeles/.

Beachy, Robert. *Gay Berlin: Birthplace of a Modern Identity*. New York: Vintage Books, 2015.

Berenbaum, Michael, and Abraham J. Peck, eds. *The Holocaust and History: The Known, the Unknown, the Disputed, and the Reexamined*. Bloomington: Indiana University Press, 1998.

Bessmann, Alyn, and Insa Eschebach, eds. *The Ravensbrück Women's Concentration Camp: History and Memory*. Exhibition catalogue. Berlin: Metropol, 2013.

Bonnet, Marie-Jo. *Les relations amoureuses entre femmes, du XVIe au XXe siècle*. Nanterre, France: Editions Odile Jacob, 1995.

Bonnet, Marie-Jo. *Plus forte que la mort: Survivre grâce à l'amitié dans les camps de concentration*. Rennes, France: Editions Ouest-France, 2015.

Buber, Martin. *I and Thou*. Translated by Walter Kaufmann. New York: Charles Scribner's Sons, 1970.

Buber Agassi, Judith. *Jewish Women Prisoners of Ravensbrück: Who Were They?* Lubbock: Texas Tech University Press, 2014.

Buber-Neumann, Margarete. *La révolution mondiale: L'histoire du Komintern (1919–1943) racontée par l'un de ses principaux témoins*. Translated by Hervé Savon. Casterman, 1971.

Buber-Neumann, Margarete. *Milena*. Translated by Ralph Manheim. London: Collins Harvill, 1989.

Buber-Neumann, Margarete. *Under Two Dictators: Prisoner of Stalin and Hitler*. Translated by Edward Fitzgerald. London: Pimlico, Random House, 2009.

Černá, Jana. *Kafka's Milena*. Translated by A. G. Brian, with introduction by George Gibian and selection of works by Milena Jesenská. Evanston, IL: Northwestern University Press, 1993.

Černá, Jana. *Kafka's Milena, by her daughter*. Translated by A. G. Brian. London: Souvenir Press Ltd., 1985.

Černá, Jana. *Vie de Milena*. Translated by Barbora Faure, with postface by Jan R. Černý (Milena's grandson). Clamecy: Éditions La Contre Allée, 2014.

Chombart de Lauwe, Marie-José. *Toute une vie de résistance*. Paris: FNDIRP, 1998.

Despoix, Philippe, with Marie-Hélène Benoit-Otis, Djemaa Maazouzi, and Cécile Quesney. *Chanter, rire et résister à Ravensbrück: Autour de Germaine Tillion et du Verfügbar aux Enfers. Le Genre Humain* 59. Paris: Seuil, 2018.

Des Pres, Terrence. *Writing into the World: Essays 1973–1987*. New York: Viking, 1991.

Duma, Veronika. "Zum Ring von Rosa Jochmann." *Material—Beziehung—Geschlecht: Artefakte aus den KZ Ravensbrück und Sachsenhausen*, August 2018. https://www .kz-artefakte.de/zum-ring-von-rosa-jochmann/.

Eschebach, Insa, ed. *Homophobie und Devianz: Weibliche und männliche Homosexualität im Nationalsozialismus*. Berlin: Metropole Verlag, 2012.

Eschebach, Insa. "Milena Jesenská and Ravensbrück: A contribution to the history of remembrance of the women's concentration camp." From *Milena Jesenská: Biography—Contemporary History—Memory*. Edited by Pavla Plachá and Vera Zemanova. Prague: Aula, 2016.

Faderman, Lillian. *Odd Girls and Twilight Lovers: A History of Lesbian Life in 20th-Century America*. New York: Columbia University Press, 1991.

Fischer, Erica. *Aimée & Jaguar: A Love Story, Berlin 1943*. Translated by Edna Mc-Cown with Allison Brown. New York: Harper Perennial, 2015.

Hájková, Anna. "Between Love and Coercion: Queer Desire, Sexual Barter and the Holocaust." *German History* 39 (March 2021), 112–33.

Hájková, Anna. "Sexual Barter in Times of Genocide: Negotiating the Sexual Economy of the Theresienstadt Ghetto." *Signs* 38, no. 3 (Spring 2013), 503–533.

Helm, Sarah. *Ravensbrück: Life and Death in Hitler's Concentration Camp for Women*. New York: Nan A. Talese/Doubleday, 2015.

Hockaday, Mary. *Kafka, Love and Courage: The Life of Milena Jesenská*. Woodstock, NY: Overlook Press, 1997.

Iggers, Wilma A. *Woman of Prague: Ethnic Diversity and Social Change from the Eighteenth Century to the Present*. Providence, RI: Berghahn Books, 1995.

Jesenská, Milena. *The Journalism of Milena Jesenská*. Edited and translated by Kathleen Hayes. New York: Berghahn Books, 2003.

Jesenská, Milena. *Lettres de Milena Jesenská 1938–1944: De Prague à Ravensbrück*. Edited by Hélène Belletto-Sussel and Alena Wagnerová. Villeneuve d'Ascq, France: Presses Universitaires du Septentrion, 2016.

Jesenská, Milena. *Vivre*. Edited by Dorothea Rein. Paris: Éditions Cambourakis, 2016.

Jirásková, Marie. *Kruzer Bericht über drei Entscheidungen: Die Gestapo-Akte Milena Jesenká*. Frankfurt: Neue Kritik, 1996.

Johnson, Ian Ona. *Faustian Bargain: The Soviet-German Partnership and the Origins of the Second World War*. New York: Oxford University Press, 2021.

Kafka, Franz. *À Milena*. Translation from German to French by Robert Kahn. Caen, France: Nous, 2021.

Kafka, Franz. *Letters to Milena*. Edited by Willy Haas. Translated by Tani and James Stern. UK: Penguin Modern Classics, 1983.

Kafka, Franz. *Letters to Milena*. Translated by Philip Boehm. New York: Schocken Books, 1990.

Kafka, Franz. *The Trial*. Translated by Breon Mitchell. New York: Tribeca Books, 2011.

Kundera, Milan. *The Unbearable Lightness of Being*. Translated by Michael Henry Heim. Boston and London: Faber and Faber, 1984.

Lévy, René. *Margarete Buber-Neumann: Du Goulag à Ravensbrück*. Paris: L'Harmattan, 2015.

Marhoefer, Laurie. *Sex and the Weimar Republic: German Homosexual Emancipation and the Rise of the Nazis*. Toronto: University of Toronto Press, 2015.

Meusen, Isabel. *Unacknowledged Victims: Love between Women in the Narrative of the Holocaust. An Analysis of Memoirs, Novels, Film and Public Memorials*. PhD diss., University of South Carolina, 2015. Retrieved from https://scholarcommons .sc.edu/etd/3082.

Neiberg, Michael S. *Dance of the Furies: Europe and the Outbreak of World War I*. Cambridge, MA: Harvard University Press, 2013.

Noiville, Florence. *Milan Kundera: "Écrire, quelle drôle d'idée!"* Paris: Éditions Gallimard, 2023.

Plachá, Pavla. "Muses in Ravensbrück: Cultural and artistic activities of Czech women prisoners." *Memory and History* 11, no. 2 (2017), 3–17.

Plachá, Pavla. *Zpřetrhané životy: Československé ženy v nacistickom koncentračnom tábora Ravensbrück v letech 1939–1945* (*Torn Lives: Czechoslovak women in the Ravensbrück Nazi concentration camp in 1939–1945*). Prague: Ústav pro studium totalitních režimů, Puchra, 2021.

Półtawska, Wanda. *And I Am Afraid of My Dreams*. Translated by Mary Craig. UK: Hodder & Stoughton, 1987.

Rautenberg, Uta. *Homophobia in Nazi Camps*. PhD diss., University of Warwick, October 2021.

Riding, Alan. *And the Show Went On: Cultural Life in Nazi-Occupied Paris*. New York: Vintage Books, 2010.

Rigoulot, Pierre. "Margarete Buber-Neumann (1901–1989), Portrait." *Actualités* 40 (January 2010), 99–104.

Schoppmann, Claudia. *Days of Masquerade: Life Stories of Lesbians During the Third Reich*. Translated by Allison Brown. New York: Columbia University Press, 1996.

Schoppmann, Claudia. "Denounced as a Lesbian: Elli Smula (1914–1943), Working Woman from Berlin." *Témoigner: Entre histoire et mémoire* 125 (2017), 91–94.

Schoppmann, Claudia. "'This Kind of Love': Descriptions of Lesbian Behaviour in Nazi Concentration Camps." *Témoigner: Entre histoire et mémoire* 125 (2017), 82–90.

Société des Familles et Amis des Anciennes Déportées et Internées de la Résistance. "Les Survivantes de Ravensbrück, Leur Libération par les Alliés et la Croix Rouge Suédoise et leur Retour en France." *Voix et Visages*, Paris, France, June 2020.

Tillion, Germaine. *Ravensbrück*. Paris: Éditions du Seuil, 1988.

Wachsmann, Nikolaus. *KL: A History of the Nazi Concentration Camps*. London: Little, Brown, 2015.

Wagnerová, Alena. *Milena*. Translated by Jean Launey. Anatolia: Éditions du Rocher, 2006.

Weil, Jiří. *Life with a Star*. London: Flamingo, Fontana Paperbacks, 1990.

Weisz, George M. "Starvation Genocide in Occupied Eastern Europe 1939–1945: Food Confiscation by and for the Nazis." *Journal of Law and Medicine* 28, no. 4 (December 2021), 1105–1113. PMID: 34907689.

Weitz, Eric D. *Weimar Germany: Promise and Tragedy.* Princeton, NJ: Princeton University Press, 2007.

LIST OF ILLUSTRATIONS

INDEX

ABOUT THE AUTHOR

Brice Toul

Gwen Strauss is the author of *The Nine, The Night Shimmy, Ruth and the Green Book,* and a collection of poetry, *Trail of Stones*. Her poems, short stories, and essays have appeared in numerous journals, including *The New Republic, Catapult, The Jewish Chronicle, New England Review,* and *The Kenyon Review.* She was born and spent her early years in Haiti. Strauss lives in southern France, where she is the executive director of the Dora Maar Cultural Center.